Business Continuity and the Pandemic Threat

Learning from COVID-19 while preparing
for the next pandemic

Business Continuity and the Pandemic Threat

Learning from COVID-19 while preparing for the next pandemic

ROBERT A. CLARK

it gp™

IT Governance Publishing

IT Governance Publishing Ltd
Unit 3, Clive Court
Bartholomew's Walk
Cambridgeshire Business Park
Ely, Cambridgeshire
CB7 4EA
United Kingdom
www.itgovernancepublishing.co.uk

First edition published in the United Kingdom in 2022 by IT Governance Publishing

ISBN 978-1-78778-291-4

ABOUT THE AUTHOR

Robert Clark describes himself as a business continuity consultant, author, trainer and visiting university lecturer. During his career, he has been presented with three professional fellowships – Fellow of the Institute of Business Continuity Management (FIBCM), Fellow of the British Computer Society (FBCS) and a Fellow of the Institute of Strategic Risk Management (F.ISRM). Buckinghamshire New University awarded him a Master of Science degree in Business Continuity, Security and Emergency Management in 2012.

Robert joined IBM (Big Blue) as a trainee computer operator in 1973. Big Blue was one of those forward-thinking organisations that practised business continuity management (BCM) long before the expression had even been coined. But back then, in the 1970s, with the exception of periodic fire evacuation drills, BCM was simply referred to as disaster recovery, and was entirely focused on protecting the IT environment, along with the associated electronic data.

It was less than 12 months into his 15-year IBM career that Robert first became exposed to BCM. Both local and overseas disaster fall-back trials were regular features in the IBM calendar, and often involved testing its recovery capability by transferring UK operations to Germany or the Netherlands. During his time with the corporation, the closest the operation came to a real disaster fall-back was in 1974, during the UK miners' strike, when power interruptions became common place.

Robert's 15 years with IBM were followed by a variety of positions, including 11 years with Fujitsu Services (formerly

About the author

ICL), working with clients on BCM-related assignments. In 2005 he was tasked with validating Fujitsu's own BCM state of readiness across Europe. He is now a freelance business continuity consultant and spends much of his time working with clients in Malta and the Middle East.

In 2014 Robert became a part-time associate lecturer at Manchester Metropolitan University, where he has been delivering BCM to both undergraduate and postgraduate students alongside his consultancy commitments. It was in the same year that his first publication *In Hindsight – A compendium of Business Continuity case studies* was published and reached the Number One spot in the Amazon bestseller's lists.

Since that early success, Robert has published a further three books, including the bestselling prequel to this book – *Business Continuity and the Pandemic Threat – Potentially the biggest survival challenge facing organisations.*

For more information about the author, please refer to his website: *www.bcm-consultancy.com.*

ABOUT THIS BOOK

This book is a companion to the bestselling book *Business Continuity and the Pandemic Threat – Potentially the biggest survival challenge facing organisations* published by ITGP in 2016. For your convenience, a list of contents of the original book has been included in chapter 18.

As it first hit the bookshelves almost four years before the proliferation of coronavirus, it was primarily a prediction of the detrimental effect that a severe pandemic could have on organisations. That prediction has proved to have been incredibly accurate. By comparison, this book very much considers the harsh realities and the lessons the world has been learning about the SARS-CoV-2 virus and its associated disease, COVID-19, often referred to in this book simply as 'COVID'.

Having read it early in 2020, Robert Preininger CBCP very kindly said of my original book:

> *"Bob Clark is the real deal. His book demonstrates a predictive understanding of our current threat environment as well as our personal and corporate vulnerabilities to it. Knowledge is power, read and prevail."*

Posting on LinkedIn in November 2020, honorary Fellow of the Business Continuity Institute (BCI), Joop Franke, also observed:

> *"The text on the cover of the book from 2016, 'Business Continuity and the Pandemic Threat –*

Potentially the biggest survival challenge facing organisations' *became very true in 2020."*

Dr Jonathan Quick commented:

"Bob's book, Business Continuity and the Pandemic Threat does a spectacular job filling a gaping void in the pandemic preparedness and response literature. It should be required reading for every CEO concerned with keeping their business in business and every corporate risk manager, regardless of the type of business. He's written with an engaging, rare combination of hard-nosed business survival strategy and insightful human stories of pandemic experiences."

As I write, we are now more than eighteen months into the coronavirus pandemic. I have reread the original pandemic book to re-evaluate the predictions I made back then and, in line with Robert Preininger's remarks, there is actually very little that I believe needs changing in the interest of accuracy. In that original book, I could only draw on the past to help us prepare for the future. But with COVID-19, we are able to draw on the 'here and now' while we learn from almost daily experiences that various organisations are having around the globe.

There are, of course, lessons that we have learned and continue to learn about COVID-19, which have been captured and reflected in this book. However, while it has occasionally been appropriate to cross-reference the original book, I have endeavoured to avoid just repeating its contents in this companion.

Anecdotes and injects

About this book

A series of injects and anecdotes have been included in this book usually contained within a 'box' like this one. They are intended to enhance the readers' appreciation of the broader impact of the pandemic by relating to various relevant published reports and events that have occurred.

DEDICATION

On 27 September 2020, COVID-19 claimed its one millionth victim, exactly 200 days after the World Health Organization had declared a pandemic. In that time, more than 33 million had been infected by the virus, which maintains its relentless march across the planet as the number of cases and fatalities continues to grow. As we reached year end 2021, the number of globally declared cases had passed 288 million while the recorded number of fatalities was approaching 5.5 million.

This global emergency has shone a light on the selfless devotion and bravery of health workers the world over. Sometimes labouring with inadequate personal protective equipment (PPE), in traumatic conditions, while frequently putting their own lives in jeopardy, they continued to do their absolute best for their patients.

This book is dedicated to them …

… and to Vic Robinson, who sadly lost his battle with COVID-19 on 25 January 2021, aged 69 years. A great guy who will be much missed.

ACKNOWLEDGEMENTS

I would like to take this opportunity to express my sincere thanks and appreciation to the following individuals. They have each played some part in helping me to initially understand the enormity of the threat severity associated with pandemics, in addition to supporting me in the subsequent writing of this book:

Dr Natasha Azzopardi Muscat, Director of the Division of Country Health Policies and Systems at the World Health Organization.

Dr Jonathan Quick MD, MPH, Managing Director, Pandemic Response, Preparedness and Prevention, The Rockefeller Foundation.

Dr Lisa M Koonin DrPH, MN, MPH, a US public health official and medical researcher associated with the development of social distancing as a strategy to prevent the spread of viral diseases.

Dr Fergus O'Connor FRCS Lon, FRCS Ed.

Dr Martyn Hinchcliffe BM MRCP FRCR.

Catherine Feeney MSc FIH JP, Overseas Lecturer at Edinburgh Napier University.

Katy Watt Holder of two MSc degrees, Researcher.

Alan Cain BSc FSyI FSRM, Resilience Manager, NHS Greater Manchester Shared Services.

Robert Preininger CBCP, Business Continuity, Incident Response & Disaster Recovery Consultant, Nashville, USA

Acknowledgements

Sarah Alzaid, Business Continuity Manager, HSBC Bank, Riyadh, Saudi Arabia.

Warren Goodall, Emergency Management Officer, NSW, Australia.

Wong Siu-leung, Hong Kong Centre for Health Protection.

Diana Yue, Hong Kong Mass Transit Railway (MTR) Corporation.

Geoffrey A Clark, Technical Artist.

Philip J Clark, Teacher of English as a Foreign Language.

Simon Lockyer, Headmaster, Royal Hospital School.

Simon Marsh, Director of Development and Alumni Relations, Royal Hospital School.

Lucy Pembroke, Primary and secondary education specialist in alumni relations and event management, Royal Hospital School.

Polly Honeychurch, Headteacher, Cottage Grove School, Portsmouth.

Andrea Springmann, MA, Destination Management, Sustainability Trainer, Hong Kong.

Fiona Aucott, Bournemouth Symphony Chorus.

David Claypoole, Founder and artistic director of the Virtual Light Opera Company.

Margo Dodd, Supporting the performing arts.

Martyn Parkes, Impromptu Opera.

Debbie Gallimore, Nutritional Therapist and Wellbeing Coach.

Acknowledgements

Anne Jobson, OBE, Barrister at law at Rougemont Chambers.

Clare Martin, Director of Community Projects, Pompey in The Community (PiTC), Portsmouth Football Club.

Joseph Lightfoot, Results Inc Gymnasiums.

Jane and Gavin Gosnell, Mustard Diner.

Damian Clarkson, The London Kitchen.

Hilary Bennis, Professional Granny.

Elizabeth Peacock, last but by no means least, a very good, long-standing, friend who had a sad story to tell.

I would also like to sincerely thank those individuals who chose to remain anonymous, but whose help and contribution towards the writing of this book has been significant. By remaining namelessness, I appreciate you were able to be more open about your observations and experiences.

FOREWORD

Previous pandemics have reshaped societies in profound ways. The 1918 influenza pandemic changed the course of history – millions died and suffered, and many believed that the event was so severe and unique that it could never happen again.

In 2005, experts were alarmed at the emergence of the novel H5N1 avian influenza virus as it spread among wild and domestic birds in Europe and Asia. Although it rarely affected humans, when it did, it caused a very high mortality rate. The World Health Organization (WHO) warned that between 2-7.4 million people could die if an avian virus mutated to become a human pandemic (Cheng, 2005). This concern sparked active pandemic planning in many countries, national plans were developed and rehearsed, stand-by vaccine stocks were developed and some businesses invested in pandemic planning.

As everyone remembers, in 2009, an influenza pandemic struck – not from the expected H5N1 bird flu, but from a novel H1N1 virus. Because an ancestor of this virus had once circulated, some people had partial immunity to the new virus. The severity of this pandemic varied in populations and countries, but overall, its impact was far less severe than anticipated. After the pandemic subsided, a number of businesses who had developed earlier plans that focused on H5N1, relegated those plans to their archives, assuming that future pandemics would be equally mild and not disruptive to business continuity. However, experts, including this author in his book *Business Continuity and the Pandemic Threat (2016),* advised that businesses and business organizations should include pandemic planning in their business continuity plans.

Now we are facing the most severe pandemic experienced since 1918. On December 31, 2019, the detection of the SARS CoV-2 virus was initially reported to the WHO (WHO, 2020) and on January 9, 2020, the WHO announced the emergence of a novel coronavirus-related pneumonia in Wuhan, China (WHO, 2020). No one could have predicted how the emergence of this novel coronavirus would explode to become a worldwide pandemic, creating illness and deaths in unprecedented numbers and with unexpected and long-lasting impact. Millions of people have suffered and succumbed, especially among vulnerable populations. An alarming number of businesses have closed or sustained severe financial and personnel impacts, as the virus rages on in almost every corner of the world. As of this writing, over 500,000 people have died in the U.S. from this disease, over 125,000 deaths in the UK, and there have been more than 2.5 million deaths worldwide. Thankfully, COVID-19 has had a relatively low impact on young children. Although several vaccines to protect people against this virus are being distributed and administered, there is a long way to go to get back to 'normal'.

This outbreak has presented business responders with many unexpected twists and turns. Whereas pandemic planning had previously focused on a threat from influenza, this coronavirus pandemic is different in several key ways. Unlike their preparations for influenza, business leaders had never factored into their contingency plans that the pandemic would be largely spread by those who were mildly ill or asymptomatic. Nor did they consider that the emergence of multiple virus variants or transmission of disease through aerosols may require additional mitigation measures. We have witnessed the prolonged need for use of face coverings for non-medical personnel in community settings. We also realize the heightened risk of disease transmission in indoor compared with outdoor spaces and the pivotal role that building ventilation and filtration can play. Mandates for prolonged business closures have become commonplace with consequential severely disrupted supply chains. Business leaders need also make provision for employees suffering with residual symptoms and disabling conditions that can persist in some people long after the initial illness.

This pandemic, with all of its terrible surprises, has tested and strained response and continuity plans, bankrupted some businesses, and affected the lives and livelihood of almost all companies. We have seen inequities in outcomes and access to care and learned that the risk of exposure to this virus is not the same for everyone. A sizable proportion of the workforce has been identified as "essential workers" because of the criticality of their roles and because they have greater risk and exposure to the virus, and thus, need enhanced protection.

In this book, Robert Clark updates recommendations for business pandemic planning and emphasizes the importance of the continued development and maintenance of business continuity plans to include robust pandemic planning. It is critical for business leaders to carefully assess their organization's response to COVID-19 to understand 'lessons learned' and incorporate those insights into ongoing pandemic planning. For those who did not have a pandemic plan before COVID-19, this book can inform the key pieces of a plan. We have learned that business pandemic plans must be flexible and adaptable, because it is not possible to plan for all contingencies. Readers of this book would be wise to follow Mr Clark's advice to create or update their pandemic plans, as it has become evident that pandemics can emerge without warning. Preparing and planning can lessen the blow while bolstering business resilience.

We are not 'out of the woods' yet with this pandemic. In addition, the occurrence of a coronavirus pandemic does not diminish in any way the spectre of a future pandemic from influenza or another pathogen. We can learn about how to be better prepared from the recommendations in this book.

Lisa M Koonin DrPH, MN, MPH

Public health researcher associated with the development of social distancing as a pandemic mitigation strategy.

lisakoonin@healthpreparednesspartners.com

PREFACE

As I am not a clinician or a virologist, I have been asked on a number of occasions how I got involved with pandemics and what inspired me to write not just one book on the subject but two. I honesty cannot remember when I first became aware of the word pandemic being used during a threat analysis exercise or appearing on a risk register. But it was more than a decade ago.

People may well remember the H5N1 bird flu outbreak in 2006 and the H1N1 swine flu outbreak in 2009. They may well also recall the panic that accompanied the Severe Acute Respiratory Syndrome (SARS) in 2002-2003, which was the first novel contagion of the new millennium. These events certainly helped to raise my own level of awareness.

Then in 2010, I was facilitating some risk management workshops for the Ministry of Health in the Republic of Malta. In case you are not familiar with Malta's location, it is a group of five islands right in the middle of the Mediterranean Sea – about 100 kilometres to the south of Italy.

During the workshops, I noticed that when the subject of a pandemic was raised, people got very serious, and their body language suggested that we were talking about a threat that made them feel rather uncomfortable. When we had finished the exercise, the threat of a pandemic was not so much at the top of their list of priorities, but it was way out in front.

Before we all headed off in our respective directions, I took the opportunity to talk to the then Chief Medical Officer for Malta, Natasha Azzopardi Muscat, about pandemics. She left me in no doubt about just how dangerous they could be and why they needed to be at the top of a nation's risk register. Natasha has since moved on and is now the Director of the Division of Country Health Policies and Systems at the World Health Organization (WHO).

In June 2015, I was invited to prepare and present a masterclass, first in Hong Kong and then again in Dubai. The subject was to be business continuity and pandemics. Having accepted the invitation, I duly started to design the delivery structure, when it occurred to me that there would be more than enough material to actually write a book on the subject and *Business Continuity and the Pandemic Threat* was published in 2016. Needless to say, I was delighted that the publication became a bestseller.

So why only five years later am I now writing a companion book? The simple answer is COVID-19. Instead of predicting what could happen during a serious pandemic, we are now living through one.

I am no stranger to business continuity, having received peer recognition over my many years of involvement in the discipline, which stands alongside my corresponding academic qualifications. This book is also my fifth business continuity related publication. Moreover, the pandemic threat is primarily (although not exclusively) about people and how to manage your business with a substantially depleted workforce. Human resources (HR) management departments will need to take a leading role in dealing with the pandemic issues that affect their employees. Here I have been able to draw upon the experience I gained during the five years I spent as the resourcing director for Fujitsu Consulting for Northern Europe. During this time, I had responsibility for managing approximately 1,500 consultants across five countries.

Like its prequel, writing this book has naturally necessitated undertaking a great deal of research, although this has been while we were in the middle of a pandemic rather than before or after the event. This time, the focus has been specifically on the virus SARS-CoV-2 and its associated disease COVID-19. I can tell you that as my research progressed, my appreciation of the enormity of the pandemic threat has increased beyond measure. So too has my genuine concern about the conceivable damage that is being inflicted on life as we know it – both professionally and personally.

In writing this book, in general I have used the United Kingdom (UK) as the benchmark for pandemic preparedness. I also make several references to the UK National Risk Register (NRR), which is in the public domain. I do naturally accept that other countries around the world may be more or less well prepared than the UK. That said, the pandemic threat is taken very seriously in this country, and is considered to be a Tier 1 threat to its security and economy, ranking alongside terrorism, war, cyber threats and natural disasters.

Since this book considers the pandemic threat primarily from a business continuity context, it is certainly not full of jargon that an infectious diseases clinician or virologist would thrive upon. Instead, while it has been necessary to make appropriate references to various bacterium and viruses, it also looks at what history has taught us and how we can apply those lessons to better protect our businesses, and ourselves, from what is an inevitability – the next pandemic.

LIST OF FIGURES

List of figures

CONTENTS

Contents

Contents

CHAPTER 1: INTRODUCTION

Something I have come to realise in writing this book while the coronavirus pandemic is still raging, is that it must be a bit like trying to paint a picture of the shifting sands in a desert – things keep moving. It seems that almost every day we learn something new about the virus. The media is forever carrying fresh stories, some of which are very relevant to the context of this book, while other items have the potential to serve as nothing more than a distraction. At the very least, any one of us following the progress of coronavirus too closely could end up with a severe case of information overload. In extreme cases, consequential paranoia could be the outcome of the menacing nature of some content.

I recently heard someone say that *"Breathing while we are in this pandemic is dangerous – we are dammed if we do and dammed if we don't"*. But, as with any potentially fatal pandemic, we entered its clutches armed more with the hope that it would soon be over rather than comfortable in the knowledge that there was a vaccine or cure. If mankind is fortunate, this will be sooner rather than later. In fact, the first vaccination outside of a controlled test was administered in the UK on 8 December 2020, just 272 days after the original pandemic declaration. Many organisations around the world have been working tirelessly to develop safe and effective vaccines. Others have endeavoured to find a successful means of treatment or cure from existing licensed medication. To date there has been some, albeit limited, success in that respect too.

1: Introduction

During the 2007-2008 global financial crisis, an official-looking announcement appeared on an organisation's intranet informing employees that:

"During the current financial crisis, the light at the end of the tunnel will be switched off until further notice."

Perhaps many have been echoing a similar sentiment about the pandemic crisis we have been facing. Just how long is this nasty dark tunnel we have found ourselves in, and when will we get to the end? It is certainly not encouraging when new and potentially threatening virus variants are discovered with Omicron being the latest. While scientists have been engaged in endeavouring to establish the characteristics of the new variant, it has quickly become clear that it has spread across the globe much faster than its predecessors.

In the early days, journalists kept asking politicians '*how long will the pandemic last?*'. Eventually, they came to realise that, like themselves, the politicians and even all the clinicians and scientists who found themselves on camera had no idea either. In fact, nobody did.

But one alarming statistic that the financial crisis certainly appears to have in common with the pandemic is an excess number of collateral fatalities. Published in *The Lancet*, one paper focuses on the inordinate number of additional cancer deaths associated with increased unemployment and reduced public sector spending on healthcare.

"We estimate that the 2008-10 economic crisis was associated with about 260,000 excess cancer-related deaths in the Organisation for Economic Co-operation and Development alone."

(Maruthappu, et al., 2016)

1: Introduction

Although it is too early to quote specific corresponding figures for the pandemic, a trend appears to be developing that goes beyond cancer and includes other life-threatening illnesses, such as heart conditions and strokes. There are those individuals who perhaps could have benefitted from timely medical intervention, but may have succumbed to non-COVID life-threatening conditions, primarily for two reasons:

1. They are too afraid to seek medical intervention for fear of catching COVID. But, as UK Chief Medical Officer, Chris Witty, said at a government COVID press conference:

   "The NHS is absolutely open for business and is not just there for emergencies, but for cancer care and all other kinds of care."

   (Whitty, 2020)

2. In some regions of the UK, hospital capacities have been severely stretched, especially when experiencing a rapid increase in COVID cases. Moreover, seasonal influenza was expected to add to the burden although the number of cases recorded was relatively few in 2020-21. But, even in those more developed countries with health services that may well be the envy of the world, their resources are still finite. Consequently, I believe it is inevitable that some people with non-COVID life threatening conditions may well become collateral fatalities.

It's official – it's a pandemic!

It was 11 March 2020 when Dr Tedros Adhanom Ghebreyesus, Director General of the World Health Organization (WHO), classified the novel coronavirus outbreak as a pandemic. This declaration came just 70 days after the WHO had first been notified of a pneumonia of unknown cause, detected in the city of Wuhan in Hubei province, China. At the time of notification, there had been no associated deaths reported. However, it has since been revealed that the WHO had originally learned of the novel virus via social media rather than through official channels (Hawley, 2021).

The world had been expecting a severe pandemic, although it was anticipated that it would be a novel influenza virus rather than an emerging disease in the form of a coronavirus. One month before the WHO pandemic declaration, this novel coronavirus had been named 'Severe Acute Respiratory Syndrome Coronavirus 2' (SARS-CoV-2) and the disease it causes was named 'COVID-19' (WHO, 2020(a)).

It was also around this time that I am sure that many people living in Europe and the Americas were lured into a false sense of security, perhaps believing that this was not their problem. After all, neither of the two previous coronaviruses, SARS and MERS, with the exception of Toronto, Canada, had really represented a threat to the Western world. Moreover, initially, outside of China, the only other significant report of any cases related to the cruise ship, Diamond Princess. This ship was quarantined in Yokohama, Japan with more than 3,700 passengers and crew on board.

We found ourselves facing a global crisis

For those individuals who really had no idea what a life-threatening pandemic was, the arrival of the coronavirus SARS-CoV-2 in 2020 was soon to provide the answer. Its associated disease, COVID-19, has been systematically working its way around the globe, testing the resolve and preparedness of each country it has touched. One fairly obvious observation is that the resultant societal and economic effects of the virus have been devastating.

COVID-19 very quickly proved to be indiscriminate in who it attacked, with many well-known individuals being infected. High-profile personalities have included Hollywood actor, Tom Hanks and his wife Rita Wilson. Three generations from a Bollywood dynasty, with actor Amitabh Bachchan, his son Abhishek, daughter-in-law Aishwarya and granddaughter Aaradhya all testing positive.

In the UK, Prime Minister Boris Johnson and Prince Charles, heir to the British throne, both tested positive. World-renowned opera singers Placido Domingo and Andrea Bocelli, plus Brazilian President Jair Bolsonaro were also infected. Former US President Donald Trump and his First Lady Melania tested positive. The list goes on. One US politician to die from COVID-19 was Luke Letlow, 41, a Republican congressman-elect. He died just a few days before he was due to be sworn-in. In October 2021, former US Secretary of State, Colin Powell, also succumbed to what was described as "COVID-19 related complications".

In reality, we soon discovered that we were being confronted by a world-wide emergency which, to begin with, was of largely indeterminate parameters. To the rest of the world, it seemed that the coronavirus had originated in China, although, now almost two years since the pandemic was first declared, that allegation remains unproven.

Every country can expect to face civil emergencies periodically, and needs to be prepared to effectively and efficiently manage the associated crises. The same is true of organisations, both large and small, and each will be judged on not so much the nature of the crisis, but how well it was managed. In this instance, chapter 5 looks specifically at whether organisations do or do not have a pandemic plan prepared. Running a business in lockdown, including protecting and preserving the well-being of employees, is covered in chapter 7.

Chapter 6 considers the management of a crisis which, in addition to pandemics, can equally apply to a variety of causes, such as a natural disaster, cyber attack, IT failure, supply chain failures, availability of skilled staff, etc. Every plan, whether an IT disaster recovery plan, a crisis management plan or a pandemic plan, should be exercised to ensure it is fit for purpose. This might be just a series of tabletop exercises, and chapter 8 provides some validation exercise examples to help organisations in this respect.

Although the WHO did have a war plan that the 2002-2003 SARS outbreak had provided an opportunity to exercise, many countries and businesses simply did not have a script to follow. Some country leaders took swift action and were criticised for not allowing sufficient time for people and organisations to get ready. Others were criticised for reacting too slowly, thereby giving the pandemic the opportunity to establish itself.

The UK government was accused by some of ineptitude for allowing the Cheltenham horse racing festival to proceed in March 2020, along with the Liverpool versus Atletico Madrid European Champions League soccer match. An estimated 250,000 attended Cheltenham, while 52,000, including 3,000 travelling Spanish fans, watched the match at Liverpool. Even though the WHO pandemic declaration came on the second day of the four-day Cheltenham Festival, the event was still permitted to continue unabated. It is believed that these two events led to an avoidable spike in COVID-19 deaths in both localities (Frodsham, 2020).

We have also witnessed an abundance of pop-up pandemic experts suddenly materialising. While the advice they collectively offered was often conflicting (e.g. lockdown, don't lockdown, wear masks, don't wear masks, etc.), the commonality of their messages seemed to be 'strong on the destructive but very weak on the constructive criticism'.

As with other past major incidents and crises, the conspiracy theorists have been only too ready to contribute towards the rhetoric surrounding the pandemic, something which I discuss in chapter 3.

Why weren't we warned?

The annual Business Continuity Institute (BCI) Horizon Scan Report is usually published in the first quarter of each year. It relies upon organisations providing data about the actual incidents they have experienced over the previous 12 months and the future threats they anticipate. A study of the BCI's 2020 publication reveals that the word *'pandemic'* is mentioned just once and COVID-19 three times (BCI, 2020), suggesting that the threat of a pandemic was not keeping business leaders awake at night at that time. Conversely, *'pandemic'* appears 63 times in the 2021 Horizon Scan Report and COVID-19 on 102 occasions (BCI, 2021). Not surprisingly, *'pandemic'* had become the standout threat facing most organisations.

Perhaps this might suggest that the world had not been alerted to the threat of an impending pandemic. However, as chapter 4 demonstrates, very few seemed to be listening to the ever-increasing multitude of warnings that had been growing in number ever since the start of the new millennium.

Lockdowns – The economic and societal impact

Disruption on a massive scale gathered momentum as the virus spread, and almost 20% of this book has been allocated to chapter 7 which considers the implications of lockdowns across the world. This includes an insider's account of the world's first ever mass lockdown that followed the Wuhan coronavirus outbreak.

As countries were locked down, millions were quarantined while economies suffered. Unemployment became widespread and stories of consequential hardship became common place, while health services struggled to keep pace with the rising COVID-19 case load.

Vulnerable industry sectors quickly suffered the effects of the pandemic with tourism, hospitality and events finding themselves in the forefront of the chaos. In fact, referring to an American Trade Group report, *The New York Times* stated that, in the six months from 1 March to 31 August 2020, the US tourism industry alone had sustained $341 billion in losses (Wolfe & Takenaga, 2020).

Schools, restaurants, theatres and cinemas were closed down, while holiday bookings, concerts, festivals, such as Glastonbury 2020 and major sporting events, were all cancelled. Not least of all the most prestigious of sporting events, the 2020 Olympic Games, was postponed until 2021. Some professional sports, such as soccer, cricket and tennis were able to later recommence, although matches had to initially be played behind closed doors.

Taking a holiday has become less likely to mean going away somewhere for some rest and relaxation, but instead, taking a break from paying the monthly bills, mortgages and credit card repayments.

Some companies have scaled back their operations, while others closed down all together, resulting in millions joining the unemployment statistics. *The Economist* believes the overall global economic toll to be incalculable. However, it suggests the figure will be in the order of $10.3 trillion in forgone GDP over 2020-2021 (*The Economist*, 2021).

Marketing events, exhibitions and trade expos designed to showcase companies' products and services have also found themselves falling foul of the pandemic. The list is extensive and varied from cars and commercial vehicles, pleasure boats, wedding services, tourism and travel, business-to-business marketing, security services, etc. The premier Dutch flower gardens at Keukenhof, an indispensable shop window for local bulb growers, can attract as many as 1.5 million visitors to see the 7 million spring flowers. In 2020, the garden was closed, although a virtual tour was organised by the promoters and posted on YouTube. The internationally renowned Crufts dog show, which attracts as many as 22,000 dogs each year, just managed to beat the UK lockdown.

In some countries, religious gatherings have been severely restricted or even banned altogether, while the number of people permitted to attend funerals has been strictly curtailed. The annual Hajj pilgrimage performed in Saudi Arabia by Muslims from around the world was dramatically scaled back because of the pandemic. Normally around 2 million pilgrims would travel to Mecca, but numbers have been restricted to as few as 10,000 and attendance qualification required that all participants had to reside within the Kingdom.

1: Introduction

Here in the UK, the lockdown has been far less draconian than the measures applied in some other countries. One consequence of intended lockdowns being announced, appears to have been panic buying around the world, with certain food types and hygiene products being the preference. Also, within the UK, government public information campaigns reminded everyone to wash their hands, wear a face mask and observe social distancing protocols. All very sensible advice. However, we must remember that face masks will put deaf people reliant on lip reading at a distinct disadvantage. Moreover, the visually impaired may find it difficult to comply with social distancing regulations, especially as guide dogs are unlikely to have been trained to manage these situations.

We must not forget the stress that people will have experienced due to their respective government's lockdowns by staying at home for most, if not all, the time. The personal impact across the world has been extensive, with many tragic stories unfolding. Although there are those who have found the situation far from easy, there are stories of some people being very happy about being locked down who have made good use of their time.

Across much of the world, people have been compliant in following their respective government's directives, although there have been some examples of civil disorder as people have protested against these measures. What concerns me is that these so far isolated incidents could become more widespread if the pandemic continues for an extended period. There is already talk of the expectation of post-traumatic stress disorder (PTSD) developing among frontline health workers, paramedics and care home workers, along with food store employees, the police, etc. These are the people on the front line who put their personal safety at risk every day.

My own personal observations have also led me to conclude that, despite the rising case numbers and death counts, there are some people who are just not taking the situation seriously. Others, like the ostrich with its head buried in the sand, seem to be in total denial about what is really happening.

Did business continuity management make a difference?

The twentieth century witnessed three influenza pandemics – Asian flu (1957-1958), Hong Kong flu (1968-1969) and Spanish flu (1918-1919). The deadliest of these outbreaks was the latter, which killed an estimated 50 million people worldwide. Indeed, this was more than the total number of victims claimed by World War I.

The first two of these twentieth-century pandemics occurred even before the existence of anything that could have been remotely referred to as business continuity. The third happened in the late 1960s, just as organisations were beginning to appreciate the need for IT disaster recovery, the forerunner to business continuity management (BCM). Even so, at that time there were no yardsticks or best-practice guidelines to refer to, until the arrival of the business continuity industry standards. These included the BCI's Good Practice Guidelines, PAS 56, BS 25999 and, in 2012, ISO 22301. Finally, over 40 years after the Hong Kong flu, BCM had come of age, thereby providing organisations with a framework to help build and improve their resilience.

Ironically, while public health pandemic planning had previously been very reactive, in 1976 in the US, authorities initiated efforts in order to be better prepared for future pandemics. In this respect, the concept of pandemic planning has been a couple of decades ahead of the evolution of business continuity.

It was while the Hong Kong flu was spreading across the world that so too was information technology. Third generation computers, such as the IBM System/360 and the ICL 1900 series were beginning to oil the wheels of commerce. Moving onto the twenty-first century, surveys and horizon reports often point to ICT failure, along with cyberattacks, as being among the most common cause of business interruption. Even so, during a pandemic, ICT can now often be the solution rather than the cause of the problem, as explored in section 7.4. This has certainly been the case with COVID-19. After all, this is one type of virus that computer systems are not susceptible to, even if the IT department staff are.

There is no doubt in my mind that anyone involved in those early days of business continuity was a pioneer – they were simply trailblazing! But with that outbreak of Hong Kong flu being more than 50 years ago, before COVID-19 took the world by storm, there were very few individuals left in the business world who had any first-hand experience of managing a business through a pandemic. Even so, I believe that organisations that have seriously embraced BCM, in addition to preparing pandemic contingency plans, will have only helped to build themselves a more resilient enterprise. Moreover, their chance of coming out intact on the other side of the pandemic can only have been improved by these actions.

CHAPTER 2: WHAT EXACTLY IS A PANDEMIC?

Historically, pandemics can be traced back many centuries. A simple definition that has been used to describe them is "*a contagion that has gone global*". Although a pandemic can also affect the animal and bird populations, this book focuses on the human-to-human spread of potentially fatal contagions.

The WHO tells us that this worldwide spread of a novel disease will initially have no vaccines or known cures available, and neither will people have any immunity. Generally, the most common cause of pandemics has been influenza, although in the past 75 years, almost 400 new infectious diseases have been discovered. Since 1971, scientists have identified 25 new pathogens for which we have no vaccines and no treatment, although most have not developed into a pandemic (Quick, 2018, p 41).

Influenza in its various viral forms certainly deserves more than just a passing mention in the history of pandemics. Most notable is the 1918-1919 Spanish influenza outbreak, which alone is estimated to have killed more than 50 million. History has taught us that we can expect an average of three influenza pandemics each century.

In the Middle Ages, caused by the *Yersinia pestis* bacteria, the **bubonic plague,** or Black Death as it became known, killed close to 20% of the global population. It ran from 1347-1351, and resulted in an estimated 75 million fatalities out of a world population of 450 million. Localised plague outbreaks do still occur in various parts of the world, but they are generally controlled by antibiotics.

One exception is **HIV/AIDS,** which was identified around 1980 and has killed almost 40 million in the four decades since its discovery. It is estimated that as many people, primarily in sub-Saharan Africa, are also living with the disease. The origin of HIV/AIDS has been traced back to Cameroon in Africa, as early as 1910. The disease had been in existence for around 50 years before it finally exploded onto the global scene. There is still no vaccine or known cure, but it is now treatable by using what is known as antiretroviral medication.

Perhaps also worthy of mention, although maybe not in the same league as the aforementioned pandemic causes, since first spreading from its origin in the Indian sub-continent around 200 years ago, over an extended period **cholera** has also killed millions. The WHO has estimated an annual case diagnosis of up to five million, with as many as 120,000 associated deaths. Cholera is treatable and a combination of rehydration and antibiotics are usually prescribed. However, if left untreated, cholera can kill in a matter of hours.

"The Covid-19 pandemic has made clear that our health is inextricably tied to larger environmental issues. Increased population density, global travel, deforestation, large-scale farming and melting of the permafrost has disrupted animal habitats, bringing them in closer contact to humans. This has raised the risk of more frequent zoonotic disease outbreaks and therefore a higher potential for another pandemic."

(Morrin, 2020)

In 2020, the threat from the novel virus subsequently named SARS-CoV-2 appeared. We now know that this causes the potentially fatal disease that was named COVID-19.

2: What exactly is a pandemic?

Depending upon the nature of a contagion, it can be transmitted from human to human in any one of a number of ways, including:

- **Airborne infection** – usually caused by organisms that can survive suspended in the air for long periods.
- **Droplet infection** – occurs usually from the droplets generated by coughing or sneezing.
- **Vector-borne** – e.g. carried by mosquitoes, fleas, mites, ticks.
- **Direct contact infection** – can result from skin-to-skin contact or exposure to contaminated body fluids.
- **Indirect contact infection** – can occur by touching a contaminated surface (e.g. door handles, handrails or elevator call buttons).

2.1 Known diseases that could cause a pandemic

The WHO has listed a number of diseases on its website that it believes have the potential to develop into epidemics and pandemics. Some of those listed already have achieved epidemic or pandemic status, and their names will no doubt be familiar to readers. Our business continuity and pandemic response plans should be prepared and maintained with these in mind.

It is also worth noting that, over time, the WHO will keep that list updated to reflect any emerging infectious diseases, such as COVID-19, as and when they are identified. In the meantime, I have broken these particular threats that we are facing into three sections. Those that are:

1. Capable of causing a global pandemic.
2. Capable of causing devastating regional epidemics.

3. Those that have the potential to be used in the pursuit of biological warfare and bioterrorism, to which section 2.2 has been devoted.

2.1.1 Global pandemic contenders

These include respiratory viruses, such as pandemic influenza, coronaviruses (between 2002-2019 there have been three), Nipah virus and a small number of others, including as yet unidentified emerging infectious diseases.[1]

2.1.2 Devastating regional epidemic candidates

This would typically include Ebola, Zika, Yellow Fever and Dengue.[2]

2.2 Biological warfare and terrorism

Although many politicians and scientists have pointed at a Wuhan wet market as the source of the coronavirus, other theories understandably serve to contradict. One such alternative relates to biological warfare or bioterrorism. Before discussing the origin of the virus in more detail in chapter 3, I wanted to consider the implications and history of such a theory.

Also known as germ warfare, the concept of biological warfare has been around for at least three millennia, and examples can be traced back to the fourteenth century BC (Barras & Greub, 2014). There is a distinction to be made between biological warfare and bioterrorism. The former would usually constitute a country-on-country attack, while

---

[1] Ebola, AIDS, Zika and SARS were all unknown infectious diseases before they exploded onto the scene.
[2] Some, but not all of which, now have safe, effective vaccines.

the latter would be performed by a terrorist group that is likely to be working to a different agenda.

One biological weapon that has been used in a number of terrorist attacks is anthrax, although, to date, it has only been used in very small quantities. Even so, concern remains over the potential long-term effects of a large-scale anthrax terrorist attack on a metropolitan area. This is presumed likely to be more devastating than a nuclear attack.

During World War II, the British tested the effectiveness of anthrax on the Scottish island of Gruinard. It was concluded that had, for example, Berlin been bombed with anthrax-based biological weapons, it would still have been uninhabitable at least 30 years later (Cole, 1988). By comparison, the rebuilding of Hiroshima after the dropping of the first atomic bomb in 1945, started within four years (Blackford, 2007). Estimated casualties from a mass bioterrorism attack using agents, such as anthrax, smallpox or plague vary considerably from half a million to 30 million (Clark, 2007) and (Richardson, et al., 2007).

In the 1970s, the United Nations initiated the Biological Weapons Convention (BWC), which came into force in 1975. This BWC was better known as the Convention on the Prohibition of the Development, Production and Stockpiling of Bacteriological (Biological) and Toxin Weapons and on their Destruction (United Nations, 2017). However, this did not really address any ambiguities, doubts or suspicions that countries may have harboured regarding other countries biological warfare capabilities and their subsequent compliance with the BWC.

"Only 16 countries plus Taiwan have had or are currently suspected of having biological weapons programs: Canada, China, Cuba, France, Germany,

2: What exactly is a pandemic?

Iran, Iraq, Israel, Japan, Libya, North Korea, Russia, South Africa, Syria, the United Kingdom and the United States.

There is widespread consensus against the possession and use of biological weapons. Most countries are party to the Biological and Toxin Weapon Convention, but there is no way to know whether countries are complying with their commitments."

(NTI, 2015)

Regardless of whether a biological warfare or terrorist attack was launched on a specific target using a biological agent, such as anthrax, apart from perhaps the scale of the attack, the end result would be the same. For the purpose of this chapter, the terms biological warfare, germ warfare and bioterrorism should be considered as interchangeable.

"Bioterrorism is the deliberate release of viruses, bacteria, or other agents used to cause illness or death in people, animals and plants. They (the virus and bacteria, etc.) are typically found in nature."

(Costgliola & Quaqliata, 2008, p 7)

Biological terrorism is something that has captured the imagination of television and movie producers. In the BBC series 'Spooks', Season Six, Episode One, saw MI5 operatives racing to stop a member of a rogue government unleashing a bio-weapon in the UK. Similarly, the third season of the US production of '24', followed the exploits of Jack Bauer and the fictitious Counter Terrorism Unit, while the team attempted to prevent the release of a deadly virus in Los Angeles. Various movies followed the bio-terrorism theme, the first of which I remember seeing was entitled 'The

Satan Bug', which is just one of several from that genre now listed on IMDb.

Terrorism that attacks a target using weapons of mass destruction (WMD) as its modus operandi, is still in its infancy, with few examples recorded to date of actual incidents. Such an attack would involve chemical, biological, radiological or nuclear (CBRN) based weapons. However, within the UK, the country's risk register specifies that a small-scale WMD attack, which could include a bioterrorism attack, is considered to have a 'medium' probability over the next five years. Moreover, the corresponding relative impact is also recorded as 'medium'.

2.2.1 Historical use of biological weapons

There is evidence of Russia allegedly targeting defected former KGB officers on UK soil. Using the chemical nerve agent, Novichok, Sergei Skripal was targeted in 2018. In 2006, the lethal radiological agent polonium-210 was used to kill Alexander Litvinenko. Moreover, while working in London, dissident Bulgarian Georgi Markov was also assassinated, allegedly by his country's security services. A micro engineered pellet containing ricin that was fired into his leg from an umbrella. Of these three state-enacted examples, only the use of ricin was actually a biological attack.

Statistically, the use of WMD by terrorists has averaged eight per annum globally since 1970. To date, if the single terrorist objective was mass casualties, then a combined total of 640 fatalities over that 50 year period (>13 per annum) does not represent a major success. The bomb and bullet still remain much more accessible to terrorists than WMDs, although an increase in the use of knives and vehicle-ramming attacks has certainly been noted.

The UK's National Counter Terrorism Security Office (NaCTSO) position on the threat of WMD-related terrorist attacks is:

> *"The likelihood of a Chemical, Biological or Radiological attack remains low, largely due to the difficulty of obtaining the materials and the complexity of using them effectively."*
> (Clark, 2012)

However, as an aside, perhaps it is worth noting that NaCTSO makes no such similar claim about nuclear weapons. UK security services endorse the NaCTSO view, and its website says of chemical, biological and radiological devices:

> *"To date, no such attacks have taken place in the UK. Alternative methods of attack, such as explosive devices, are more reliable, safer and easier for terrorists to acquire or use. Nevertheless, it is possible that Al Qaida, ISIL or other terrorist groups may seek to use chemical, biological or radiological material against the West."*

(MI5, 2020)

To date, chemical weapon attacks appear to have been terrorists' preferred WMD. Since 1974, there have been close to 400 WMD terrorist attacks chronicled, although, to date, no nuclear attacks have been documented. Fatalities have resulted from the chemical and biological but none from radiological terrorism (US Department of Homeland Security based at the University of Maryland, 2019).

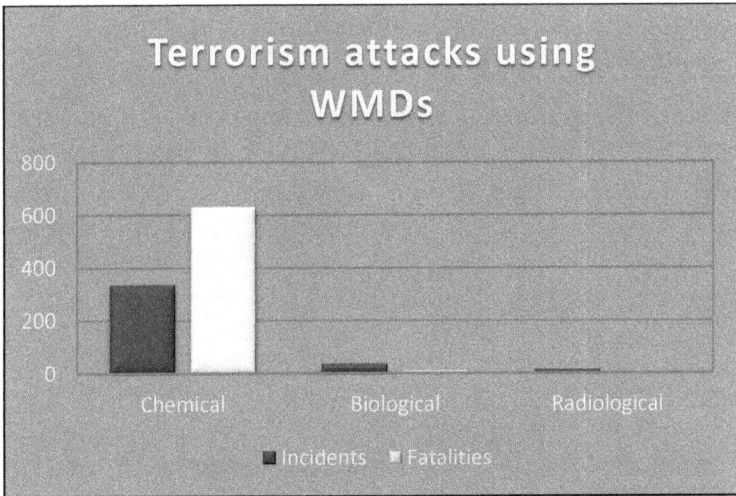

Figure 1: CBRN terrorist attacks from 1974-2018

Anthrax is just one of several lethal biological agents. Its use by terrorists immediately following the 9/11 Twin Towers terrorist attack in eight separate incidents in the US, killing six, accentuated the existence of a bioterrorism threat (Brett, 2003). Anthrax can be found in nature and is common in livestock that can pass it to humans. However, unlike other biological agents, anthrax cannot be passed from human to human. To be effective, the victim must inhale or ingest anthrax spores, or an open wound be contaminated.

The UK National Risk Register (NRR) for 2017, 2015 and 2012, while recognising the threat, only posted a threat rating of 'medium' for small-scale CBRN attack and 'medium-low' for a large-scale CBRN attack. However, the more recently published 2020 UK NRR has split the CBRN threat into 'small', 'medium' and 'large' CBRN attacks. Furthermore, while the 'small' and 'medium' attacks have been classified as 'medium-low', the large-scale attack has been upgraded to 'medium'. The 2020 version is available from:

www.gov.uk/government/publications/national-risk-register-2020.

Since 1981, several examples of bioterrorism using anthrax have been recorded in the US. In addition, there have also been cases where ricin, botulinum, salmonella and HIV/AIDS were used. While the majority of incidents occurred in the US, Israel and Japan were also targeted (US Department of Homeland Security based at the University of Maryland, 2019).

An alternative bioterrorism weapon is ricin, which is a naturally occurring toxin extracted from castor beans. In November 2011, the FBI announced the arrest of four US citizens who planned to manufacture ricin and expose other US citizens to the deadly toxin (Federal Bureau of Investigation, 2011).

Palestinian suicide bombers have been known to regularly combine the traditional use of explosives with biological and chemical agents (Cole, 2007). AIDS-contaminated blood, rat poison and hydrogen cyanide have been used to maximise the effect of the terrorist acts. This puts not only any survivors of the blast at greater risk, but also first responders, too. Cole also highlights the psychological effects generated by the biological anthrax attacks in the US in 2001, demonstrating that the fear factor associated with this type of terrorist weapon is substantial.

More recently, concern was expressed in Forbes during 2014, regarding the bioterrorism intentions of the so-called Islamic State using the Ebola virus. Either a lone wolf or groups infected by the Ebola virus would act as carriers of the contagion:

2: What exactly is a pandemic?

"ISIS may already be thinking of using Ebola as a low-tech weapon of bio-terror, says a national security expert, who notes that the "Islamic State of Iraq and Syria" and terror groups like it wouldn't even have to weaponize the virus to attempt to wreak strategic global infection."

(Dorminey, 2014)

Although ISIS has since lost some of its power base in Syria and Iraq, it would be premature to dismiss its presence as a terrorist threat.

Writing in *Scientific American*, also in 2014, Dina Fine Maron posed the question: "Weaponized Ebola: Is it really a bioterror threat? What would it take to hijack the virus in West Africa and turn it into a bioterror agent elsewhere?" This train of thought was further supported in 2015 when it was reported that the UK's top-secret military research unit at Porton Down had been assessing the use of Ebola as a bioweapon.

"The heavily redacted document, which has been released under the Freedom of Information Act, reveals that the unit was asked last October to provide 'guidance on the feasibility and potential impact of a non-state actor exploiting the Ebola outbreak in West Africa for bioterrorism'."

(Clark, 2016, p 245)

2.2.2 Classification of biological agents

The Centre for Disease Control (CDC) has created a set of criteria for categorising biological agents. They are grouped into categories A, B or C based on the ease of transmission, severity of morbidity and mortality, plus the likelihood of use.

2: What exactly is a pandemic?

Agents can be delivered via food or water, and in some cases by airborne transmission. While the majority of the agents listed may result in the death of anyone being exposed, some, such as smallpox, are contagious, while others, such as anthrax, are not.

One has to keep in mind that if a biological attack uses an agent that is a contagion, it may well be difficult to control, and any subsequent infection proliferation could develop into a pandemic. If this attack is state sponsored, one can only assume that the originating state not only has the biological weapon capability, but also a stockpile of vaccines and appropriate medications (e.g. antivirals, antibiotics, etc.) that would be used to protect its own citizens.

The highest threat level in the CDC's criterion, Category 'A', contains the biological agents anthrax, botulinum toxin and ricin, which have already proved to be terrorist weapons of choice. Also included in this category is the Plague (*Yersinia pestis*), Smallpox (variola major), plus viral haemorrhagic fevers, such as Ebola (CDC, 2018).

CHAPTER 3: AND THE ORIGIN OF THE CORONAVIRUS WAS...

So, where did this coronavirus pandemic really originate?

"A leak from a laboratory, a scientist doing field work, or a hunter infected in the wild?"

(Gracie, 2020)

Initially, it appeared that Wuhan was Ground Zero for the coronavirus. The official Chinese explanation linked the outbreak to the Huanan wet market in Wuhan, where meat, poultry and seafood were sold alongside live animals. However, it wasn't very long before conspiracy theories started to circulate, often supported by nothing more than anecdotal evidence.

State-sponsored bio-terrorism has been one of the more popular hypotheses I have come across. It was, after all, only two years earlier that the indiscriminate attempted poisoning of Russians Sergei and Yulia Skripal happened in Salisbury, UK. The use of the deadly nerve agent, Novichok, necessitated some areas of the city being locked down. Meticulous decontamination was essential, a process that took 12 months, while requiring the expertise of up to 800 military personnel. The decontamination of just the Skripal's former home took 13,000 man-hours to complete (Forces Net, 2019).

Despite the use of a WMD, the Salisbury episode was actually conducted using a chemical rather than a biological weapon. There is, however, very compelling and credible evidence associating the event with the state-enacted terrorism theory. It is perhaps also worth reiterating that between 1974-2018, non-state adversaries conducted as many as 336 terrorist attacks using chemical weapons and 35[3] using biological-based weapons (START, 2019). Anthrax, botulinum toxins and ricin were listed among the biological agents of choice. So, could SARS-CoV-2 be a weaponised biological agent?

"Is China the hero or the villain of this pandemic?"
(Sacker, 2020)

There is both trustworthy plus unsubstantiated voluminous quantities of information in the public domain that challenges the Chinese version of events. There does seem little doubt that Wuhan is where the coronavirus burst onto the world stage. But, just maybe China has been accused of a 'crime' it did not actually commit and Wuhan was a victim rather than the miscreant. For example, we now know that HIV/AIDS had been around for more than 60 years before it made its grand entrance when it exploded onto a totally unprepared world in the 1980s.

I have also been made aware of several people from various parts of the world who claim to have experienced COVID-19-like symptoms long before the virus even had a name. This alone suggests that the coronavirus may have been in circulation well before the Wuhan outbreak. Relating to his own experience, BBC journalist Fergus Walsh said:

"My experience of testing positive for coronavirus antibodies clearly struck a nerve. Two weeks ago I wrote that I'd had no recent symptoms but dismissed a

---

[3] 20 September 2020, it was reported that a package containing ricin addressed to former President Trump had been intercepted before reaching the White House (Feuer, 2020).

bout of pneumonia in January because it was weeks before the first confirmed cases of Covid-19 in the UK."

(Walsh, 2020)

In fact, the *International Journal of Antimicrobial Agents* carried a report that claimed that "*SARS-CoV-2 was already spreading in France in late December 2019*". (Deslandes, et al., 2020)

Moreover, an unsubstantiated report published by the *South China Morning Post* (SCMP), a Hong Kong-based publication, claimed that China's first confirmed COVID-19 case had been traced back to 17 November 2019. This firmly contradicts the Wuhan fish market story (Ma, 2020). The SCMP report also alleged that Chinese authorities had further identified at least 266 coronavirus cases in 2019.

"*A significant proportion of undiagnosed and asymptomatic carriers shed SARS-CoV-2 in stool[s].*"

(Chavarria-Miró, et al., 2020)

Although it may have initially been benign, as the '*Chavarria et al.*' quote implies, the reality is that the virus may have been around far longer than originally thought. *Reuters* carried the report of the Spanish study conducted by the University of Barcelona that goes some way to substantiating this possibility. The study claimed that traces of the coronavirus were apparently found in samples of local sewage as early as March 2019. This was nine months before the Wuhan outbreak (Allen & Landauro, 2020).

Several countries have since adopted wastewater testing to check for the presence of coronavirus in the wider population, in addition to searching for the existence of virus variants. By May 2021, in the UK, a sewage testing programme covered approximately two-thirds of England's 56 million population.

Researchers from the University of Sienna, Italy, engaged in a lung cancer screening trial, detected SARS-CoV-2 antibodies in 111 of the 959 participants. Approximately 14% were detected from blood samples taken in September 2019, five months before Italy's first official case (Apolone, et al., 2020).

More recently, when the world was alerted to the coronavirus Omicron variant in November 2021, evidence also emerged that it was in global circulation for weeks if not months beforehand (Brean, 2021).

"A lie gets halfway around the world before the truth has a chance to get its pants on."

(Winston Churchill)

They can of course go by different names, but misinformation, half-truths, falsehoods, rumours, fake news and conspiracy theories are nothing new. The practice has been around for centuries, and it became very apparent during the 2002-2003 SARS and the 2014-2016 Ebola outbreaks, not to mention the 9/11 and 7/7 terrorist attacks on the US and the UK respectively. Today, in fact, some people make a great deal of money in peddling COVID-19 conspiracy theories and anti-vaccination misinformation.

When the Spanish influenza pandemic spread across the world as the First World War was drawing to a close, with radio broadcasting still in its infancy, the primary source of information was through newspapers. 100 years on, the media is hardly recognisable, with multiple communication channels now available and the capability of information circumnavigating the planet in a matter of seconds. The advent of social media has undoubtedly aided and abetted the spread of misinformation.

We are certainly seeing plenty of contributions from what I would call the disciples of modern *'flat earth societies'* promoting their unconventional and often controversial pandemic theories. One article I came across claimed that modern flat earth societies had supporters all around the globe, which seems like a bit of an oxymoron to me. Having been censored by mainstream social media platforms, accused of distributing fake news, some have since relocated onto independent distributed server platforms that are subsidised by donations and crowd funding.

One rather 'tongue-in-cheek' social media post about the pandemic that caught my eye seemed very much like a frustrated plea about who and what to believe.

The author began by acknowledging the multitude of trained doctors, nurses, virologists, epidemiologists, and researchers who have been continually warning us about the dangers of COVID-19. However, he then proceeded to inform readers that he had become confused by the plethora of pop-up experts and their alternative views that suddenly appeared alongside the pandemic. Many have expressed their often controversial 'expert' opinions, when in reality they had quite possibly struggled to attain their basic science grades at school.

Personally, I think this author makes a very valid point. We do seem to have had rather a lot of pop-up pandemic and pseudo-scientific experts appear on the scene since COVID-19's began its march across the planet.

There have also been conspiracy theories circulating about the so-called *'vaccine agenda'*. This has prompted social media platforms to act to either prevent their proliferation or to add warnings that the content contains 'false or misleading information'. Social media organisations were heavily criticised after appearing to be helpless in preventing the constant flow of fake news during the US 2016 presidential election. In the UK, GCHQ, part of the country's security services, has been conducting an offensive cyber operation to disrupt anti-vaccine propaganda allegedly being spread by hostile states. (Fisher & Smyth, 2020). Published by *The Lancet, Correcting COVID-19 vaccination misinformation,* also makes its own contribution towards addressing what is seen as a growing body of misinformation about these vaccines (Lancet, 2021).

Oh, and we must not forget the 5G conspiracy theory that it's not really a virus we are dealing with but the radiation from 5G transmissions. Despite major health organisations categorically stating that 5G is safe, this conspiracy theory continues to persist.

To add to the mix, I have regularly come across other conspiracy theory reports that I believe are, shall we say, of dubious origin. Yet, despite the supposedly best efforts of the various social media platforms to supress and remove fake news, they still seem to proliferate. In some instances, as fast as controversial videos are removed from Facebook, Twitter and YouTube, users are uploading the clips again. Those of us who have been fortunate enough to have attended university, if we learned nothing else, it should have been to validate our sources of information when researching. I wish more people would do the same before just instinctively hitting the 'share' or 'retweet' buttons.

BBC specialist disinformation reporter, Marianna Spring, maintains that videos posted on YouTube by fringe groups with extreme ideas are influencing users' views. The pandemic has pushed misinformation to new levels, with false reports about the coronavirus that are often finding a much larger audience than trusted sources.

"A man who would like to remain anonymous got in touch with us [the BBC] after his Mother decided to go along to a demonstration in London. It was promoting some of the more popular conspiracy theories mainly seen online. She was first taken along by conspiracy theories on YouTube and has now been radicalised. It is so hard to have a normal conversation with her now."

(Spring, 2020)

I have also found it annoying, to say the least, after having watched a pandemic-related press conference, to then see a subsequent associated media report mis-quoting or being 'economical' with the truth, all in the interest of politicising or sensationalising the story. While I understand this tactic is intended to sell more newspapers or attract readers to a website in an attempt to maximise affiliate marketing revenues, I still find it an unethical practice.

"Our greatest enemy right now is not the virus itself. It's fear, rumours and stigma. And our greatest assets are facts, reason and solidarity."

(Tedros Adhanom Ghebreyesus, Director General of the WHO, 28 February 2020)

Tedros Adhanom Ghebreyesus added that the world was not just fighting a pandemic, it was also fighting what he referred to as an 'infodemic'. In attempting to counter rumours and misinformation, the WHO has a team of 'myth busters' working with social media platforms to counter the spread of what they classify as fake news. Some individuals who have expressed alternative opinions contrary to the mainstream pandemic viewpoint have subsequently found themselves censored by the behemoth social media platforms.

A dubious information source would typically display one or more of the following traits: an extreme bias, the systematic endorsement of propaganda or conspiracies, little or no reference to credible sources of information, a complete lack of transparency and/or is fake news. The United Nations (UN) advises that people consider the Five 'W's before they share an online post:

1. WHO made the post?
2. WHAT is the source of the information?
3. WHERE did it come from?
4. WHY are you sharing it?
5. WHEN was it published?

The UN's message is simple: #TakeCareBeforeYouShare. Further information about this programme is provided via the article "5 ways the UN is fighting infodemic of misinformation" (United Nations, 2020).

One noticeable characteristic of the information age is the demand for quality reliable news, which has soared in recent times. Moreover, dependable and trusted news outlets have become a precious commodity. So, what sources of information can we actually trust? I have taken a look at several surveys conducted in the US about which are the most trusted and least trusted sources of news. As *Business Insider* remarked:

> "*The most trusted news outlets in America, according to a new study from Pew Research Center, are actually British.*"

The Economist and the BBC consistently appear at the top of survey results. Also referring to the Pew Research Center survey, the MediaPost added:

> *"The U.S. lacks a single news source that people trust."*

In the UK, the Office of Communications (Ofcom) is the government-approved regulatory and competition authority for broadcasting, telecommunications and postal industries. In its 2020 News Consumption Report for the UK, it lists the BBC News TV channel and website as the primary 'go to' information source.

But, surely there must be other reliable information sources than just the BBC or *The Economist*? Well yes, there are, and while there are a number of short courses available to help people tell the fake from the genuine news article, there are some other checks that you can do to help make an informed decision about an article's credibility. For example:

- Is a story carried by multiple websites? While this does not guarantee its accuracy, it is an encouraging indication.
- Does the website that is posting a particular story have a reputation for validating its information sources (e.g. the BBC, etc.)?
- How old is the story? We are learning more about COVID-19 almost every day that passes, so could the information on a website have been superseded?
- If the website is trying to sell you something, be suspicious, especially if it's *Dr John's Magical COVID cure* or *Big Chief Dodgy Deal's miracle snake oil*. There is also a subtle sales ploy know as *'framing'*, which might ask a question, such as *"have you tried the new*

amazing XYZ supplements?" Caveat Emptor – buyer beware!!

- If the website has a suffix of .GOV or .ORG, it will be a government or a not-for-profit website and is likely to be more reliable.
- Similarly, if the suffix is .AC (in the UK), .EDN (US) or .EDN.AU (Australia), these are examples of academic institutions, and the information is also much more likely to be credible. There will, of course, be many other credible academic institutions out there that can also be taken seriously.

"Everything we hear is an opinion, not a fact. Everything we see is a perspective, not the truth."

(Marcus Aurelius)

In January 2021, the WHO began investigating the virus's origins in Wuhan. Since the city was initially declared as 'Ground Zero' for the COVID-19 outbreak, China appears to have been caught holding a smoking gun. But, with evidence emerging of the SARS-CoV-2 virus being present in at least three European countries before the Wuhan outbreak, perhaps the WHO will need to consider asking, '*Who actually pulled the trigger?*' A 120-page report was subsequently published and although it considered the possibility of a laboratory accident as being one of the potential causes of the pandemic, it concluded that it was extremely unlikely (WHO, 2021). However, several countries, including the US and the UK, have sharply criticised the report, implicitly accusing China of *"withholding access to complete, original data and samples"* (Beaumont, 2021).

3: And the origin of the coronavirus was...

2021 ushered in a change of administration in the White House. The incoming President Biden ordered that efforts to establish the origin of the virus should be intensified, including a re-examination of the theory that it originated from a Chinese laboratory. Concern had also been independently raised that research scientists in China were carrying out unsafe research activities on SARS-CoV-like novel viruses. In one way or another, they did not take the appropriate actions to work safely with SARS-CoV-2 or a precursor virus (Bostickson & Ghannam, 2021).

Moreover, in their paper entitled *A Reconstructed Historical Aetiology of the SARS-Coronavirus-2 Spike*, Sørensen et al., claim that the SARS-CoV-2 virus has no credible natural ancestor. They further argue that it is highly likely that this coronavirus was actually the creation of a Chinese laboratory (Sørensen et. al, 2021).

Survivors (1975-1977) was a television series about the aftermath of a deadly plague. The opening sequence establishes that the plague originated in a laboratory in the Far East and was accidentally released after a beaker was dropped. Commercial aviation helped the flu-like disease spread quickly around the world and wipe out 99.98% of humanity. The series focuses on a community of survivors that struggle to stay alive in the wake of this global pandemic More information about the series can be found at IMDb.

So, to conclude my thoughts on the contents of this chapter, whilst I do acknowledge their existence, despite my rant, I am sorry if I am now going to disappoint. Fascinating though some of these claims and counter-claims may be, in writing this book, it is not my intent to present any further arguments that either support or refute their rationale. Indeed, I have elected to leave that to the conspiracy theorists, who will no doubt be writing their own versions of what, where, when and how. Meanwhile, I intend to focus on the here and now of dealing with COVID-19, and whatever other future nasty contagions we have the dubious pleasure of anticipating.

CHAPTER 4: WHY DID NOBODY WARN US?

"Diseases know no boundaries. They threaten us all."
Former US President Clinton, 1996 (WP, 2020)

The truth is, we had been warned – on numerous occasions and from several different sources. I guess maybe not many people were listening in either government or business circles around the world. Very few people in the workplace today will have lived through a serious pandemic. Consequently, I believe the truth is that before the SARS-CoV-2 virus arrived, many were living in a state of ignorance or denial.

"At some point, we are likely to face another pandemic."

George W Bush, 1 November 2005 (WP, 2020)

Long before he became US President, Barack Obama was endeavouring to raise the profile of the pandemic threat. In 2005 he said:

"When we think of the major threats to our national security, the first to come to mind are nuclear proliferation, rogue states and global terrorism.

But another kind of threat lurks beyond our shores, one from nature, not humans – an avian flu pandemic. An outbreak could cause millions of deaths, destabilize Southeast Asia (its likely place of origin), and threaten the security of governments around the world."

Barack Obama, 2005 (McLeigh, 2017)

4: Why did nobody warn us?

Two years earlier, the speed at which SARS had proliferated across 26 countries should have started alarm bells ringing. Furthermore, in 2012, a second emerging and potentially fatal coronavirus, MERS, ought to have complemented any cacophony that SARS had managed to create. However, it seems that only some of those countries in Asia that had found themselves caught in the 'crosshairs' of SARS and MERS actually sat up and took notice.

In 2005, *The New York Times* published an article jointly written by Barack Obama and Richard Lugar in which they quoted Dr Julie L Gerberding. She was, at the time, the Director for the Centers for Disease Control and Prevention. In referring to the possibility of an avian flu identified as H5N1 spreading from South East Asia, Dr Gerberding said:

"A killer flu could spread around the world in days, crippling economies in Southeast Asia and elsewhere. From a public health standpoint, Dr. Gerberding said, an avian flu outbreak is "the most important threat that we are facing right now."." (Obama & Lugar, 2005)

Originally identified in 1976, the 2014-2016 West Africa Ebola outbreak was contained. This was thanks to thousands of selfless health workers. A global spread of the disease was avoided, but not before more than 11,000 had died. It was while this outbreak was in full flight in 2015 that Bill Gates gave the TED talk entitled *"The next outbreak? We're not ready"*. Did no one see and react to this talk? According to the TED website, around 43 million did view the recording, while the YouTube posting of the talk has at this time of writing, logged a further 36 million views. So, did no one take Bill Gate's warning seriously?

Other warnings have come and gone, and have been largely ignored, except perhaps by the medical profession, which knows only too well the health implications of a severe pandemic.

4.1 The coronavirus family

Coronavirus was first discovered by the Scottish virologist, Dr June Almeida, in her laboratory at St Thomas' Hospital, London in 1964. The virus owes its name to the crown or halo that surrounds it, which Almeida observed through an electron microscope (Brocklehurst, 2020).

The CDC has listed seven coronaviruses that can infect humans, although four, 229E, NL63, OC43 and HKU1 only result in relatively mild symptoms. However, the remaining three SARS-CoV, MERS-CoV and SARS-CoV-2 can be fatal to humans and have all been identified since the start of the new millennium (CDC, 2020).

Although COVID-19 has spread globally, SARS and MERS only reached 26 and 27 countries respectively. Their mortality rates also differ, with MERS measured at 34.4%, SARS at 9.50% and COVID-19 the lowest of the three coronaviruses at 5.06%.

Figure 2[4] provides a snapshot comparison of these three coronaviruses, although, at the time of writing, the world was still very much in the clutches of the COVID-19 disease.

---

[4] The number of cases, fatalities and mortality statistics quoted for SARS, MERS and COVID-19 were as of 31st December 2021.

Coronavirus name	Name of associated disease	Emerged	Cases	Deaths
SARS-CoV	Severe Acute Respiratory Syndrome (SARS)	2002	8,098	774
MERS-CoV	Middle East Respiratory Syndrome (MERS)	2012	2,494	858
SARS-CoV-2	COVID-19	2019	288, 599, 268	5,454,998

Figure 2: SARS, MERS and COVID-19 statistical comparison

The three conditions present similar symptoms, although COVID-19 can affect different people in different ways. Some will be asymptomatic, but most infected people will develop mild to moderate illness and recover without hospitalisation. Those typically presented symptoms might include, although are by no means limited to, fever, dry cough, tiredness and breathing difficulties. As we have learned more about COVID-19, more symptoms have been identified. For an up to date list, please refer to a credible source, such as the WHO, CDC or your national disease control centre, such as Public Health England, ECDC, China CDC and African CDC, etc.

For some people, COVID-19 results in symptoms that last for weeks or even months after the infection has gone. Often referred to as post-COVID-19 or 'long COVID', the typical symptoms are not dissimilar to COVID-19 itself. As in the previous paragraph, for an up to date list of these symptoms, please refer to one of these reliable sources.

What the world cannot afford to overlook, is the frequency with which these potentially fatal coronaviruses have appeared since the arrival of the new millennium. Ten years between SARS and MERS, followed by seven years between MERS and COVID-19. Does that mean that we can expect another coronavirus to appear on the scene during the current decade?

4.1.1 Severe Acute Respiratory Syndrome (SARS)

"Severe Acute Respiratory Syndrome (SARS) is the first new disease to show the damage possible in a globalized world."

(Mary Kay Kindhauser, WHO, 2003), (Clark, 2016, p 43)

4: Why did nobody warn us?

The virus, SARS-CoV, which causes the severe acute respiratory syndrome, was the first novel virus and wake-up call of the new millennium. It demonstrated how quickly a novel virus could spread across the world assisted by modern commercial aviation. It was spreading even before the WHO knew of its existence.

SARS originated in Guangdong province in China in November 2002, although initially the Chinese authorities treated the situation as a state secret. Consequently, when it spread to Hong Kong in February 2003 and from there on to Singapore, Hanoi, Toronto and Taiwan, people erroneously believed that Hong Kong was the initial source (Feeney, 2014).

SARS was contained by isolating the infected and quarantining those believed to have been exposed to the disease. In Toronto, 25,000 were quarantined and 18,000 in Beijing. At least this lesson was not wasted, and has been employed again in dealing with COVID-19. Even so, when the numbers quarantined during the SARS outbreak are compared with the many millions of people quarantined as entire cities were locked down in response to COVID-19, SARS almost fades into insignificance. However, there is still no known cure or a vaccine available for SARS, so a comeback is not beyond the realms of possibility.

"The psychological reaction in Hong Kong was the generation of fear, panic and paranoia. Moreover, putting the situation into context, of the 7,000,000 inhabitants of Hong Kong, less than 2,000 were infected with SARS and around 300 died. That represents less than 0.029% of the population who actually caught the disease. Even so, approximately 80% of the population

took to wearing face masks, in what some have called an unnecessary knee-jerk reaction."

(Clark, 2016, p 74)

In just a few months, SARS is known to have infected less than 10,000, with 776 recorded associated deaths. Despite this, it was referred to as an economic tsunami and cost the global economy an estimated $50 billion (TASW, 2011).

In Hong Kong, tourism, hospitality and retail industries were all badly affected, along with their supporting industries and associated supply chains. Airlines cancelled flights to and from the territory, as passenger numbers plummeted by as much as 77% in April 2003. Hong Kong-based carrier, Cathay Pacific, went from reporting a $505 million 2002 operating profit to losing $3 million per day.

Nervous customers were staying away as restaurants, bars and cinemas generally remained empty, while the wearing of protective face masks became the norm. Between March-May 2003, average hotel occupancy rates dropped from 79% to 18%, which necessitated some drastic action. Among the more elite hotels:

- The Hyatt Regency sacked 130 staff, while another 470 staff took ten days unpaid leave per month.
- The Grand Hyatt closed some floors and all staff had to take unpaid leave.
- In the Regal Hotel Group, every employee in its five hotels took eight days unpaid leave per month.
- At the Marriott, voluntary unpaid leave was encouraged. The CEO took the month off as a '*leading by example*' show case.

(Lee & Warner, 2008)

4: Why did nobody warn us?

"The world should brace itself for an increase in infectious diseases like SARS because of a fatal under-estimation of the power of viruses and bacteria ...

"Humans tampered with the environment to the extent that the effects were now being seen in the form of mutated viruses.

"I believe that the next ten to 15 years will see a substantial increase in infectious disease," Prof Curson said."

Professor Peter Curson, Historical Epidemiologist at Sydney's Macquarie University (Curson, 2003)

Of the many novel diseases discovered since the end of World War II, if we only consider the three potentially fatal coronaviruses that have emerged this century, Curson's prediction has so far proved remarkably accurate. In 2012, ten years after SARS, the Middle East Respiratory Syndrome (MERS) was identified, and COVID-19 followed seven years later.

4.1.2 Middle East Respiratory Syndrome (MERS)

Unlike SARS and COVID-19, which were first identified in China, MERS is believed to have originated in Saudi Arabia. It is also likely to be the least well-known of the three. Compared with its two coronavirus relations, MERS is rare, and well under 3,000 cases have been diagnosed since it emerged. Although cases have been recorded in 27 countries, it is most common in the Middle East.

Sometimes referred to as 'camel cough', as it is believed to be carried by camels, its symptoms are similar to SARS and COVID-19, and it can be transmitted from human to human by cough droplets. Approximately one-in-three cases prove to be fatal.

In 2015, there was an outbreak in South Korea, which has, to date, been the largest outbreak outside of the Middle East, with 185 cases diagnosed and 38 deaths. Having faced both outbreaks of SARS and MERS, South Korea is certainly one country that appears to have been better prepared to deal with COVID-19.

While MERS has not spread with the same intensity of either SARS and especially COVID-19, it did provide the world with another reminder that emerging diseases should be taken seriously.

4.1.3 SARS-CoV-2 (COVID-19)

As I write, we are in the middle of a pandemic, and COVID-19 is the here and now. Hardly a day passes when we do not learn something new about the disease.

Like SARS and MERS, we know that the symptoms are similar, and it can be transmitted from human to human in the same way. However, two symptoms not presented by SARS or MERS patients have been noted – loss of taste and smell. We also know that, unlike SARS and MERS, it is more than just a respiratory infection, and, as a multi-systems disease, it can attack just about any organ within the body.

We have also learned that it can leave infected patients with scarring on the lungs, along with possible side effects on the heart and kidneys, and it may even have a neurological legacy, too. The UK Sepsis Trust is concerned that COVID-19 survivors could subsequently develop sepsis. This condition can be triggered when the body overreacts to an infection, causing the immune system to turn on itself – leading to tissue damage, organ failure and potentially death.

In August 2020, the UK's Office of National Statistics (ONS) published a report possibly linking polluted air and COVID-19 mortality. Corresponding studies in the US, Northern Italy and the Netherlands have revealed similar results (ONS, 2020).

For some people, COVID-19 does not present a linear recovery path. In fact, a victim's recovery time can be significantly prolonged by post-viral fatigue, which in some instances could last for many weeks and delay a return to work. Moreover, evidence has also been found suggesting that Black, Asian and Minority Ethnic (BAME) groups can be twice as much at risk from COVID-19 than the white population. UK scientists are receiving millions of pounds of government funding to research why people from an ethnic minority background are at greater risk from COVID-19.

Clearly, a major priority was to find a vaccine, and more than 100 worldwide laboratories joined the challenge to find a safe and effective solution. What is more, it is as yet unclear whether infected patients gain any long-term immunity once they have recovered from COVID-19. In addition to the search for a vaccine, work has also been focusing on whether any existing medication can help with the treatment of the disease. So far, work in the UK has discovered that the inexpensive and readily available drug, dexamethasone, can speed up recovery time. Remdesivir is also being used in an attempt to accelerate a patient's recovery from COVID-19.

4.2 H5N1 2006 and H1N1 2009

Although they were mild outbreaks, influenza reminded us it was still around with the avian flu and swine flu outbreaks of

2006 and 2009. The reality is that, scary though many may consider COVID-19 to be, it is possibly just a trial run for the severe influenza pandemic that many NRRs are predicting (see section 4.5).

4.3 Bill Gates – "The next outbreak? We're not ready"

The Bill and Melinda Gates Foundation works with partners across the globe to tackle five different programme areas. Of specific interest to readers of this book will be the Global Health Division, which aims to reduce inequities in health by developing new tools and strategies to reduce the burden of infectious disease (Gates Foundation, 2020).

In his 2015 Ted Talk, Bill Gates told the audience that when he was a child, the disaster that people worried about most was a nuclear war. But today, a global disaster is much more likely to come from an influenza pandemic than a nuclear apocalypse. If anything is likely to kill millions of people, it is most likely to be a virus.

Gates argued that the world is simply not ready for the next epidemic and he uses the 2014-2016 Ebola outbreak to illustrate the point. Moreover, Ebola was largely contained across three West African countries – unlike COVID-19, which has achieved global proliferation. That said, Ebola was active primarily in rural communities, but had it spread to densely populated areas, the outcome could have been very different. He also adds that the virus could be a natural occurrence or it could be the result of bio-terrorism (Gates, 2015).

4.4 *Business Continuity and the Pandemic Threat*

Having already been convinced of the high probability of a severe pandemic occurring, when my own publication first hit the bookshelves in 2016, I did hope that it would add some support to the other pandemic wake-up calls that had gone before. Consequently, I was delighted to discover that the medical fraternity embraced it and were taking it very seriously.

Since its initial launch, to my knowledge, at least two US clinicians have referenced my book in their own publications, Dr Jonathan Quick (Quick, 2018) and Dr Lisa (Koonin, 2020).

In writing the book, I was very grateful for guidance from Dr Martyn Hinchcliffe BM MRCP FRCR and Dr Fergus O'Connor MD FRCS (Lon) FRCS (Edin) who also very kindly said:

> *"I know you had the business community in mind when you wrote this book, but everyone should read it, it could save lives."*

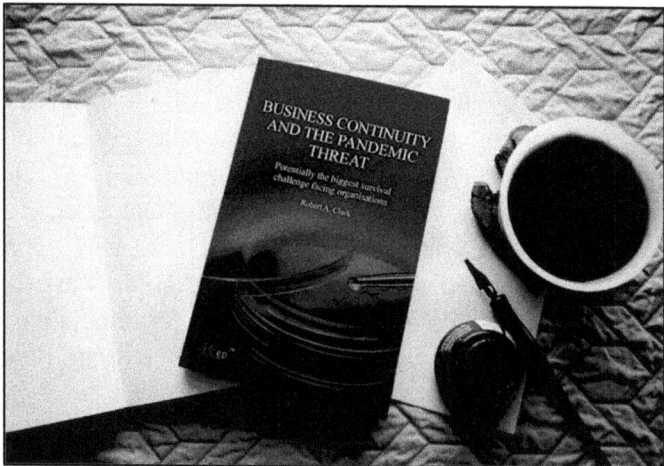

Figure 3: Business Continuity and the Pandemic Threat – Potentially the biggest survival challenge facing organisations

Sadly, the same was not true of people involved in business continuity or crisis management, who were actually the target audience I originally had in mind. Some thought the subject matter was too morbid. Others just laughed at me and said a severe pandemic was never going to happen. "Don't worry, the health services have this one covered", was a typical response.

In July 2017, I also took the opportunity to speak at the Business Continuity Institute's (BCI) North East forum meeting in Leeds. My presentation was entitled *"Is a pandemic potentially the biggest survival challenge facing organisations?"*, but disappointingly my talk received a very cool reception.

Even though *Business Continuity and the Pandemic Threat* ultimately became a bestseller, I have taken no pleasure in being proved right, especially as I watched the daily toll of new cases and fatalities continuing to grow across the world.

Figure 4: There's going to be a pandemic – you're having a laugh?

4.5 National risk registers

I have had the opportunity to examine a number of NRRs from different countries over a period that stretches back well over a decade. They all have one thing in common – severe influenza pandemics were seen as the 'Number One' threat.

In writing this book, I will refer to the UK NRR of Civil Emergencies (UK NRR) as it is in the public domain and can be downloaded for reference (UK Cabinet Office, 2017). This document is reviewed and republished periodically.

The UK NRR explains that it is difficult to forecast the spread and impact of a new flu strain or new emerging infectious diseases until they start circulating. However, consequences may include up to 50% of the UK population experiencing symptoms, potentially leading to between 20,000-750,000 fatalities and high levels of absence from work.[5]

If a global estimate is calculated from a simplistic extrapolation from the projected worst case UK scenario, this would result in an approximate global figure in excess of 85 million deaths.

In the context of a pandemic, there are two risks that need consideration, 'pandemic influenza' and 'emerging infectious diseases' – COVID-19 falls into the latter category.

---

[5] Before the end of August 2021, UK fatalities had exceeded 131,000, more than any other European country and, at that time, globally exceeded only by the US, India, Brazil and Mexico.

4: Why did nobody warn us?

The UK NRR also warns of the possible spread of vector-borne diseases, such as Dengue, Yellow Fever, West Nile virus and Zika, which are carried by mosquitoes. Except for Zika, they are not known to be transmitted from human to human, they are typically found in the tropics and have previously not bothered countries with temperate climates. However, with the ever-growing threat of global warming, there is evidence that these diseases are already expanding their range both north and south. The *aedes aegypti* mosquito has already established itself in Florida and other areas, such as the Mediterranean Sea basin, could prove to be an ideal climate, too.

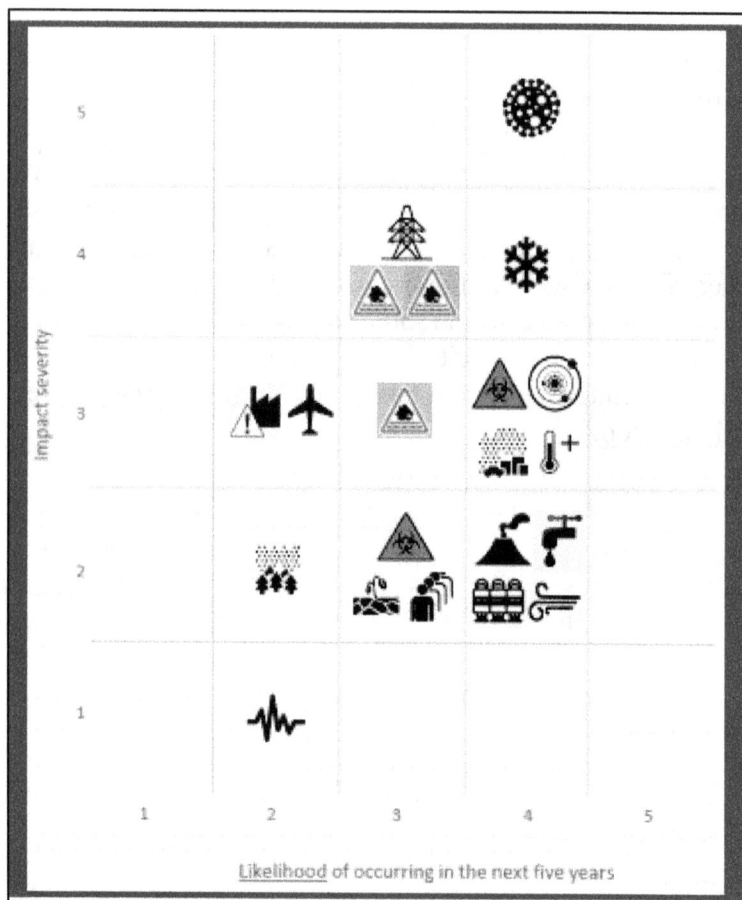

Figure 5: Hazards, diseases, accidents and societal risks (UK Cabinet Office, 2017, p 9)[6]

Figure 5 illustrates the UK NRR risk prioritisation, while Figure 6 provides the key or legend.

---

[6]*https://assets.publishing.service.gov.uk/government/uploads/system/up loads/attachment_data/file/644968/UK_National_Risk_Register_2017.*

4: Why did nobody warn us?

Using a '5 x 5' matrix to calculate the risks in Figure 5, the maximum score possible is 25 (i.e. if you have a risk that scores a '5' for the impact severity and another '5' for the likelihood of occurring, '5' x '5' gives you that maximum score of '25').

KEY

Natural hazards	Diseases
Coastal flooding	Pandemic influenza
River flooding	Emerging infectious disease
Surface water flooding	Animal disease
Storms and gales	
Cold and snow	Major accidents
Heatwave	Widespread electricity failure
Drought	Transport accidents
Space weather	Industrial and urban accidents
Volcanic eruptions	System failures
Poor air quality	Societal risks
Earthquakes	Industrial action
Wildfires	Public disorder

Figure 6: Hazards, diseases, accidents and societal risks legend (UK Cabinet Office, 2017, p 9)[7]

The pandemic influenza risk scores 20 out of 25, placing it in the 'Number One' risk position. This is followed in second

---

[7] https://assets.publishing.service.gov.uk/government/uploads/system/up loads/attachment_data/file/644968/UK_National_Risk_Register_2017.

place by 'cold and snow', four points behind. 'Emerging infectious diseases', the classification for COVID-19, scores a comparatively much lower score of 12 out of 25. The UK NRR goes on to explain that:

> *"The emergence of new infectious diseases is unpredictable but evidence indicates it may become more frequent.*
>
> *This may be linked to a number of factors such as: climate change; the increase in world travel; greater movement and displacement of people resulting from war; the global transport of food and intensive food production methods; humans encroaching on the habitat of wild animals; and better detection systems that spot new diseases.*
>
> *No country is immune to an infectious disease in another part of the world. In light of evidence from recent emerging infectious diseases such as Ebola and Zika, the likelihood of this risk has increased since 2015."*

(UK Cabinet Office, 2017, p 7)

It is worth noting that the risk value of 'emerging infectious diseases' in the UK NRR published in 2015 was 9/25 (UK Cabinet Office, 2015, p 13). In the 2017 UK NRR publication, while the projected impact of 'emerging infectious diseases' remains the same as its 2015 equivalent, the probability of occurrence has increased. The relative likelihood of occurring in the next five years increased from between '1-in-200 and 1-in-20' to '1-in-20' and '1-in-2'. The events of 2020 have clearly shown this revision of the risk assessment to have been justified.

Adding strength to the UK NRR, in his 2018 publication, *The End of Epidemics*, Dr Jonathan Quick states that close to 400 new infectious diseases have been discovered in the previous 75 years. This includes HIV/AIDS, Ebola and Zika. He adds that since 1971, scientists have discovered at least 25 new pathogens for which we have no vaccine or treatment. Quick further argues that:

"Given the rate at which population, deforestation, global warming, urbanization, climate change, international travel, and emergence of new pathogens are accelerating the risk of pandemics, it's reasonable to ask: Are we entering the century of pandemics?"

(Quick, 2018, p 41)

4.6 The fragility of tourism in the face of a pandemic

In November 2018, I was invited to present a paper at the Budapest Business School (BGE) entitled *"The fragility of tourism and hospitality in the face of a pandemic"*. This invitation was extended to joining the panel discussion on Sustainable Tourism – Best Practices.

With COVID-19 raging around the world, two of the most vulnerable industry sectors have been reeling – tourism and hospitality. There are other industries of course, but these were the two my paper focused on in Budapest.

The World Travel and Tourism Council maintains that tourism directly accounts for 3.2% of the global economy, along with a further 10.4% indirectly. However, some countries are far more dependent on tourism income than others. In the Maldives, almost 40% of its GDP is tourism generated. At 14.2%, Malta is the European country with the highest GDP tourism dependency compared with 3.7% for the UK and 2.6% for the US (Smith, 2020).

Using the lessons learned from Hong Kong's experience in 2003 with SARS, I was able to relate the type of actions that hotels and restaurants would need to take to stand a chance of surviving a severe pandemic.

Figure 7: Delivering at the BGE

The Sustainable Tourism panel, which followed the seminar, included Catherine Feeney (Edinburgh Napier University), Balazs Kormany (Board member of the Hungarian Hotel and Restaurant Association), Professor Melanie Smith (Corvinus University of Budapest), Robert Clark (Consultant, Trainer and Author) and moderator Dr Németh Tamás (BGE).

The venue was full, thus presenting an opportunity, albeit limited, to promote the threat of a pandemic to the attention of the academia. In a positive response, Dr Sara Csillag, Head of Institute at the BGE, expressed her intent to implement a programme of hygiene across the school, which would need to be one of the key actions required in the event of a pandemic.

4.7 Leading virologist warns top corporations

In 2019, world-expert virologist, Nathan Wolfe, warned top corporations that a severe pandemic could have multi-trillion dollar implications. Unfortunately, the warning seems to have fallen on deaf ears (Machell, 2020).

A similar warning had been previously issued by economist, Dr Sherry Cooper, some 11 years earlier, who stated that the cost to the global economy from even a moderate pandemic would be measured in trillions of dollars.

4.8 International Security Expo – December 2019

I guess the last irony, from a personal point of view, was the International Security Expo, London, which was held in December 2019. I had originally been invited to present a paper entitled *"Evaluating the multi-faceted threat from a pandemic that will confront the business world"*. By chance, the timing of the Expo coincided with the embryonic stages of what was to become the coronavirus pandemic. Yet, what would have been my last opportunity to address a large audience about the pandemic threat before it actually occurred never happened. The promoters, as was their right, opted for an alternative speaker who spoke about computer viruses instead. Life is so full of irony!!

4.9 So, was anyone really listening to the warnings?

Speaking on the BBC Breakfast programme in April 2020, Bill Gates believes that despite all the warnings most governments were simply not ready for the coronavirus. He also remarked that:

4: Why did nobody warn us?

"Very few countries are gonna to get an A-grade for what that scrambling looked like and now here we are, we didn't simulate this, we didn't practice so both the health policies and economic policies, we find ourselves in unchartered territory."

(Gates, 2020)

In October 2019, the world-renowned Johns Hopkins University published its Global Health Security Index. It marked every country out of 100 for its effectiveness across six criterions. In the section measuring *'Rapid Response to and Mitigation of the spread of an Epidemic'*, the UK came top with 91.9% and the US was in second place with 79.7% (Johns Hopkins University, 2019, p 20). The implication of Johns Hopkins's findings was that the UK and the US were both prepared to react to a pandemic. Ironically, when considering their respective responses to COVID-19, neither country has been a shining example of best practice in managing a pandemic.

Seized by the gravity of the COVID-19 crisis, the World Health Assembly in May 2020 requested the Director-General to review lessons learned from the WHO-coordinated international health response to COVID-19. The Director-General asked Her Excellency, Ellen Johnson Sirleaf and the Right Honourable Helen Clark to convene an independent panel for this purpose. They, in turn, invited 11 highly experienced, skilled and diverse people to form the panel. These include other former heads of government, senior ministers, health care experts and members of civil society. Referred to as The Independent Panel for Pandemic Preparedness and Response (TIP), it spent eight months reviewing evidence of the spread, actions and responses to the COVID-19 pandemic. Although not mentioning either the UK or the US specifically, TIP observed that:

> *"**Country wealth was not a predictor of success.** A number of low- and middle-income countries successfully implemented public health measures which kept illness and death to a minimum. A number of high-income countries did not."*

(TIP, 2021)

So, which countries might be in line for that elusive Bill Gates 'A-grade'? If we consider those countries that experienced SARS and/or MERS, in the main they have fared better than most countries that are experiencing a coronavirus outbreak for the first time.

As I write, the pandemic continues its march across the planet with the Omicron variant currently leading the charge. Consequently, it will only be in the final analysis that we will be able to accurately conclude which countries did well, which could have done better and which were a complete disaster. But, we can look at those countries that have got off to a good start and try to understand why.

A rather important point to remember is that the WHO has not provided any guidelines on how countries should report their COVID-19 cases and related fatalities. Therefore, each country has been left to decide how its figures are presented, and it is not always possible to accurately compare statistics. Moreover, some countries in the developing world do not necessarily have the means to diagnose every COVID-19 case. Charles Parton spent 22 years of his 37-year diplomatic career in China, Hong Kong and Taiwan. Commenting on China's COVID-19 case and fatality count, he remarked:

4: Why did nobody warn us?

"I don't think anyone believes that the statistics coming out of China are accurate. Clearly politics comes into this and the party wishes to show that it has done a far better job at containing it (the Coronavirus) than it really has."

(Gracie, 2020)

Russia is another country where case and fatality statistics seem rather out of step. By 9 September 2020, it had declared more than one million cases, but only 18,000 fatalities, circa 1.7% of its total case count. This was seen by many experts as totally implausible. With a global average mortality rate of around 6%, a more realistic Russian death count should have been in the region of 67,000. However, by the end of 2020, *The British Medical Journal* (BMJ) reported that Russia had come clean. It had admitted that its death toll was more than 180,000, making it the third highest in the world at that time (BMJ, 2020). In fact, by 31 December 2021, Russia had declared around 10 million cases with over 300,000 fatalities. Meanwhile, Iran's statistics have attracted interest, too. With a declared death toll of 17,000 as of 1 August 2020, leaked official Iranian government papers revealed the actual figure is likely to have been more than 42,000, 2.5 times higher than officially declared. Like Russia, Iran also appeared to be reporting a more realistic figure of 131,606 fatalities as year end 2021 approached.

That said, it does appear that, generally, South-East Asian countries that have had experience of SARS or MERS have made a good start and I would like to focus on three of them.

4.9.1 Hong Kong

I have been a frequent visitor to Hong Kong in recent years, including the time I spent there researching the impact of

SARS for my previous pandemic book. What has always impressed me is that it is clearly ready for a pandemic, as a consequence of the devastating effect that SARS had on the territory. As people arrive in Hong Kong, thermal imaging has been used to discreetly measure their temperatures since the SARS outbreak. Many other countries only started doing this after the COVID-19 pandemic materialised.

Some countries' leaders have been giving out mixed messages regarding whether people should wear masks or not. Even before the pandemic, in Hong Kong, if someone had a cold or some other infection, they automatically wore a mask so as not to pass it on to others. Remember that we should all wear masks to reduce the chance of passing infections onto others.

Walk into a shopping mall and you will see hand sanitising dispensers for peoples' use. Although public transport and airlines around the world have started regular, deep cleaning, this has been routinely done in Hong Kong since SARS.

Hong Kong is semiautonomous, and it is the fourth most densely populated country or territory in the world, with a population of around 7.5 million. Yet, by mid-July 2020, it had recorded less than 2,000 cases of COVID-19, and around a dozen deaths in the first wave of the pandemic. Seventeen months later, those figures had risen to a comparatively low 12,667 and 213 respectively. I believe the world can learn a lot about managing pandemics from Hong Kong, especially in the way it appears to have used SARS as a dress rehearsal for COVID-19.

4.9.2 South Korea

I have never been to South Korea, and unlike Hong Kong, its experience of SARS was minimal. However, in 2015 it did suffer the largest outbreak of MERS outside of the Middle East. Many companies and individuals looking to purchase face masks for protection during the MERS epidemic found that they very quickly sold out. This was an experience to be repeated in various parts of the world when COVID-19 appeared on the scene. Even so, its highest first pandemic wave daily peak of 851 new COVID-19 cases occurred more than a week before the WHO's global pandemic declaration on 11 March 2020.

Although its case and fatality statistics are not as impressive as Hong Kong's, what has caught the attention of many observers is South Korea's apparent ability to track and trace the spread of the virus.

Four years before the MERS outbreak, South Korea had introduced the Personal Information Protection Act, which imposed strict compliance on any organisation that collects individuals' personal data. This would typically include mobile phone tracking and credit/debit card transaction recording. However, in the event of a national emergency, government agencies can collect and use this data without needing to seek authority.

"The ability to collect, process and widely disclose personal data has enabled health authorities to conduct contact-tracing with military precision."

(Chan, 2020)

What sets South Korea apart from other democracies is its willingness to use widely available advanced technology that almost gives it a kind of 'Big Brother' persona, normally considered synonymous with totalitarian regimes.

But sadly, South Korea's 2021 year end assessment presented a worrying development. While previous daily new cases' statistics had shown the maximum spike size of 3,200 new case diagnoses in October 2021, within two months, a cluster of new cases had appeared with each spiking at more than double the October figure.

4.9.3 Taiwan

One of the six SARS hotspots in 2003, with a population of around 24 million, Taiwan is certainly the country to watch. While some countries have been seeing daily new case counts measuring in the tens of thousands, by year-end 2020, Taiwan had never exceeded 27.

In the eight months since the pandemic outbreak, in a population of almost 24 million, Taiwan has recorded only 817 cases and just 7 deaths. This rose to 17,000 and 850 respectively by December 2021. Its approach has been simple. Initially, the border was closed to non-residents in March 2020. It has since followed a strict quarantine procedure for all arrivals, plus a targeted testing process, coupled with a very efficient contact tracing programme. The population are also complying with social distancing and wearing face masks, resulting in Taiwan, unlike so many other countries, not needing to implement a major lockdown. It did, however, introduce tougher measures by closing entertainment venues and limiting the size of gatherings to deal with a spike in cases between May and July 2021.

4.9.4 The Hare and the Tortoise?

Having mentioned Taiwan, South Korea and Hong Kong in this way, I feel I must add a caveat. We must not forget that we are in a marathon, not a sprint, as each country battles with coronavirus. It will only be after the pandemic is declared 'over' that we will be able to look back and make an accurate and fare assessment on how each country has performed.

Despite their excellent starts, whether these three countries will remain among the front runners, achieving one of those coveted 'A' ratings that Bill Gates spoke of, remains to be seen. Or perhaps the moral of *The Hare and the Tortoise* may yet prove to be more appropriate.

So how had these countries fared by year-end 2021?

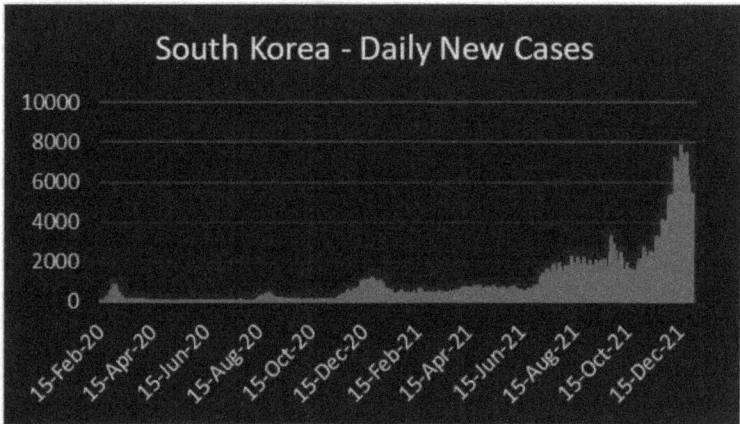

Figure 8: South Korea – Daily new cases 31 December 2021

For South Korea, after the initial surge of daily new cases at the end of February 2020, Figure 8 illustrates a low steady flow of cases with a modest peak during August and September. Moreover, the maximum number of daily cases in the second peak was only around half the number recorded during the original peak. But by November, things started to go wrong. and we see a massive third wave of new daily cases, peaking at more than 1,200 and then doubling by August 2021. Fuelled by the arrival of the Omicron variant, 2021 ended with South Korea's daily new case count more than doubling the peaks witnessed some four months before.

In stark contrast, after a comparatively small first wave that peaked at just 82 new daily cases, Hong Kong presented signs of a much bigger second wave that threatened to overwhelm its health services. Even so, its current peak of 145 daily new cases on 27 July 2020 is still considerably smaller than South Korea's highest daily figure of 851 registered on 3 March 2020. Moreover, South Korea has registered 4.4 times as many deaths as Hong Kong.

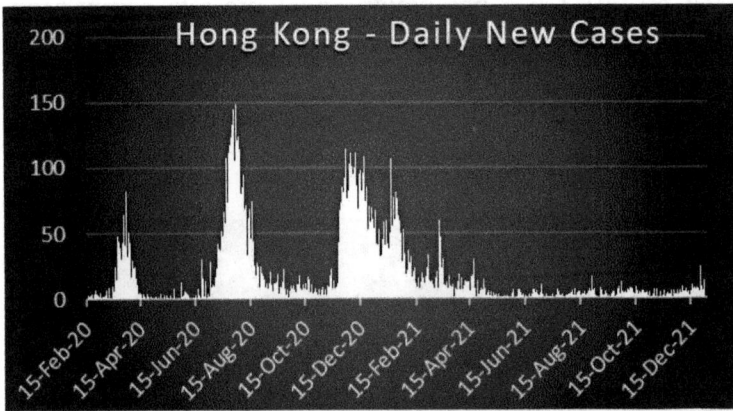

Figure 9: Hong Kong – Daily new cases 31 December 2021

Despite the comparatively modest daily new case count peak, the BBC reported that:

> In a statement on 29 July 2020, the Chief Executive of Hong Kong, Carrie Lam, warned the local population that the city was on the *"verge of a large-scale community outbreak, which may lead to a collapse of our hospital system and cost lives, especially of the elderly."* (BBC News, 2020)

Like South Korea, Hong Kong had also experienced a third peak before year-end 2020, although its peak was lower than the second wave, reaching only just over 100 daily new cases.

An interesting comparison can be made between Hong Kong, France and the UK. The populations for each of the two European countries are approximately nine times greater than Hong Kong's. But as of 15 October 2020, the highest daily new case counts for France and the UK were 206 and 136 times greater respectively than Hong Kong's highest peak of 149. On a population count pro-rata comparison, Hong Kong was in a considerably much better position than either France or the UK.

But still very much on course for that elusive 'A' grade that Bill Gates talked of is Taiwan.

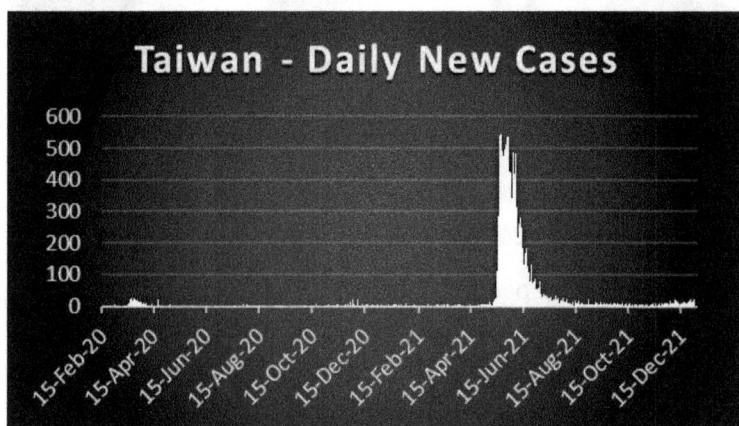

Figure 10: Taiwan – Daily new cases 31 December 2021

Apart from a handful of minor spikes in December, its first and only wave, from 11 March[8] to 10 May 2020, recorded only 393 positive cases of COVID-19. Over the same period,

---

[8] 10 March 2020 was the date the pandemic was declared by the WHO.

South Korea reported 3,361 cases, while Hong Kong reported 927.

By year-end 2020, it had still only recorded 817 cases of COVID-19 and just seven deaths, while Hong Kong had reached 9,050 cases and 153 deaths. South Korea brought up the rear of this trio with 64,979 and 1,007 respectively. However, Taiwan certainly saw a brief but uncharacteristic blip around June 2021 when new daily case declarations hovered around the 500 mark.

4.10 The pop-up hospitals

In reacting to the rapid increase of COVID-19-related hospital admissions, the world did seem better prepared to face the pandemic than it did in many other respects. Like other countries, in England the NHS freed up around 15,000 beds by cancelling elective (planned) operations. Another 15,000 were freed by discharging patients primarily into care homes, while a further 8,000 were purchased at cost from the private sector. However, social distancing necessitated extra space between beds thereby reducing the total number that could be accommodated across the hospitals.

Pop-up hospitals started appearing – sometimes as a reaction to an immediate demand for extra beds and intensive care capability, other times as a contingency measure.

The day after the Wuhan lockdown in China (refer to section 7.1), work started on constructing the Huoshenshan and Leishenshan Hospitals. With the names of the hospitals meaning Fire God Mountain (Huoshenshan) and Thunder God Mountain (Leishenshan), these two 25,000 square metre pop-up hospitals were constructed using prefabricated units. providing a combined capacity of 2,300 beds.

4: Why did nobody warn us?

The project was completed in around 10 days, and was based on Xiaotangshan Hospital, which was constructed in Beijing to help manage the SARS virus in 2002-2003. The Xiaotangshan was in fact reopened during the COVID-19 crisis, although other pop-up hospitals were also planned.

Other countries activated their contingency plans, too. The UK quickly converted a number of existing buildings into what were referred to as 'Nightingale Hospitals', adding around 12,000 extra beds in England alone. This included a former railway terminus – 'Manchester Central'. On two previous occasions, the UK had temporarily commandeered and converted operational railway stations (Kings Cross in London and Manchester Victoria) into triage centres to manage casualties following terrorist attacks.

In the US, the hospital ships, the USNS Mercy and Comfort, were deployed to Los Angeles and New York respectively, while field hospitals were erected, such as the one in Manhattan's Central Park, to provide hospitals with overflow capacity.

The healthcare system in Italy was in serious trouble at the height of its first wave. The country turned to shipping containers converted into intensive care facilities to complement the country's hospital capacity.

Although there are other examples from around the world, the last example I would like to mention is in the Netherlands. With the Eurovision Song Contest 2020 being cancelled, the Rotterdam Ahoy concert venue was converted into an emergency hospital to help in the battle against COVID-19.

There is one final fundamental point that must not be overlooked vis-à-vis pop-up hospital strategies. It is certainly a very positive step that some countries are able to react in this way. However, at the risk of stating the obvious, they must not forget they still need to find the trained resources to man these hospitals without leaving other parts of their health services dangerously exposed.

In some countries, it was not always possible to locate a 'pop-up' hospital close to existing health facilities. This often presented the challenge of finding sufficiently trained staff to operate them without leaving other areas of their respective health services exposed. However, as the pandemic ebbed and flowed, the need to keep the pop-up facilities permanently operational all but disappeared.

Nevertheless, the alarming proliferation of the Omicron variant towards the end of 2021 re-emphasised the need for 'pop-up' hospitals. In some countries, including the UK, purpose-built structures were erected in the grounds of existing hospitals. This made it easier to manage the extra demands that the pop-up facilities placed on trained staff.

4.11 Risk managers criticised

"I am constantly amazed by the number of executives who dismiss potential disasters as being too unlikely to consider, or who put off dealing with known risks because they have other things to worry about."

Martin Caddick, Former Head of Resilience, PwC, UK (Clark, 2014, p 8)

As this chapter has established, the writing was clearly on the wall vis-à-vis the pandemic threat, supported by a plethora of multi-source, high-profile warnings. I find it inconceivable that so many organisations seemed utterly unprepared. It would also appear that some countries did not appear to believe in their own NRRs and the veracity of the pandemic threat.

Tracey Skinner, Director of Insurance and Risk Financing for the BT Group, was critical of risk managers and said:

> *"With hindsight, risk managers could have done a better job of identifying pandemics as a threat before Covid-19 hit."*

(Norris, 2020)

4.12 The final word on global preparedness

TIP, whose formation was explained in section 4.9, spent eight months reviewing evidence of the spread, actions and responses to the COVID-19 pandemic. It has produced a definitive account of what happened and why, and has analysed how a pandemic can be prevented from happening again.

In its 2021 report, "COVID-19: Make it the Last Pandemic – A Summary", TIP observed that:

> *"Years of warnings of an inevitable pandemic threat were not acted on and there was inadequate funding and stress testing of **preparedness**, despite the increasing rate at which zoonotic diseases are emerging."*

(TIP, 2021)

It seems appropriate that the head of the WHO has the final word on just how ready the world was:

> *"None of this should come as a surprise. Over the years there have been many reports, reviews and recommendations all saying the same thing: – the world is not prepared for a pandemic."*

4: Why did nobody warn us?

(Ghebreyesus, 2020)

4: Why did nobody warn us?

CHAPTER 5: IS IT TOO LATE TO WRITE A PANDEMIC PLAN?

With the world's first COVID-19 vaccine having been approved by the UK in early December 2020, the more optimistic among us who believe that COVID-19 will soon be just a distant memory, might feel justified in asking this question. Now to remind you that I am not a clinician or a virologist, but in my humble opinion as a Fellow of the Institute of Strategic Risk Management, **COVID-19 is not the severe pandemic that the world was expecting.**

That might surprise you, but as I explained in section 4.5, the various NRRs I have had sight of have all flagged a severe influenza pandemic as their biggest concern. While the custodians of these NRRs may well choose to re-examine their assessment of emerging infectious diseases, such as coronaviruses, I see no reason why they would want to change their thinking regarding influenza pandemics. Also, keep in mind that with COVID-19, it could be several days after being infected that symptoms start to present, assuming the infected individual is not asymptomatic. Conversely, when the 1918-1919 Spanish influenza pandemic was raging, people could look a picture of health at breakfast time but be dead before dinner time.

"Are we entering the Century of Pandemics?"
(Dr Jonathan Quick, 2018)

History has taught us that periodically we will be threatened by the onset of a severe influenza pandemic. Maybe it will be this year, perhaps next year or conceivably sometime in the next ten years. If you take a look at the UK NRR, which, to remind you, is in the public domain, you'll see that the probability of a severe influenza pandemic occurring in the next five years is between 1-in-20 and 1-in-2. The truth is we may not know for sure when that will be until it is virtually breathing down our necks. Unfortunately, the bad news is that Mother Nature does not publish a useful timetable of forthcoming dangerous and disruptive events. As consolation, I should add that the WHO has created a global influenza surveillance response system. Even so, we also only need look at the COVID-19 proliferation timeline to see how fast the disease has spread. Yet, until the case count exploded in China, most of us had never heard of it. Moreover, China had recorded almost 45,000 cases with over 1,100 associated deaths before this novel coronavirus had even been given a name.

Now let us contemplate the plethora of unregulated organisations that had either never given pandemic planning a thought, or had opted to prepare only when they were warned that one was imminent. So, consider this:

- On 1 February 2020, there were around 14,500 known coronavirus global cases and 300 associated deaths.
- One month later, those numbers had increased to 88,000 and 3,000 respectively.
- Within two months, the count was 1,000,000 cases with 50,000 fatalities.
- After three months, the case count was up to 3,356,391 and fatalities had reached 244,917.

So, had your organisation been one of the "let's wait and see what happens" brigade, or "we will create a plan when we know the threat of a pandemic is looming", at what point would you have hit the panic button? Moreover, how long do you think it will take to actually develop a plan – it certainly is not an overnight task. Moreover, you will have no doubt found that many of the consumables that you were invariably going to need (e.g. PPE, hand sanitiser, cleaning products, etc.) were in very short supply.

Some organisations may argue that they have engaged with business continuity and have a validated BCP. That is clearly good news, but is that sufficient when you are facing a serious pandemic? Those organisations that are familiar with the BCI's Good Practice Guidelines (GPG), will appreciate that:

"The business continuity plans are not intended to cover every eventuality as all incidents are different. The plans need to be flexible enough to be adapted to the specific incident that has occurred and the opportunities it may have created. However, in some circumstances, incident specific plans are appropriate to address a significant threat or risk, for example, a pandemic plan."

(BCI, 2018, p 62)

I believe it is safe to assume that, in addition to a BCP, the GPG is recommending that organisations develop and maintain a contingency plan specifically for pandemics.

And here is some more bad news. SARS-CoV-2, to use its viral name, is the third potentially fatal coronavirus to have emerged since the turn of the millennium. That makes it three coronaviruses inside 17 years. If they keep coming at that rate, then we have at least one more novel coronavirus to look forward to before 2030.

To return to the question 'Is it too late to write a pandemic plan?', when considering the ever-present influenza threat plus emerging infectious diseases, the answer is most emphatically '**NO**', it is not too late.

Other sources of information out there that can help organisations prepare to face a pandemic include the Arizona State University (ASU). It has published *"A comprehensive survey on how companies are protecting their employees from COVID-19"*. Using survey data collected from more than 1,000 companies across 29 countries, it reveals the stark challenges in navigating the pandemic (ASU, 2020). Supported by the Rockefeller Foundation, more recently ASU has also prepared a very useful resource entitled *"Back to the Workplace: Are we there yet?"* (ASU, 2021).

5.1 Did you have a pandemic plan in place?

5.1.1 Yes, we had prepared a pandemic plan

For those organisations that had a pandemic plan in place before COVID-19 arrived, you need to be asking yourselves some serious questions, such as:

- Did the plan work?
- What went well, what could have been done better and what went badly?
- What lessons did you learn?
- Did your organisation find itself facing any unexpected risks? In which case, are there any future mitigation actions or contingency activities you should consider?
- What incorrect assumptions did you make in originally preparing the plan?
- Did government legislation and regulations help or hinder your ability to conduct your business?

You may not know all the answers to any issues arising until after the pandemic is over. But there is no harm in making any changes to the plan that you realise are necessary.

5: Is it too late to write a pandemic plan?

5.1.2 No, we didn't have a pandemic plan

The first thing to remember about a pandemic plan is that, like a BCP, one size does not fit all. For example, there is little point in using a plan that was perhaps developed for a financial institution if you are, say, a manufacturing outfit. That said, your pandemic plan should work in conjunction with your BCP.

In the prequel to this book, I devoted around 70 pages to how to go about writing a pandemic plan. In the following subsections, for your convenience, I have included an overview of some key points that you will need to consider while preparing your own plan. Please keep in mind that the shape of your plan will be very much influenced by whether your country considers your business to be essential or non-essential. In the latter case, in the event of a total lockdown, you are likely to be unable to operate from your premises until the restrictions are lifted.

While accountability must lie with senior management, where in your organisation should you position the responsibility for developing your pandemic plan? Ideally, this should be managed from the same area of the organisation that deals with your business continuity planning or within risk management. However, it would be wise to seek medical expertise to advise and provide independent validation of your plan. Your HR team can also expect to play a key role in the plan's development.

5.1.2.1 First and foremost, your employees

a. Where possible and practical, if your staff can work from home (WFH), then this should be encouraged. You will need to ensure that staff are properly equipped and, if appropriate, they have an acceptable Internet bandwidth. Keep in regular contact with them either via online meetings or phone calls. Be aware of the potential for both mental health and well-being issues, plus musculoskeletal disorders resulting from long periods of using display equipment.

b. You should try and make allowances for those employees who are more vulnerable to the pandemic, perhaps because of underlying health issues.

c. Be prepared for staff absenteeism, which could be for any one of a number of reasons (e.g. sickness, childminding, sick parents needing care, transport issues, in isolation, fear, etc.)

d. Ensure staff know what to do if they develop any pandemic-related symptoms, whether they are at home or work. This will invariably be based upon in-country medical guidance. While an individual's COVID-19 symptoms can deteriorate over a period of days, other illness can develop very quickly, such as influenza.

e. Develop a process for dealing with workers who may be taken ill at work, which minimises the threat of cross infection to other workers. Although it hasn't been necessary with COVID-19 as the symptoms develop relatively slowly, in the event of an influenza outbreak, having a medical room available can be a useful means of helping to manage sickness at work. Ensure that procedures are in place to follow-up with cleaning any areas of the workplace potentially infected.

f. Allow sick staff sufficient time to recover from the pandemic, keeping in mind that some may suffer from an extended period of post-viral fatigue (e.g. long COVID – see section 3 etc.).[9]

g. Consider enlisting the service of trauma counsellors should staff be severely affected by the death of any colleagues. You may choose to extend this service to include the death of their loved ones, including close friends.

5.1.2.2 Making the workplace safe

Various governments have published guidelines about keeping both staff and customers safe in the workplace. In the event that you cannot locate any relevant documents for your own country, I have included a number of useful URLs on my website: *www.bcm-consultancy.com/pandemicthreat*.

There are several recognised ways in which your employees and customers can be infected by the virus in and around the workplace. This can include:

- Employees coming to work when they are presenting symptoms that can be for any one of a number of reasons (e.g. they will not be paid if they stay at home, a sense of loyalty – letting the team down, etc.). This type of situation needs to be addressed by your HR team before it becomes an issue in the workplace.
- When hands are not washed or washed adequately.
- Workers not observing coughing and sneezing etiquette, including not wearing face masks, especially when

---

[9] Some countries are not very generous with paid sick leave allowance. Staff may be tempted to return to work while they are still infectious because they cannot afford to remain at home if they are not being paid. I know of at least one country that permits only two weeks paid sick leave even when an extended period of hospitalisation is necessary.

working indoors.

- Cross infection occurring in potentially high traffic areas, such as toilets, canteens, ingress and egress points.
- Inadequate cleaning regime in the workplace.
- Contravening social distancing regulations.
- Inadequate ventilation in the workplace.
- Insufficient supplies of PPE, handwash and hand sanitiser.
- Workers co-habiting and/or car sharing when travelling to and from work.

The following actions should be considered as part of your workplace safety plan:

a) Introduce a process that ensures employee's and visitor's temperatures are taken regularly and, if required, log the results. Forehead thermometers are ideal for this, although there are more sophisticated alternatives that are less intrusive, such as those deployed in airports. Remember that whoever is responsible for monitoring temperatures should also record their own, too.

b) Educate staff in handwashing plus coughing and sneezing protocols. Prominently display posters around the workplace to act as constant reminders. Where one does not already exist, foster a culture of wearing face masks.

c) Ensure that ample supplies of PPE, especially face masks and hand sanitisers are available. Consider allocating staff with their own bottles of hand sanitiser. Do not wait for a pandemic to be declared before ordering supplies – they ran out when the comparatively minor 2015 MERS outbreak occurred in South Korea.

When COVID-19 arrived, the global demand quickly outstripped the supply.

d) Perform a risk assessment with the primary objective of identifying:
    i. Areas where people tend to congregate;
    ii. Bottlenecks, especially where social distancing might be difficult to maintain;
    iii. Surfaces that are likely to be touched repeatedly; and
    iv. Indoor areas with poor ventilation.

e) Frequent cleaning of the workplace is essential, especially infection traps, such as elevator buttons, handrails, door access keypads, door handles, telephones, etc. This list could be extensive, and is also likely to vary from organisation to organisation. Special attention should be paid to cleansing any high-traffic areas identified by your risk assessment.

f) In the event that workers or visitors are taken ill on your premises, ensure that procedures are in place to follow up with cleaning those areas of the workplace potentially infected.

g) Prohibit cultural greetings that involve any form of physical contact.

h) Discourage face-to-face meetings if possible and encourage the use of online conference platforms. even if it is two or three people who work in adjacent offices. Keep in mind that staff may need training in the use of your chosen platform.

i) Travel, especially internationally, may become difficult if not impossible. Unessential travel should be avoided.

j) If staff cannot WFH, ensure your plan allows for accommodating all social distancing regulations.[10]

k) Consideration may need to be given to workplace ventilation, especially if windows cannot be opened.

l) Engage in dialogue with those workers who cohabit and/or travel to work together. Determine how to reduce the risk of them being vulnerable to infection and/or instrumental in the virus spreading.

m) Put in place one-way systems to reduce potential congestion and, if possible, designate staircases going up and others going down. Ideally nominate ingress/egress as either just an entrance or an exit from your premises.

n) While it may not be easy, it is also worth discouraging gossip in the workplace, especially if it specifically references pandemic conspiracy theories. The proliferation of misinformation could serve to undermine your efforts to keep the workplace safe.

5.1.2.3 Communications

Whenever you are faced with a crisis, your ability to communicate effectively can make the difference between a successful outcome or a major catastrophe. Having a well-rehearsed communication plan in place is an essential part of business survival, regardless of the nature of the crisis you

---

[10] Social distancing recommendations have not been applied consistently globally, with some countries opting for one metre while others have chosen two. Your social distancing plans may need to be flexible, especially as recommended distance may be increased or decreased as more is learned about the virus. There have been incidents where it has been revealed that social distancing has not been adequately observed (e.g. food processing plants, etc.) but workers have been reluctant whistleblowers for fear of losing their jobs.

are facing. Just to be clear, this communication is not specifically for a pandemic, it should be for any type of crisis that comes your way.

So, what needs to be in your plan?

Let's start with the basics, how are you going to mobilise your crisis management team (CMT) and any other supporting team you may need (e.g. business continuity, IT disaster recovery, emergency preparedness, etc.). Crises can happen at any time and for those organisations that still enjoy the luxury of working from 9 am to 5 pm, Monday to Friday, then statistically a crisis is more likely to occur outside of your normal working hours.

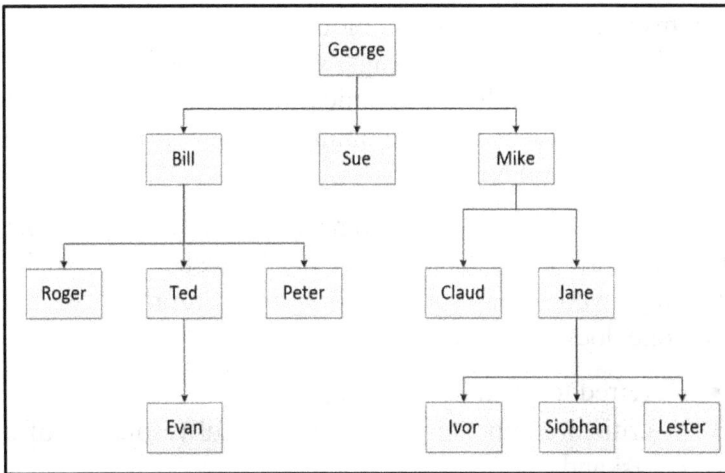

Figure 11: Telephone message cascade approach

Some, usually small- to medium-size organisations, may opt to use the telephone message cascade approach. In the preceding illustration, George calls Bill, Sue and Mike. Bill then calls Roger, Ted and Peter, while Mike calls Claud and

Jane, etc. But the more links there are in the chain, the greater the chance of the chain breaking.

In one crisis rehearsal exercise case I researched, it was acted out over a weekend. The scenario was a plane crash at an airport and the local hospital was involved. It was an unannounced exercise, and they used the message cascade approach, but the person responsible for alerting the hospital catering manager, failed to make the call. The catering team were expected to keep the emergency workers fed and watered over the weekend. But, owing to the message cascade failure, no field kitchen facilities were deployed and there were no refreshments available for the entire weekend.

What is becoming more popular are mass notification systems which, in addition to mobilising your teams, can be used for emergency warnings, too (e.g. active shooter, tsunami threat, wildfires, chemical spills, etc.). The better examples on the market certainly remove the risk of a cascade call chain breaking.

Your communications will also need to take account of your stakeholders, and an obvious pre-requisite is actually knowing who your stakeholders are. Surprisingly, not everyone does, but they may be:

- Referred to as an 'interested party';
- A critical component in the successful resolution of a crisis; and
- An individual person, a group or an organisation.

You must know **WHO** you will need to communicate with, **HOW** you are going to communicate with them and **WHAT** you are going to tell them. Also, keep in mind that communication is a two-way thing, so you must be set up to monitor and react to inbound messages, too.

So, let's think about the **WHO**. For example, your stakeholders could include the following:

- Authorities/government
- Competitors
- Customers and suppliers
- Emergency contacts
- Employees
- Local communities
- Media
- Regulators/legislators
- Shareholders
- Financiers

There may well be others that you will have to factor into your plan accordingly. On occasions, you may need to consider the order in which you communicate with your stakeholders. This begs questions, such as: 'Is there anyone we should be telling first?'

Next, **HOW** are you going to communicate with your stakeholders? You will need to define your communication channels and decide on the most appropriate for each stakeholder group, such as:

- Mass notification systems
- Internet/website
- Radio/television
- Local/national newspapers
- Media advertisements
- Trade journals
- Telephone/SMS texting/fax
- Email
- Social media

Now here is the thing. Communication channels can be compromised by the very crisis you are trying to manage. Consequently, I would strongly recommend that you include some contingency measures in your plan that would enable continuity of communications by using alternative channels.

It is also worth remembering that when a crisis starts, people will expect answers and quickly. For example:

- The 2002-2003 SARS outbreak happened while social media was very much in its infancy. Over the three days, 8-10 February 2003, the SMS text message: 'There is a fatal flu in Guangzhou' was sent 126 million times just from mobile phones in the city of Guangzhou alone (Brahmbhatt & Dutta, 2008).
- The week following the 2007 bombing, Glasgow Airport website received 130,000 visits compared to 6,000 the previous week. (Crichton, 2007, pp 18-23)
- When the 2009-2011 Toyota product recall crisis reached its peak, circa 14,000 daily inbound phone queries were received in the UK alone. (Duncan, 2014, p. 252)
- After the 2015 Paris terrorist attacks, approximately 10.7 million tweets were posted in a 24-hour period. Twitter is just one of many social media platforms. Much of this Paris-focused information was incorrect or arguably 'economical with the truth'. (Whitten, 2015)

So, WHAT are we going to communicate?

For each threat scenario that has been included within the crisis management scope, it should be possible to construct a set of communication templates to speed up the process of responding. These templates should be subject to a programme of continual improvement, as more experience is gained by the organisation.

Keep in mind that an organisation's chief executive officer is not always the best person to stand up in front of the media.

5.1.2.4 Supply chain management

Examine your upstream supply chain, especially if it has more of global rather than local dependency and reflect on just how vulnerable to a pandemic it could be. When China went into lockdown, many organisations found products that they depended upon were no longer easily obtainable. This very much impacted global health services and their urgent need for PPE.

A friend needing to ship a small package from Australia to the US was informed that the transit time (normally just a few days) would now take several weeks. Oh, and the price had gone up 10-fold, making the shipment more expensive than the value of the product.

Those organisations operating a just-in-time (JIT) supply chain model could find they are especially vulnerable. Many passenger airlines effectively closed down, which meant their cargo holds were no longer available for shipping products quickly around the world. You should also consider your downstream supply chain – your customers. If your operation is interrupted, maybe because of a lockdown, how will you inform your customers that you are back in business? Or, if you are able to continue operations during a lockdown, how will you tell them 'we are still here', always assuming of course that your customers are still in business, too.

One example I rather liked was Amazon originally created a 'COVID-19 Information' page on its website. This kept customers up to date about how Amazon was dealing with the pandemic and, more importantly, was reassuring them that it was still open for business.

And a final thought. Do your suppliers have BCPs and pandemic plans in place and are they prepared to share them with your organisation? In the interest of being reassured, there is no harm in asking – some of your customers may ask you the same question.

5.1.2.5   Resources to help you create your plan

If you don't already have a copy of the prequel to this book, just to remind you that it has around 70 pages devoted to writing a pandemic plan.

You will also find a number of useful pandemic-related resources, including sample plans, case studies, videos and useful links on my website:

www.bcm-consultancy.com/pandemicthreat.

CHAPTER 6: MANAGING THE CRISIS

Whenever an organisation finds itself facing a crisis, the cause can be varied – a cyber attack, civil unrest, industrial action, legislation changes, hurricanes, earthquakes, ICT failure, head office fire, etc. – the list goes on. It could even be a crisis that is multifaceted, resulting from two or more threats materialising simultaneously. It is certainly worth remembering that because you may be dealing with one crisis, other crises can and sometimes do happen concurrently.

In its *Global Crisis Survey – Building resilience for the future*, published in March 2021, PwC reported that 95% of the worldwide survey respondents believed their crisis management capabilities needed improvement (PwC, 2021).

Today, and for the foreseeable future, we are facing a global civil emergency in the form of a pandemic, which, in addition to the human aspect, has very serious implications for just about every organisation on the planet. We are being strongly encouraged to practise social distancing, both in our personal as well as our professional lives. The parameter has varied from country to country, but ideally, we should keep a distance of two metres (six feet) between ourselves and work colleagues or passers-by in the street. This can understandably make the traditional round-table crisis management meeting logistically very difficult to conduct. Fortunately, technology is at hand to help resolve that challenge, and these meetings can now easily be conducted online. Consequently, members of the CMT can be at home or theoretically anywhere in the world, but are still able to engage in a meeting providing they have a suitable Internet connection.

Make no mistake, a severe pandemic presents organisations with a crisis that should be managed by senior management. But, anyone in an organisation, including senior management, could become a victim of COVID-19 and replacements for every member of the CMT should be named. As a point in case, one need only look to UK Prime Minister Boris Johnson when he was hospitalised with COVID-19. He already had a nominated successor in Foreign Minister, Dominic Raab.

Enter the age of Zoomtopia

After being hospitalised and treated for COVID-19, UK Prime Minister Boris Johnson encouraged online meetings within the government. Other members of the UK Cabinet had also tested positive for COVID-19, including the then Secretary of State for Health, Matt Hancock and the UK Chief Medical Officer, Professor Chris Witty who also self-isolated with COVID-19 symptoms.

6.1 The crisis management leadership profile

During periods of crisis people look to a strong leader. When the Russian submarine 'Kursk' sank on 12 August 2000, President Vladimir Putin caused a public relations disaster by keeping a very low profile, as he continued to enjoy his vacation. Conversely, in the immediate aftermath of the 9/11 terrorist attacks, New York Mayor Rudy Giuliani was lauded for presenting a very high and effective media profile.

The UK's war time Prime Minister, Winston Churchill, in addition to the Monarch, King George VI and Queen

Elizabeth, would regularly visit UK cities that had been bombed by the German Luftwaffe to help lift morale. This was much appreciated by the people. So, in short, in times of crisis, an organisation's leader needs to be very visible, unless they are actually the cause of the crisis (see section 6.2).

Organisations would do well to remember the words attributed to Warren Buffett: *"It takes 20 years to build a reputation and five minutes to ruin it. If you think about that, you'll do things differently."* With Buffett's words in mind, you would typically expect a good leader to be able to:

- Quickly take responsibility, plan, monitor and communicate;
- Assume a proactive, transparent and accountable position, while demonstrating adaptability and creativity in the face of adverse conditions;
- Act quickly and make bold decisive decisions when necessary. Hesitation can be seen as a sign of weakness;;
- Seek first to understand the situation,[11] then ensure that you get ahead of the story and 'own it';
- Be ready for a social media backlash, although remember it could be the original cause of the crisis;
- Even if it is not the organisation's fault, before taking action, be prepared to apologise and show empathy, especially if there have been injuries or fatalities. Never engage in a finger pointing blame-game;
- Always listen to the team before making decisions and avoid 'knee-jerk' reactions. This can be a tough call for

[11] When you are not sure exactly what has happened, be prepared to issue a holding statement. 'No comment' or ignoring the media must be avoided otherwise it may well concoct its own version of events.

politicians. In normal times, they may be used to taking months or even years of deliberation over a decision. Suddenly, in the midst of a pandemic, they have to be able to react in a matter of hours, which can be seen as a 'knee-jerk' reaction;

- Where practical, turn off the fan. The classic example is in 1982, Johnson and Johnson recalled the entire worldwide stock of the company's flagship product, the painkiller, Tylenol. Seven people had died in Chicago after taking tablets from a small batch of the drug that had been contaminated with cyanide; and
- Be prepared to break the rules when necessary. Rules, budgets and policies are seldom made with a crisis in mind.

6.2 When an organisation's leader is the crisis

Although not specifically pandemic related, there have been occasions when organisations have found themselves facing a crisis that has been caused or aggravated by their own leadership. This has often resulted in C-Suite individuals losing their position, with many deciding to *fall on their swords* before they were fired. Three classic examples taken from a 'rogues' gallery' include:

- Tony Hayward, former BP CEO, who made one of the biggest public relations gaffs of all time regarding the 2010 Deepwater Horizon oil rig disaster. People died in the explosion and others lost their livelihoods. Hayward said on camera that "I'd like my life back", as dealing with the crisis was taking up too much of his time (Reuters, 2010).
- Gerald Ratner was the former CEO of the jewellery company, 'Ratners'. He achieved notoriety when

speaking at a dinner engagement in 1991. He jokingly said that many of his company's products were so inexpensive because "it's total crap". That joke was reported in the UK media and wiped £500 million (sterling) off the value of the company more or less overnight (Ratner, 1991).

- The late Warren Anderson presided over the 1984 Bhopal toxic chemical disaster that led to in excess of 10,000 fatalities. An arrest warrant was issued by Indian authorities, but Anderson managed to leave the country.

As the pandemic progresses, we may also find more and more examples of organisational leadership that was found lacking. This could just as easily be in the public as well as the private sector. Maybe some politicians' handling of the pandemic crisis will place them in line for similar condemnation as our preceding rogues' gallery.

6.3 Who should be on the crisis management team?

For large organisations you would generally expect the CMT to be made up of members of the 'C-Suite'. Executive level managers, such as the chief executive officer (CEO), chief financial officer (CFO), chief information officer (CIO), etc. Other C-suite job titles can be added to the list as appropriate.

In the current pandemic-generated crisis, while the titles of the various senior management roles will vary from organisation to organisation, a CMT might look something like this:

- CMT leader – usually the CEO would take the lead role.
- HR director – a pandemic is first and foremost a human issue.

- CFO – will invariably be expected to control the funding of any initiatives that are required during a crisis. The CFO would also be expected to consider how the organisation could benefit from any government economic stimulus packages.
- CIO – with responsibility for information technology.
- Chief operations officer – representing what the organisation does or its 'raison d'être'.
- Company doctor (assuming the organisation has appointed a medical representative).
- Media communications manager – this role may sometimes be handled by the CEO, although some organisations will appoint a specialist in public and media relations.

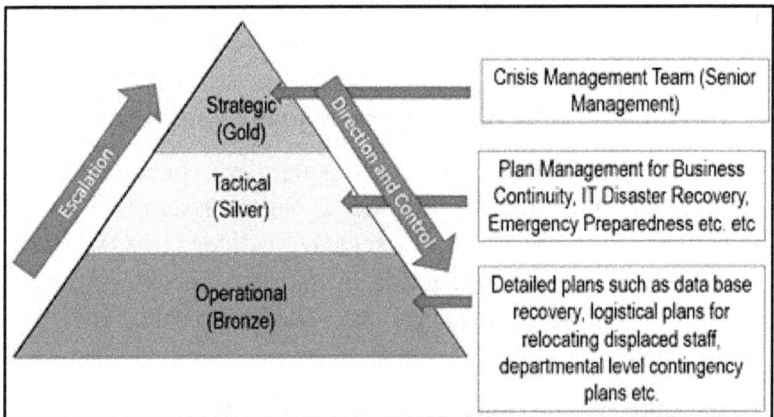

Figure 12: Typical three-tier crisis management structure

"A company-wide social media crisis communication plan allows you to respond quickly to any potential issue. Instead of debating how to handle things, or waiting for senior managers to weigh in, you can take action and prevent things from getting out of control."

(Newberry & Dawley, 2019)

In a typical three-tier command model, while a CMT would generally operate at the 'Strategic' level (sometimes referred to as 'Gold' or 'Command' level), the team may also decide to co-opt others who would normally be expected to function at the second level – the 'Tactical' level ('Silver'). For example, this could include those individuals with responsibility for managing business continuity and emergency preparedness.

For small- and medium-size enterprises (SMEs), because they have probably not reached a critical mass, they may only need to adopt a two-tier or even a single-tier command structure. Furthermore, it is entirely possible that the chief executive is also the individual who wears several other 'hats', including, perhaps, HR director, catering manager and receptionist. Consequently, SMEs should make sure that, even if some individuals are responsible for multiple aspects of the 'business', they still have sufficient representation for all appropriate parts of the organisation.

Regardless of the size of an organisation, what is also important is that every member of the CMT has at least one named backup who can stand-in as and when necessary. If it is logistically possible, they should also be in attendance at CMT meetings, whether the meeting is being run as a traditional round table or an online session. Their brief may only be to observe proceedings. However, should they be called upon to take a more active role on the CMT, they will already be up to speed on what has happened and been agreed in previous meetings.

6.4 What about a CMT meeting agenda?

First and foremost, we need to accept that the agenda for just about every crisis management meeting will be event driven. Moreover, whatever the nature of the crisis, any issues pertaining to the health and safety of employees and other stakeholders should be high up, if not at the top of the agenda. A life-threatening pandemic certainly meets that criteria.

In order to be effective, while avoiding precious time being wasted, like just about any other type of meeting, a crisis management meeting needs a predefined agenda. Along with the minutes from any previous meetings, the agenda must be circulated to attendees before the meeting. Events associated with some crises will be very dynamic, and in the case of a pandemic, the crisis can be exacerbated by members of the CMT succumbing to the contagion.

I remember many years ago watching a training film that ran for about 30 minutes, entitled 'Meetings, bloody meetings'. It featured John Cleese of Monty Python fame (a trailer of the film can be found on YouTube).

The film is very amusing, but it carries a serious message, one that has stayed with me in the years that have passed, so I would recommend looking at the trailer. It shows you enough to provide a flavour of how meetings should be organised, with specific emphasis on agenda setting before the meeting starts. If you can see a full version of the film, I would recommend it. There is also a sequel called 'More bloody meetings'.

What type of things are you likely to find in that pandemic-flavoured CMT meeting agenda? It is not easy to create the definitive agenda, as I would argue that it does not exist.

However, I would suggest that you consider the mock agenda below, which should help you construct your own. You should also read the case study of a pandemic plan exercise (see section 8) that I facilitated several years before the COVID-19 pandemic.

1. You are going to need the usual standards, such as:
   a. Meeting date/start time;
   b. Location details/URL link for joining an online meeting;
   c. Requested attendees[12]; and
   d. Reviewed and approved minutes of last meeting.
2. Human issues
   a. Current absenteeism statistics, including:
      i. Reasons for absenteeism;
      ii. Update on support programme(s) for 'at risk' employees;
      iii. Status on sick employees; and
      iv. Areas of organisation affected, and potential backfill options for absent staff.
   b. Report on social distancing initiative across the organisation's premises.
   c. Home working update.
   d. Availability of counselling for traumatised employees.

---

[12] You may find that it is useful to have a nominated 'gatekeeper' whose primary role is to allow access to authorised individuals only. This would allow the meeting chairperson to focus on running the meeting and avoid interruptions that can result from latecomers or dealing with attendees who may have technical issues.

3. Financial update from the CFO, which could include relevant input from any government economic stimulus packages.
4. Supply chain management update:
   a. Upstream; and
   b. Downstream.

If your organisation uses a JIT supply chain model, should any of the products or components depend upon commercial aviation, as we saw during the 2002-2003 SARS outbreak and now during the COVID-19 pandemic, commercial aviation all but stopped. Consequently, your JIT supply chain may well be broken.

5. Facilities management:
   a. Report on state of hand gels, paper towels, personal tissues, plus PPE, such as disposable gloves and face masks, etc.; and
   b. Daily premises cleaning update.
6. Review/agree actions on escalated issues from business continuity and emergency preparedness managers, etc.
7. Agree upon any appropriate stakeholder communication, including employees.
8. Any other business.
9. Date/time/venue for next meeting.

For those organisations that have a 24/7 market presence, the frequency of CMT meetings could be daily and, in some cases, several times during a 24-hour period, especially if the media and social media spotlights are focused on your operation. The nature and gravity of the crisis will be a key driver in this.

And finally ...

For a meeting to be effective, someone needs to write the minutes. As an old boss of mine used to say: "If it isn't in writing then it didn't happen, or it was never said." He used to be very pedantic about this point, but he was absolutely right.

So, please don't forget to ensure that someone is nominated as the minute taker. Or better still, consider making a recording of the meeting, either audio or if practical use video. Online platforms like Zoom have a facility to record a session – just as long as someone presses the 'record' button. This shouldn't be used as a substitute for the traditional minutes, but it could prevent any later disputes arising should anyone choose to challenge what was said by whom and when, and what the minute taker actually wrote.

CHAPTER 7: LOCKDOWNS: SAVING LIVES, SHATTERING ECONOMIES

This chapter considers how different countries have approached lockdown. There are those that have adopted a very relaxed manner, while others have been extremely oppressive. Which are right and which are wrong, which are better and which are worse, will only truly become apparent when some kind of final post-pandemic analysis can be conducted.

"We isolate now so when we gather again, no one is missing." An anonymous Haiku

In past pandemics, the world has experienced most of the social containment strategies we have seen deployed during COVID-19, but certainly not lockdowns on anything like the scale that have been endured during the COVID-19 pandemic. In addition to other countries around the world, at one point, much of China and all of India went into lockdown, meaning billions simultaneously found themselves in this state.

Let's be clear, isolation does not kill the virus, but it can reduce the rate of infection. It has given rise to the word 'Blursday', meaning an unknown day of the week resulting from the disorienting effect of a lockdown. All that said, can this mass confinement of the world's citizens really be justified? Taking different modelling approaches and using data from 11 European countries, both Imperial College London and the University of California, Berkeley, arrived at similar conclusions – the timely lockdowns executed in March 2020 served to save over 3 million lives in those countries.

7: Lockdowns: Saving lives, shattering economies

"According to one [study] conducted by Imperial College London, wide-scale rigorous lockdowns imposed in March 2020 averted 3.1 million deaths in 11 European countries (including the UK, Spain, Italy, France and Germany)." (Schwab & Malleret, 2020)

While the 'powers that be' also argued that lockdown measures would contain the virus and save lives, there has been a cost to pay. The most obvious one is the effect on the global economy, which will invariably prove to be a millstone around the necks of future generations. Just how much of a burden will depend upon how long the pandemic lasts, although it is fair to expect a substantial rise in debt-to-GDP ratios across the globe. Furthermore, countries with high dependency on service industries, such as tourism and hospitality, are certainly at a disadvantage. Moreover, the effects on the economies of individual countries will also be determined by how successful each has been in containing the spread of the virus.

Reflecting on how economies and businesses are changing to combat COVID-19, Former World Bank Chief Economist, Paul Romer, remarked:

"An economy can survive with 10 percent of the population in isolation. It can't survive when 50 percent of the population is in isolation."

(Murray & Parkinson, 2020)

We have seen businesses go under, and many have lost their jobs. What is more, with many economies shrinking, it is also a bad time for youngsters entering the job market for the first time, as employment opportunities dry up. While there are of course those who have been protected by economic stimulus packages their respective governments have introduced, others have not had this protection. This is especially true of ex-patriot workers stranded in foreign countries, who have found they are not eligible to receive any form of local subsistence allowance. Just about the only recourse for many stranded ex-pats was to try and get home. This often necessitated travelling with the dwindling number of airlines still operating, which were often exploiting the situation by charging very inflated fares. Naturally, airlines would argue it is all justified by the principles of 'supply and demand'.

From my own UK vantage point close to Manchester International Airport, I noted a massive reduction in the number of flights passing overhead. Even so, one constant has been the reliable, daily appearance of Qatar Airways, which has continued to operate a regular service unabated.

We must also not forget the collateral casualties from the pandemic with unrelated health concerns. Some have been reluctant to seek medical treatment for fear of being infected with coronavirus. Others had urgent hospital treatment delayed because health services had to switch their attention to addressing the COVID-19 onslaught.

Hospitals also denied patient visitor access and care homes adopted a similar policy. Although in the interest of reducing the serious threat from cross infection, it has caused much distress and heartbreak, especially when families were unable to be with loved ones in their final hours. And, we must not forget those individuals who have found the whole experience of lockdown a psychologically dauting situation to manage. To them, their front doors represented the entrance to a prison rather than a sanctuary.

November 2020, Manchester UK

Hundreds of people defied the coronavirus restrictions, gathering in Piccadilly Gardens in the UK city of Manchester in protest against England's second lockdown. Many had arrived by coach from other parts of the country, and the crowd displayed a total disregard for social distancing and the wearing of face masks.

Arrests were made by Greater Manchester Police, whose resources were already stretched because 10% of the force were off work due to COVID-19 (Robson, 2020).

Finally, we have witnessed the polarisation of communities – some demanding the lockdowns continue to save lives, others insisting the economy is opened up to protect jobs. In some countries, large multitudes have taken to the streets in protest. Groups primarily, although not exclusively, consisting of millennials have also been observed blatantly ignoring local face covering and social distancing directives while they continued their social lives unabated.

7.1 Wuhan, China – The world's first mass lockdown

This section is based primarily upon the account of a Chinese citizen who has requested to remain anonymous, and who regularly travels to Wuhan to visit an elderly relative. Arriving at the beginning of 2020, they planned to remain for just a few weeks, although with the intervention of coronavirus, their stay was extended by several months.

The capital of Hubei province, with a populace in excess of 10 million, Wuhan is the most densely populated city in central China. It is situated at the confluence of the Yangtze

River and, its largest tributary, the Han River, approximately 750 kilometres west of Shanghai.

The story of the doctor unfairly dubbed the 'Wuhan whistleblower', Dr Li Wenliang, has been widely chronicled. On realising that patients being treated in Wuhan Central Hospital for a mysterious pneumonia were actually presenting SARS-like symptoms, he shared his concerns with his colleagues at the end of December 2019. In this supposedly private message, he encouraged his colleagues to take extra precautions to protect themselves from the infection. Despite requesting confidentiality, his concerns were widely circulated and were subsequently posted on social media. Although later completely exonerated, Dr Li was initially reprimanded and accused of spreading false rumours on the Internet. Sadly, he contracted the disease and died on 7 February 2020, aged just 33.

By mid-January 2020, rumours originating from the hospitals that a SARS-like disease was circulating in Wuhan started spreading among local residents. At that time, there had been no official mention of the situation, and in fact, the media and government dismissed the rumours as being false. Even so, hospitals had already started clearing the wards of patients suffering with less-urgent conditions. China, of course, had had first-hand experience of SARS in 2002-2003, and it was severely criticised on that occasion for what amounted to an attempted cover-up (Guardian, 2003). The British medical journal, *The Lancet,* reported that in the days before his death, Dr Li Wenliang was alleged to have said:

> *"If the officials had disclosed information about the epidemic earlier, I think it would have been a lot better. There should be more openness and transparency."*
> (Green, 2020)

7: Lockdowns: Saving lives, shattering economies

In its report *COVID-19: Make it the Last Pandemic – A Summary,* TIP concurs with Green's remark acknowledging that "valuable time was lost". (TIP, 2021)

Before the enforced Wuhan lockdown, the virus spread rapidly, hospitals were at breaking point and PPE for health workers was in short supply. PPE manufacturers were calling their employees back from their Chinese New Year holiday break to meet the sudden surge in demand for their products.

Wuhan residents believe the actual death toll was far higher than the official figures suggested. This alleged discrepancy may have been driven by an official need to appear to be totally in control, a compelling aspect of the 'face saving' culture common in that part of the world.

New CDC figures appear to confirm that belief. When the agency tested 34,000 people in Wuhan for coronavirus antibodies, it found a rate of 4.43%. Extrapolating that figure across a city of close to 11 million people, that means nearly 490,000 people were infected, dwarfing the official tally of 50,354 cases (Sherwell, 2021). This would suggest that only 1 in 10 cases were recorded.

Initially, there was also no means of effectively testing people for COVID-19, as it was a novel virus. Meanwhile, two vloggers who referred to themselves as citizen journalists, Fang Bin and Chen Qiushi, using VPN, loaded several videos onto YouTube that documented what was happening in Wuhan. They recorded long lines of people seeking help at hospitals. The conditions inside were desperate and piles of body bags were seen in corridors as the mortuaries overflowed. By mid-February, Fang and Chen had 'disappeared' but, for posterity, their legacy remains on YouTube.

7: Lockdowns: Saving lives, shattering economies

7.1.1 The lockdown

Following the outbreak of what we now know as COVID-19, Chinese authorities imposed a complete lockdown in Wuhan on 23 January 2020, in an effort to contain the spread of the novel virus. This included the suspension of all public transport, rail, major highways and air transport. The lockdown was eventually relaxed on 8 April 2020. But, in the hours leading up to the initial closing down of the city, an estimated 500,000 managed to beat the deadline and leave. It is highly likely that some took the virus with them.

Other Chinese provinces soon followed Wuhan and Hubei's lockdown lead, resulting in an estimated 234 million quarantined in China alone. During this time, people returning to China from overseas were routinely quarantined in hotels for 14 days. In the event that 5 or less passengers on an inbound flight to China tested positive for COVID, flights to and from that destination would be suspended for one week. Up to 10 positive cases and flights would stop running for 2 weeks. More than 10 cases and flights would be suspended indefinitely.

It is usual in Wuhan for most residents to live in high-rise apartment buildings, sometimes with as many as 50 or more floors in which several hundred families reside. It is also quite common for several of these high rises to be grouped together in what can best be described as a gated community. When the lockdown started, these gated communities were locked and, unless they were classed as essential workers, no one was permitted to leave their apartments except to be taken to hospital. Every day, residents had to report their temperature to the community management team, which would normally have one person assigned to manage each high rise. This restriction remained in place for 76 days.

During the lockdown, local food stores were only allowed to sell to the nominated representatives of each community, who would also organise any medication that their community's residents needed. This would be delivered directly to the residents' apartments. Older residents were treated as a priority, and they would receive fish and meat free of charge. All non-essential shops, restaurants and cafes were closed.

With public transport suspended, volunteer car drivers and shuttle buses were introduced to enable essential workers, especially health workers, to get to their respective places of work. The day following lockdown, China deployed an extra 1,800 doctors and medical specialists from Beijing to Hubei province, along with PPE and medical supplies. Doctors from other parts of China followed later.

Post-Thanksgiving: Massive COVID case spike observed

Both national and religious holiday periods (such as the Chinese New Year vacation) can represent a major risk of seriously propagating a contagion during a pandemic.

In another example, while the estimates do vary, around four million US citizens are known to have travelled over the 2020 Thanksgiving holiday, resulting in a massive spike in new COVID-19 cases. On 26 November, Thanksgiving Day, at just under 162,000, the new daily case count appeared to be following a downward trend. However, by 11 December, that daily new case figure had risen to 248,000.

7.1.2 Relaxing of the lockdown

When the lockdown was relaxed on 8 April 2020, although they were discouraged from doing so, residents were permitted to leave their communities, but usually for no more than two hours at a time. They were clocked out and clocked back in again by their community officials. If they used public transport, they had to present their smartphone health code (see section 7.1.4) before being permitted to board. This had to be scanned on boarding and alighting to facilitate 'track and trace' activities. Should someone who was later diagnosed with COVID-19 have travelled on the same vehicle, this would establish exactly who was on the bus at the same time. Anyone who came into close proximity with an infected person would find their health code change from green to amber. Before the outbreak, buses would be driver-only, but a second crew member was added to validate the health check status of passengers before permitting them to board.

Despite the relaxation of regulations, those individuals wanting to shop or perhaps go to their bank would need to present their health code and have their temperature taken before being allowed to enter those premises. Moreover, without exception, if they were not wearing a face mask, they would not be permitted entry or for that matter be allowed to board a bus.[13]

7.1.3 Ten million tests in two weeks

During the second half of May 2020, China mounted a massive logistical operation in Wuhan, when every one of its ten million inhabitants was tested for the virus in a process

---

[13] In October 2021, I visited the Guggenheim Museum in Bilbao, Spain. While no one was interested in my vaccination status, I was not permitted entry until my temperature was checked and I was wearing a face mask. This had been the only occasion since the start of the pandemic that anyone has been interested in my temperature.

that took around two weeks. Everyone had their test results returned within two days. With the exception of France, Germany, Italy, Spain and the UK, that is more tests than every European country had achieved in the first nine months of the pandemic. Furthermore, at least nine of the countries falling into that category have populations in excess of Wuhan.

Based apparently on a British concept, the swabs from the Wuhan exercise were tested in batches of ten at a time, and providing the combined test was negative, all ten individuals included in that batch would be flagged accordingly. If, however, the presence of the virus was detected, the ten people would be tested again individually, enabling any positive cases to be identified. The batch approach clearly increased the overall efficiency of the exercise.

7.1.4 The Alipay health code

Alipay is a mobile and online payment platform that was first introduced into Hangzhou, China, in 2004, and is now used extensively throughout the country. The company claims to have 1.2 billion users, which includes approximately 80% of the Chinese population (1.15 billion), plus international merchants who sell to Chinese consumers.

In 2020, Alipay introduced the use of the QR code to support the containment of COVID-19. By using the Alipay app on smartphones, a code turns 'red' for those who should be in quarantine. If you are waiting for test results or you have come into contact with a confirmed COVID-19 case, your code would be 'amber', otherwise, your code would be 'green'. Individuals would need to provide data, such as their Chinese ID number, phone number, residential address and their place of work.

While the virus is in circulation, citizens will only be allowed to leave their communities if their health code is 'green'. *The New York Times* conducted an analysis exercise of the software code and discovered that the app does far more than decide whether a smartphone's owner poses a contagion risk.

"It also appears to share information with the police, setting a template for new forms of automated social control that could persist long after the epidemic subsides"

(Mozur et al, 2020).

The Times's analysis found that as soon as a user grants the software access to personal data, a piece of the program labelled "reportInfoAndLocationToPolice" sends the person's location, city name and an identifying code number to a server.

The majority of buildings, including work locations, public buildings and residential compounds have security guards in situ who are responsible for measuring the temperature of anyone entering. They are also expected to check an individual's Alipay health code before allowing entrance. The 20% of Chinese citizens who do not own a smartphone are faced with a challenge, and they are generally dependent either upon their children or their local communities for support.

Although the introduction of the health code by Alipay has enabled China to relax lockdowns across the country, it has raised concerns from international human rights advocates. Known for its 'Big Brother' approach to controlling the population, the advocates fear that China will use the health monitoring software as a means to increase its ability to 'manage' its citizens.

7.1.5 The Wuhan stigma

As the lockdown was relaxed, people from Wuhan found it difficult getting work outside of Hubei province. Prospective employers were reluctant to employ anyone associated with what had been China's epicentre for the virus. Prime Minister Li Keqiang encouraged people who had lost their jobs to become street vendors.

Broadcast by the BBC, *'Three Years in Wuhan'*, Episode three tells the story of a group of businessmen from Wuhan who, after lockdown had been lifted and with government approval, went on a trip to Hangzhou, Jiaxing and Shanghai. Software entrepreneur Huang Tiesen explains that on arriving in Hangzhou, they tried to book into a hotel but were turned away. At another hotel they managed to slip in, but on later realising where they were from, they were ejected by hotel staff at 5.00 am the next morning. In desperation, they hired a car and slept in that.

"It was very difficult when others started to blame Wuhan (for causing the pandemic) and call people here idiots. It was really hurtful because people outside didn't understand what we were going through."

Huang Tiesen (*Three Years in Wuhan*, 2020)

7.1.6 The positive legacy of SARS

China had first-hand experience of the 2002-2003 SARS outbreak, particularly as the virus is known to have originated in Guangdong province. Consequently, because of the connection to SARS, unlike some people in other countries, individuals in Wuhan took the COVID-19 outbreak very seriously, especially as many had personally experienced SARS. So, just maybe, that 2002-2003 outbreak had provided a rehearsal that the vast majority of the world did not get.

All that said, local Wuhan officials were slow to understand the gravity of the early reports of hospitalised people presenting SARS-like symptoms. Instead, Dr Li Wenliang was allegedly censored (Verna Yu, 2020), and the spread of the virus gathered momentum, while any chance, however small, of preventing its proliferation was lost.

7.2 Lockdowns, saunas and vodka

Despite the world having had some limited experience of dealing with coronaviruses before, we still have much to learn about the specifics of COVID-19, especially when a new mutation is discovered such as Omicron. Consequently, there is no precise model or playbook on which countries and organisations can base their pandemic plans, mitigation measures and contingencies. Therefore, it is hardly surprising that each country is for all intents and purposes 'doing its own thing' in whichever way it thinks is best. Their respective coronavirus lockdown 'rules', country by country, include the way in which they each report their COVID-19 confirmed cases and associated fatalities. This will invariably lead to some reporting inconsistencies.

Even so, we have learned from previous epidemics and pandemics that while the world waits for a vaccine, cure or an effective treatment for the coronavirus, isolation, quarantining and social distancing are all valid responses. Moreover, changes to social behaviour can also make a big difference, such as more frequent handwashing, not shaking hands or hugging and, as the French would say, *'arreter de faire la bise'* – stop cheek kissing. The Māori traditional greeting of rubbing noses should be temporarily suspended, too.

In addition to observing a safe sneezing and coughing etiquette, we have been encouraged not to touch our face, because if we have somehow contaminated our hands, our eyes, nose and mouth are areas where viruses can easily enter our body. Some estimates show that we can touch our face as many as 20 times an hour. But, psychologist Natasha Tiwari explains "we can't help it, it's part of our DNA. We're hardwired to do it", (Tiwari, 2020).

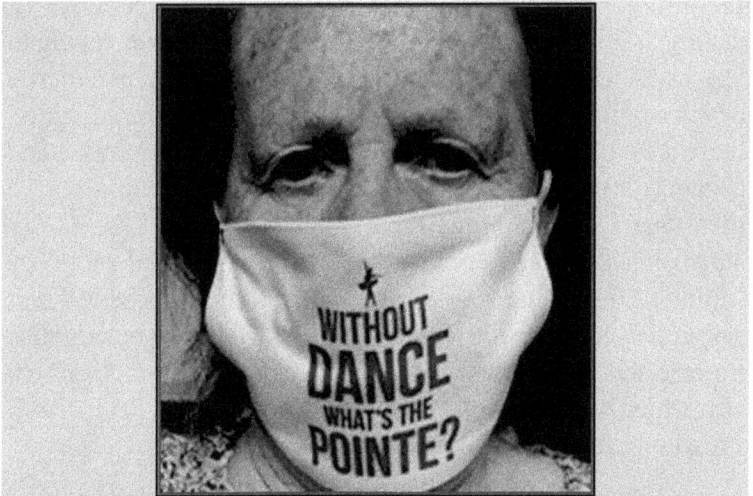

Figure 13: Pictured wearing a mask that rather appropriately makes 'A Pointe' is Anne Jobson, ballet instructor at 'Ballet for Adults' in the UK city of Exeter

Regrettably, some countries were either too slow to adopt or even chose to ignore recommendations emanating from the WHO, such as the wearing of face masks and conducting extensive testing. With regard to face masks, I make no apology for saying what some may consider to be contentious.

It has been widely reported in several countries that there are those individuals who just refuse to wear masks, even to go into a shop. To me their actions are implying that they are quite happy to be inconsiderate and really don't care if they share their germs with other people. I am equally sure that some of those individuals who claim that they cannot wear them for health reasons are not genuine. When all is said and done, there are those countries where the culture means that everyone unreservedly wears a face mask.

"Patients without medical conditions ask GPs for sick notes to exempt them from mask rules."

(Diver, 2020)

Professor Martin Marshall, Chair of the Royal College of General Practitioners, has expressed his concern that doctors' valuable time was being wasted by these frivolous requests. But as one UK nurse, very distinctly put it:

"Until you've done Cardiopulmonary Resuscitation (CPR) in scrubs, scrubs gown, plastic apron, FFP3 masks, visor, hood and two pairs of gloves, you should probably stop moaning about wearing a mask to the shops."

Staying with the point regarding clinicians wearing face masks, hospital operating theatre staff will always wear them. Edwards nicely presents the rationale behind this when he remarked:

"Surgeons and nurses performing clean surgery wear disposable face masks. The purpose of face masks is two-fold: to prevent the passage of germs from the

surgeon's nose and mouth into the patient's wound and to protect the surgeon's face from sprays and splashes from the patient."

(Edwards, 2016)

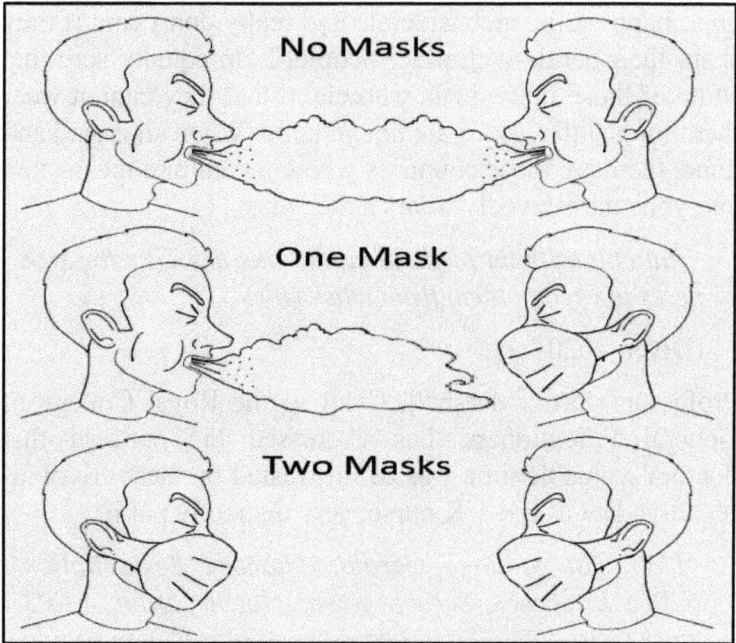

Figure 14: What a difference a mask can make
Artwork: Geoffrey A. Clark

Enter the 'COVIDiots'

One morning I heard a new coronavirus-spawned word while I was watching a Breakfast TV news programme – *'COVIDiots'*. Many airports and commercial airlines insist that travellers observe social distancing protocols and wear face masks continuously from the moment they enter their departure airport right up to the moment they walk out of their destination airport. This is as much for the safety of the individual travellers as it is to protect airport and airline employees.

The news programme reported that the face mask rules had been flouted on one particular flight from the Greek island of Zante to Cardiff, Wales. The flight was full and had around 200 passengers and crew onboard. One traveller said the flight was carrying several 'COVIDiots' who not only ignored social distancing while waiting to board, but wouldn't wear masks while on the plane. Moreover, the cabin crew appeared inept and didn't seem to care about the absence of masks. Another passenger claimed there "wasn't much" policing of the rules. At least 16 of the travellers have since tested positive for COVID-19, and every passenger has now had to go into isolation for 14 days (BBC News (Wales), 2020).

When two people are not observing social distancing protocols, figure 14 illustrates how masks can help make a difference. When neither is wearing a mask, infection can more easily pass from one to the other. Where only one wears a mask, infection can still pass from the person without the mask to the person with. In the third case, where both are wearing masks, the possibility of either infecting the other is dramatically reduced.

And what is it with those people who insist on wearing masks that cover their mouths but not their nose? Perhaps they are unaware that, like their mouths, their noses are also connected to their lungs. By not covering both, they are defeating the object of mask wearing. For anyone in doubt, the WHO provides advice on its website about 'when and how to use masks'.

Maybe this is the stuff of fantasy, but I keep coming across a report from the 1918-1919 Spanish flu outbreak. It claims that a special officer working for the US Board of Health shot a man for refusing to wear an influenza mask. The man apparently survived and after hospital treatment he was arrested for refusing to comply with the order. Could this happen today?

Born in 1933, the now 87-year-old June Selway remembers living through World War II. Immediately following the declaration of war, in the interest of their safety, many children were evacuated from UK cities. When comparing the air raids of the 1940s with the situation in 2020 and the fuss some make about wearing a face mask, June simply says:

"Try being evacuated from your home for years because of a blitz ... running to the air-raid shelter most nights. Just wear your masks ... it's little enough to do."

In the instance of the 2002-2003 SARS experience, tens of thousands were quarantined, which ultimately enabled the virus to be contained within a few months of the initial outbreak. That valuable lesson has clearly not been lost. With COVID-19, at one point in time, well over one billion people found themselves in a lockdown situation, sometimes of the most draconian nature.

The whole point of a lockdown is to contain the spread of the disease by instructing non-essential workers to remain at home. This, in turn, means fewer people are infected, and it reduces the impact on a country's health services because of reduced numbers needing hospitalisation.

Having followed the media from several different countries in researching for this book, frequent reference has been made to the 'R' number, or the 'reproduction number'. The UK government's definition of 'R' is the average number of secondary infections produced by a single infected person.

An R number of 1 means that on average every person who is infected will infect one other person, meaning the total number of infections is stable.

If R is 2, on average, each infected person infects two more people. In the following illustration, it assumes that R=2 and each individual who has become infected are themselves in an infectious state within four days.

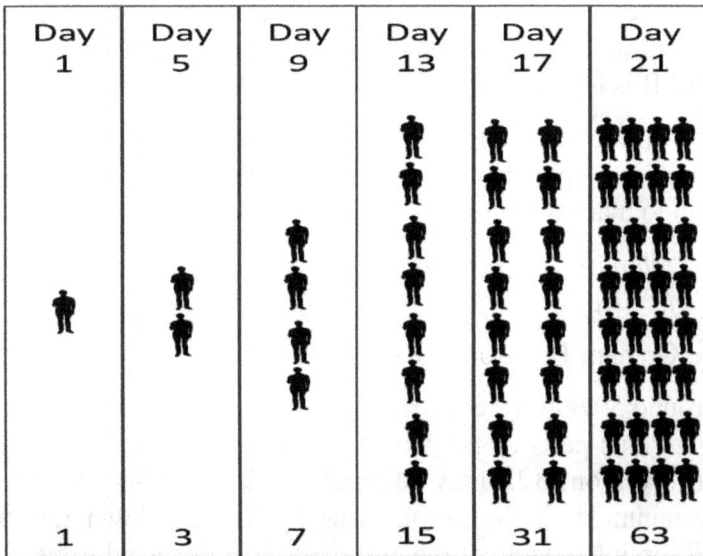

Day 1	Day 5	Day 9	Day 13	Day 17	Day 21
1	3	7	15	31	63

Figure 15: Example of unimpeded spread of COVID-19 when R = 2

Using this model, by the end of the third week, 63 people will have been infected. If this situation is allowed to continue unabated and the number of confirmed cases approximately doubles every four days, after eight weeks, that infection count will be in excess of 65,000.

These conclusions do not allow for a 'super-spreader' occurrence, and the earlier example of the flight from Greece to Wales is a point in case. Likewise, the 26 September 2020 Amy Coney Barret White House ceremony resulted in 11 people subsequently testing positive (Annett, 2020).

R has changed over time.[14] For example, it falls when there is a reduction in the number of contacts between people, which reduces transmission. Even so, by comparing various countries and their approach to lockdown, you will see variations. But, all countries should avoid exiting lockdown until R is less than '1'.

The first country to implement a lockdown policy was China, which was oppressive to the point that some may consider it akin to martial law.

> *"China's coronavirus lockdown strategy: Brutal but effective."*

> (Graham-Harrison & Kuo, 2020)

Around 50,000 were quarantined during the SARS outbreak in various parts of the world, including 18,000 in Beijing. However, on 23 January 2020, China kicked off its attempted containment of the coronavirus by locking down the 10 million inhabitants of the city of Wuhan, believed to be the origin of the outbreak. But, the lockdown coincided with the start of the Chinese New Year holiday. The country's

---

[14] With arrival of the Omicron variant, Reuters reported that scientists believe the number of new cases is doubling every 1.5 to 3 days (Nebehay, 2021).

Outbound Tourism Research Institute estimated that more than 7 million international trips were planned during this period, while many more millions would also be travelling within China. So, had the genie already got out of the bottle and was COVID-19 spreading before the Wuhan lockdown?[15]

Public transport stopped, only food shops and pharmacies could remain open, and private cars were banned, unless granted special permission. Some residents were even banned from leaving their homes, and had to rely on suppliers delivering their provisions. Quarantined arrivals from overseas were also required to follow the 'not one step' policy, which meant they literally could not step over the threshold of their apartment or hotel room for 14 days.

A very uncompromising policy of door-to-door health checks was conducted by officials. Anyone suspected of being infected with COVID-19 was forced into isolation.

The wearing of face masks became ubiquitous across the country.

With the Chinese New Year holiday period coinciding with the start of the lockdown, industry effectively shut down in China. Organisations depending on a JIT supply chain model with products sourced in China, felt the effects of the spreading virus almost immediately. Both the UK-based Jaguar Land Rover and the Italian car manufacturer Fiat were among the first to express supply chain concerns.

---

[15] When the discovery of Omicron variant was first announced by South African scientists, it is highly likely that it had already proliferated across much of the world.

The world also started scrambling to source PPE that was needed for protecting health workers from the virus. Moreover, countries that had stockpiled PPE of a type suitable for influenza, which included the UK, found this was inadequate when dealing with coronavirus. Much of the world's supply was also made in China, although the global PPE shortage was further exacerbated when President Trump banned the export of PPE from the US. At the beginning of the pandemic, the UK was producing just 1% of its PPE needs. By August 2020, that number had increased to 70%.

Staying with the UK, its devolved parliaments defined the parameters for each of the four countries making up the union. Although they were similar, there were slight variations from one to another to reflect their specific circumstances. For example, beyond its larger cities, Scotland has an average of around 67 people per square mile in contrast to the more densely populated England which has 1,010. As for Northern Ireland, it shares a land border with the Republic of Ireland, which is not part of the UK.

The procurement and distribution of PPE in England proved a major challenge. In normal times, PPE would be distributed to 151 Primary Care Trusts (PCT). But, with the coronavirus outbreak, PPE use became essential in more than 58,000 locations that extended to doctors' surgeries, clinics, residential care homes, nursing homes and dentists. This massive logistical nightmare was ultimately managed by the UK armed forces.

23 March 2020, Prime Minister Boris Johnson instructed all but essential workers in England to remain at home except for food shopping, medically related activities or to exercise for a maximum of one hour every day, such as walking in a local park. Gymnasiums, pubs, clubs and restaurants were

closed, although those restaurants that could offer take-out food were permitted to continue trading.

Individuals who could WFH were naturally encouraged to do so. It should be stressed that the chief medical officers (CMOs) from each of the four UK countries remained in regular dialogue. Moreover, COVID-19 related experiences were also shared with the CMOs of other countries outside of the UK.

Foodbanks globally have seen a massive increase in demand. In the UK, a 59% rise has been experienced and Italy opened soup kitchens in its worst hit areas. Meanwhile, foodbanks across the US are under widespread and growing pressure as they cope with an increase in the 'new needy' amid the coronavirus pandemic ensuing unemployment (Lakhani, et al., 2020).

"Just as poverty has been a propagator of the pandemic, the pandemic has become a propagator of poverty."

(Bryant, 2020)

Sweden's approach to lockdown was more relaxed, and those bars and restaurants capable of ensuring social distancing were permitted to remain open. Conversely, when compared with the more favourable case and fatality counts of its Nordic neighbours, Sweden's figures are less than impressive, and some have been critical of its seemly nonchalant cavalier approach to lockdown.

Swedish state epidemiologist, Dr Anders Tegnell, believes that the country will have achieved up to 40% exposure to the virus, while its Nordic neighbours will be around 1%. Dr Tegnell justified the relaxed approach explaining that

Sweden believed that, before the end of May 2020, between 30-40% of the population would have been exposed to COVID-19. By reaching this goal, this would have achieved a high degree of 'herd immunity'. (Tegnell, 2020).

That said, even allowing for any asymptomatic cases that have not been identified by testing, with the benefit of hindsight, it does seem that Tegnell's herd immunity aspiration was somewhat over ambitious.

Although Sweden's first wave seems longer than many other countries, it is possible that its more relaxed lockdown attitude may indeed pay dividends in the longer term. There have been examples around the world in a number of countries with citizens demonstrating against the lockdowns they are having to endure. Now Sweden, like other countries, is facing another pandemic wave, just maybe the Swedes will not be so lockdown weary as other nationalities might be. Even so, what a second wave that is proving to be which, before year-end 2020, its peak is more than ten times higher than its first. However, at just under 9,000 its 31 December fatality count is around 2% of its declared cases. But by mid-August, 2021, Sweden's death rate was reported to be 10 times higher than its Scandinavian neighbours (Bendix, 2021). However, when compared across Europe by deaths per capita (DPC), Sweden was 23rd out of the 48 countries/provinces reporting.

European DPC Ratings	Country	Total Death Count	Deaths per Capita by percentage
1	Hungary	30,114	0.313%

23	Sweden	14,688	0,114%
39	Denmark	2,614	0.045%
43	Finland	1,039	0.019%
44	Norway	828	0.015%

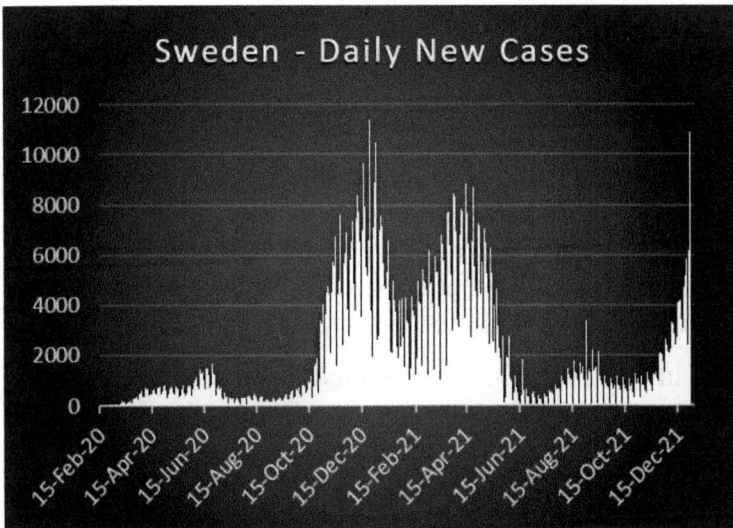

Figure 16: Sweden's daily new cases as of 31 December 2021

In the Mediterranean island republic of Malta, initially, a €1,000 fine (approximately $1,175 US) was introduced for anyone caught breaking the COVID-19 quarantine regulations. This was subsequently raised to €3,000, and it was reported that, following spot checks conducted by the police, a Frenchman based in Malta had breached quarantine on five separate occasions. He was subsequently fined

€9,000. Malta raised the fine for a third time offence to €10,000, and there have been no reported breaches since.

Failure to observe the social distancing rule of not meeting in more than groups of three was also enforced in Malta. This attracted a more modest fine of €100. By the end of April 2020, 645 fines had been recorded with 96 being issued for one single event.

On the other side of the world, the Australian state of Victoria wasted no time and declared a state of emergency on 16 March 2020. Meanwhile, Western Australia was fining people as much as $50,000 (circa US $35,000) and up to one year in jail for breaching mandatory isolation. In New South Wales (NSW), the same crime carried a less draconian $10,000 fine, with up to six months in jail. Not complying with social distancing could cost you a $1,000 fine. NSW later added a $5,000 fine for anyone deliberately coughing or spitting at an 'essential worker', with a repeat offence attracting a six-month prison sentence.

Still in Australia, 7-News reported that three young women were apprehended when trying to cross the border into Queensland, after two of them had previously tested positive for COVID-19 before leaving Melbourne. They were charged on 23 July 2020 with providing false or misleading documents plus fraud, and they face up to five years in jail plus hefty fines.

As Christmas 2020 approached, the UK ONS announced that more than 27,000 pandemic regulation-related fines had been given by police in Great Britain alone (England, Scotland and Wales). However, these fines were far from being evenly distributed.

7: Lockdowns: Saving lives, shattering economies

"The 27,000 fines, mostly for gatherings, are not evenly spread geographically. Leicester has been under the longest-standing restrictions – yet it has a far lower rate of fines than north-west England, which has faced similar challenges."

(Triggle, 2020)

The reality is that when confronted by the threat of rising COVID-19 case numbers, a country is generally dammed if it goes into lockdown and is dammed if it doesn't. Taiwan is certainly one exception worthy of note.

A lockdown will invariably be to the detriment of a country's economy and its non-essential businesses, while its population, although potentially better protected from the virus, can expect to suffer varying degrees of hardship. The more severe the lockdown, the tougher it will be on the economy, and millions may well find themselves nosediving into extreme poverty.

Conversely, if a country does not go into lockdown, that might be good news for the economy, but more of its citizens will be placed at a greater risk of becoming victims of COVID-19.

"We have seen leaders all around the world posturing, wanting to blame other countries or other individuals for what is happening."

(Davidson, 2020)

Furthermore, some leaders just seem to be completely out of their depth and are struggling to manage the pandemic consequences that their countries are suffering.

While I am sure that every country will have their own stories about how good, bad or indifferent their leaders have been in handling the situation, initially, I want to focus on just two who have not had a good press.

The first is the Brazilian President, Jair Bolsonaro who presides over a population in excess of 212 million. Even though he tested positive for COVID-19 on 6 July 2020, he has been guilty of belittling the coronavirus, while telling supporters that it was nothing to worry about.

"In a televised address last week, he repeated a now well-worn phrase. "It's just a little flu or the sniffles," he said, blaming the media once again for the hysteria and panic over Covid-19."

(Watson, 2020)

The tragedy is that by 31 December 2021, Brazil's COVID-19 case count was over 22 million, while its corresponding fatality statistics are in excess of 600,000. Even so, on 16 April 2020, Bolsonaro sacked his Minister of Health, Luiz Henrique Mandetta, after he had urged people to observe social distancing and remain indoors. Mandetta's replacement, Nelson Teich, resigned after only being in the job for one month, although without giving any reason for quitting.

To be quite cynical, Bolsonaro seems utterly determined to keep the economy open, but without any regard of the cost to Brazilian lives.

The second is Belarus President Alexander Lukashenko who has also taken a rather flippant approach to dealing with the pandemic. Belarus is a landlocked country bordered by Russia, Latvia, Lithuania, Poland and Ukraine. Its population is around 9.5 million, while the population density is 118 people per square mile (188 per square km).

7: Lockdowns: Saving lives, shattering economies

Writing for Reuters, back in April 2020, Andrei Makhovsky reported that Lukashenko had stated that nobody will die from the coronavirus in Belarus even though, at that time, there had already been 26 fatalities in the country, and by 31 December 2021, over 5,500 had died.

"It was the latest show of defiance by the strongman leader, who has dismissed worries about the disease as a "psychosis" and variously suggested drinking vodka, going to saunas and driving tractors to fight the virus.

In stark contrast to other European countries, Belarus has kept its borders open and even allowed soccer matches in the national league to be played in front of spectators."

(Makhovsky, 2020)

To juxtapose the seemingly frivolous Bolsonaro and Lukashenko styles of pandemic management with a much more divergent approach, praise has been heaped on the way New Zealand (NZ) has managed the virus to date. Moreover, it has only ever recorded one case of SARS and no cases of MERS, so, it hardly fits the same profile as the South-East Asian countries that have had first-hand experience of a coronavirus outbreak.

Prime Minister Jacinda Ardern's decision to close the border to non-national's clearly helped the country make a good start in managing the situation.

NZ has a population of around 5 million and an average density of 46 persons per square mile. The distance from Australia, its nearest neighbour, is around 2,500 miles (4,000 kilometres).

7: Lockdowns: Saving lives, shattering economies

The first confirmed COVID-19 case was diagnosed on 28 February 2020, and it closed it borders less than three weeks later, by which time the confirmed case count was still only 28. A State of Emergency (SoE) was declared on 24 March, in response to the case count having jumped by a factor seven to reach 208 in the five days since the border closure.

The SoE expired on 13 May 2020, when the country entered a National Transition Period that was due to last three months.

With the threat level raised to its highest point, 'Level 4 – Lockdown', it has meant that except essential workers, citizens have been instructed to remain at home barring vital personal movement (e.g. collecting food provisions or medical reasons, etc.).

Safe exercising was permitted within an individual's immediate locality, although any form of travel was severely curtailed. All events and gatherings were banned, while non-essential businesses and public venues were closed down.

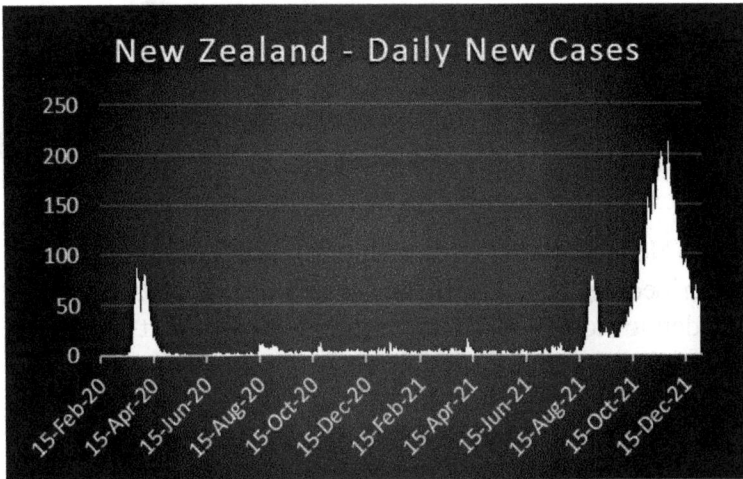

Figure 17: New Zealand's first wave COVID-19 statistics, 31 December 2021

By year end, apart from its early but fairly modest first wave, by year-end 2020, NZ, like Taiwan, had very little to report. That was until August 2021 when a second wave began to develop. However, with the new daily case count remaining below 100, this certainly compares favourably with much of the remainder of the world. Even so, while still low compared with other countries, that daily count had doubled within two months.

But despite its early and apparent continued success, not everyone has been totally convinced with NZ's pandemic management. Professor Patricia Davidson, Dean of Johns Hopkins University School of Nursing, believes that strong leadership during the crisis is essential and uses NZ's Jacinda Ardern as an example. However, during a COVID-19: Psychological Impact, Wellbeing and Mental Health – Discussion Panel, she then went on to say that:

"It's much easier to contain the virus if you are an isolated island."

(Davidson, 2020)

She may have a point about NZ, so let's compare it with another island nation, Japan, which also made a good start.

Like New Zealand, Australia also adopted what is best described as a nationalistic isolationist approach to the pandemic along with a low vaccination take up. It has tightly controlled its international borders and apart from two relatively minor surges within the first five months of the pandemic, its daily new case count (DNCC) has remained very low. However, as July 2021 arrived, the DNCC soared dramatically suggesting the country's isolationist policy was no longer working effectively.

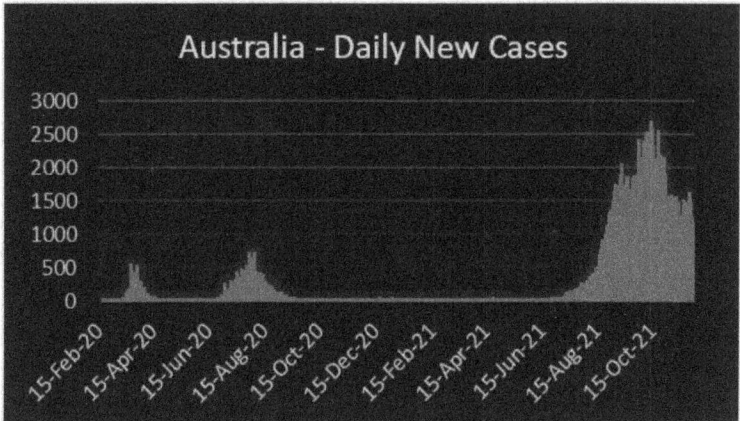

Figure 18: Australia's COVID-19 statistics, 31st December 2021

Similar to NZ, Japan is a group of islands, although at more than 126 million, its population is 25 times greater than NZ with only around 50% more land mass. But when you compare their COVID-19 case counts, Japan's is only 16 times higher than NZ, and so has a much lower confirmed cases per capita. Rather surprisingly, Japan, as yet, has also not gone into a formal lockdown, and despite the disparity of population sizes, Japan's testing count is only around 200,000 greater than NZ.

"When you look at Germany or South Korea, Japan's testing figures look like they're missing a zero."

(Wingfield-Hayes, 2020)

No movement restrictions were placed on Japanese citizens and many businesses were permitted to remain open, including shops, hairdressers and restaurants.

There are certainly a number of circumstances that may have contributed towards helping Japan to be an early contender for one of Bill Gates's 'A' grades for pandemic preparedness. However, there is no one obvious single factor that can be identified.

Before the coronavirus outbreak, Japan already had a track and trace process in place, although unlike other app-based approaches, Japan's was analogue. Even so, while other countries had to design and implement a process and then train operators, Japan was able to hit the ground running. It is unclear whether this analogue process would be scalable or not should it be required to manage greater case numbers in a future wave.

There is also a school of thought that believes that Japan learned many early useful lessons when it was presented with the *fait-accompli* of having to manage the COVID-19 crisis onboard the Diamond Princess (refer to section 12.11.1). With the world watching on, having the virus arriving on your doorstep with an infected cruise ship docking in

Yokohama, is certainly likely to have grabbed the attention of the local community.

Although there is evidence that obesity can be a factor in an individual's chances of surviving COVID-19, Japan has one of the lowest obesity rates in the world, which is likely to weigh heavily in its favour. Even so, in mid-April, a SoE was declared in response to a spike in case numbers. Japanese local governments were granted the authority to 'urge' citizens to stay inside, but unlike other countries, they could not apply any punitive measures or legal force. The number of daily new cases noticeably reduced and the SoE remained in operation for one month.

During this time, citizens were encouraged by doctors and medical experts to follow the 'Three Cs'. This meant avoiding:

- Closed spaces with poor ventilation;
- Crowded areas; and
- Close contact situations, such as close-range conversations.

Time reported that Mikihito Tanaka, a professor at Waseda University, said:

"You could say that Japan has had an expert-led approach, unlike other countries"

(Du & Huang, 2020)

With politicians being slow to react and take ownership of the crisis, perhaps Tanaka's observations hit the right mark.

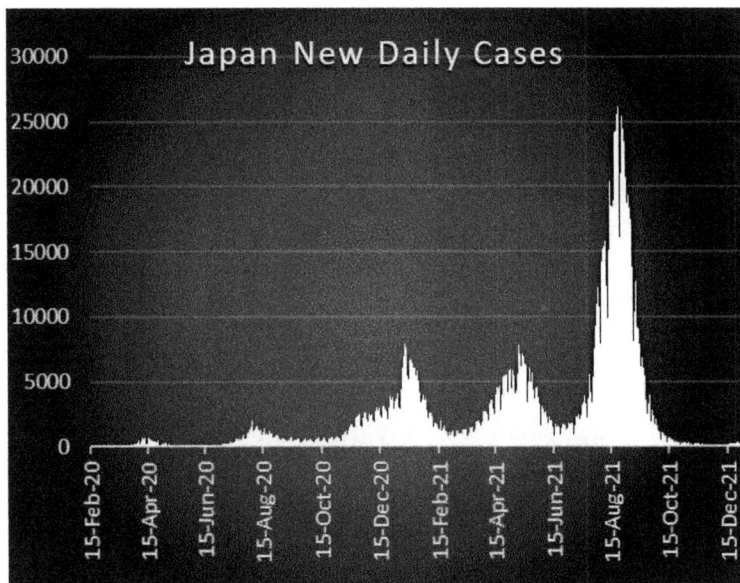

Figure 19: Unlike New Zealand, Japan has now had five waves

Regardless of which country you are in, the easing of restrictions should not be taken as a signal that the pandemic is over. As July 2020 arrived, something started to go wrong in Japan. Within a month of lifting its SoE, a new one had to be imposed. This ultimately led onto a third wave as year-end 2020 approached.

> *"Officials have begun to speak of a phase in which people "live with the virus," with a recognition that Japan's approach has no possibility of wiping out the pathogen."*

(Du & Huang, 2020)

The arrival of July 2021 saw not only the commencement of the delayed Olympic Games but also a rapid rise in new daily case counts. Even so, the Japanese government were insisting that there was no relationship between the games and the case count rise.

So, arguably, one of the few countries definitely in poll position to receive one of Bill Gates's 'A' grades (see section 4.9) for pandemic preparedness has to be Taiwan, one of the six worst hit locations from the 2002-2003 SARS outbreak. It clearly learned the lessons to be gained from that experience.

Returning to the analogy used in section 4.9.4 of the pandemic being a marathon rather than a sprint, the reality is that countries will invariably find it necessary to impose more than one lockdown. Moreover, the actual size of a country may affect whether it impose constraints on discrete parts or applies restrictions to the entire country.

After it had relaxed its initial lockdown measures, in response to a spike of new cases, China locked down Beijing, a city of 20 million inhabitants. Similarly, in England, the city of Leicester (population 330,000) was locked down at the end of June, while the remainder of the country had largely relaxed lockdown. About one month later, the UK re-established restrictions to areas in the North West of the country, including Greater Manchester, in response to COVID-19 spikes, affecting around four million inhabitants. Australia has taken comparable action in relation to the city of Melbourne (population 4.5 million), in addition to imposing a night-time curfew. In Belgium, a night-time curfew order was also imposed on the city of Antwerp, with the threat of even the capital city of Brussels following suit.

Even into 2021 some countries introduced further lockdown measures, particularly in response to the rapid spread of the Omicron variant.

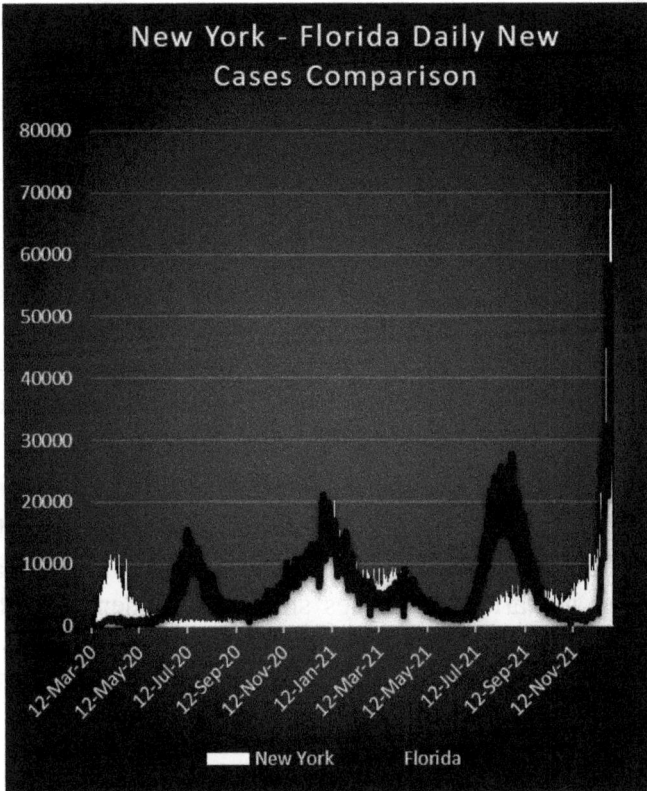

Figure 20: New York – Florida: Daily new case comparison

By making a comparison of two states in the US, New York and Florida, we can see as New York was exiting the first wave around the end of May, Florida was just entering. By year-end 2020, both states had entered a second wave almost alongside each other. Likewise, both states simultaneously entered a third wave although the Florida daily new case count was far more severe than New York's. In fact, Florida's DNCC figure was approximately five times that of New York. Even so, despite the comparison of the two sets of pandemic waves being largely out of sync, it is noticeable that the late 2021 Omicron arrival seems to be affecting both states simultaneously.

As the pandemic ebbs and flows, in response, lockdowns will be relaxed or intensified. Rather worryingly, there are those people who seem to be deluded that once the lockdown in their respective countries has been relaxed, that's it – the pandemic is over. There are also those individuals who prefer to bury their heads in the sand and pretend the pandemic isn't really happening. Should they choose to ignore their government's COVID-19-related regulations vis-à-vis staying at home, washing hands, social distancing and wearing face masks, although they may not suffer the consequences of their actions, others might.

What is also likely to have helped proliferate the spread of the disease were the number of demonstrations that have occurred in various countries since the pandemic started. Some targeted local lockdown regulations, while others were totally unrelated, such as the 'Black Lives Matter' protest supported in several countries.

'Don't kill granny!'

Whatever little children call their grandmothers – granny, grandma, nanny, etc. – it is still the same person. In August 2020, the UK city of Preston re-entered lockdown after a spike in COVID-19 cases was detected. With half of the people who tested positive being between 18 and 30 years old, the leader of the city's local government issued a stark warning to these youngsters – 'Don't kill granny'. Although young people are statistically less likely to present any serious symptoms, they can still pass the infection on to other, more vulnerable people.

In a separate example, using around 20,000 volunteers, the UK Biobank has been undertaking a study into how COVID-19 spreads. This organisation describes itself as being a major national and international health resource, and a registered charity. Its aim is to improve the prevention, diagnosis and treatment of a wide range of serious and life-threatening illnesses.

Although the Biobank study is still in progress, early results have indicated that antibodies have been detected in 1 in 14 of the participants. This means they have unknowingly had COVID-19 and were probably asymptomatic. These early results also indicate that the biggest group by far falling into this category, like the city of Preston, are in the 18 to 30 age range. If they also belong to the gung-ho 'COVID-19 won't get me' brigade, then the coronavirus version of the children's fairy-tale '*Little Red Riding Hood*' (Guenthier, 2020) may well apply to them.

Those of you familiar with the fairy-tale will appreciate the parallel of a pandemic-themed cartoon I recently saw. A little girl was walking through the woods on her way to her grandma's house when she came across a wolf called 'Coronavirus'. Confronted by the wolf, the little girl stood her ground and said "I'm not afraid of you, Mr Wolf", to which the wolf replied "Oh, I'm not interested in you little girl, I just want to follow you to Grandma's house".

So, who was ultimately infected with coronavirus in this variant of the story? Of course, it was grandma.

7.3 You can't rob us of our rights and our liberty

Many of the major democracies around the world, although not all, have been struggling to manage the pandemic crisis without upsetting the voters who elected them in the first place. That is a difficult achievement, even on a good day, because as the saying goes, 'you cannot please all of the people all of the time'. Politicians invariably want to be re-elected when their term in office comes to an end. Consequently, doing or saying anything that has the potential to upset the electorate is a big 'No-No'.

However, in the midst of the pandemic, for some it has become an impossibility, especially when the question of what to do about Christmas had arisen. Although every country that celebrates Christmas will regulate what its citizens can and cannot do, very few countries approached it in the same way. That is not unreasonable if we remind ourselves of the old adage: 'one size does not fit all'.

As year-end 2020 approached, an increase in new cases of COVID-19 was being witnessed across much of the world. With Christmas celebrations in mind, a variety of actions were being taken, and some examples are as follows:

- Germany and the Netherlands would be in lockdown.
- Italy originally had cancelled Christmas markets and imposed a 10.00 pm to 5.00 am curfew. But with less than a week before Christmas, the country opted to join Germany and the Netherlands re-entering lockdown.
- France relaxed travel restrictions over the holiday period.
- Russia told elderly citizens to self-isolate.
- Spain permitted travel and limited gatherings.
- Originally, the UK proposed introducing temporary 'Christmas Bubbles', allowing up to three households to celebrate together over a five-day period. The devolved governments in Wales and Northern Ireland imposed

tighter controls because of a dramatic rise in new cases. However, one week before Christmas, by which time the new case counts were rising rapidly across all four UK countries and a new variant of the virus was emerging, tighter restrictions were introduced. Prime Minister Boris Johnson announced that the planned relaxation of COVID rules for Christmas was to be scrapped for large parts of south-east England and cut to just Christmas Day for the rest of England, Scotland and Wales. Around 18 million people in London and the south east were effectively placed into lockdown. A further six million people, primarily from East Anglia and Hampshire, were expected to be added to these tighter restrictions on 26 December, in response to further rapid proliferation of the virus variant.

To antagonise the situation, French President, Emmanuel Macron, banned all travellers from the UK from entering France for fear of the new variant of COVID-19 spreading. Massive traffic jams resulted in both Dover and Calais, with thousands of commercial vehicles being trapped as both Eurotunnel operations and ferry crossings between the two countries were initially suspended. However, by 28 December, cases of the new variant were being reported worldwide.

- In the US, each state was defining its own restrictions. By mid-December, 22 states had travel restrictions imposed and many had up to 14-day quarantine in place. With the country still reeling from the Thanksgiving-associated spike in new cases, Christmas travel was expected to be more than double.

In the UK, in July 2020, the government imposed extra restrictions immediately before Eid al-Adha. In effect, this deprived the British Muslim community of one of their major religious festivals. At that time, the new daily case count was well under 1,000 while by mid-December, it was hovering around the 25,000 mark. Had Prime Minister Boris Johnson allowed Christmas to proceed as originally planned, this would have been seen by many as discourteous and hypocritical.

So here is the challenge. On the one hand there were those who believed Christmas should be severely curtailed or even cancelled, thereby depriving the virus of an excellent opportunity to proliferate. There is certainly some very strong evidence supporting this argument, especially when we consider the spiralling numbers being hospitalised by COVID, long before the festive season. Some health services were already stretched to their limits and thóse in the northern hemisphere would also have the fallout from seasonal flu to contend with.

The BMJ and the Health Service Journal (HSJ) jointly issued a warning that the easing of the UK COVID regulations for the Christmas holiday period *"would cost many lives"* (Godlee, 2020 and McClellan, 2020).

In referring to the BMJ and HSJ's joint statement, BBC reporter, Chris Mason, remarked that any tightening of the regulations may be seen by many as: *"Robbing us of liberties that we take for granted."* (Mason, 2020). This is, of course, a luxury that the citizens of those more autocratic countries do not necessarily enjoy.

Mason's remark takes us to the other side of the argument and those who maintained that Christmas should be 'business-as-usual'.

Those NGO's whose raison d'être is to champion a nation's civil liberties would understandably argue that governments have an obligation to protect people's lives which seems reasonable to me. This would naturally be expected to continue during a public health emergency such as the coronavirus pandemic. However, when this also involves imposing restrictions on the populace, some might consider that it erodes civil liberties. In such instances, NGOs would invariably be quick to react by protesting in the strongest possible terms.

In response to the UK's Coronavirus Act, 2020, which granted the government emergency powers, one such UK based NGO, was Liberty. It proposed its own alternative Bill to be put before parliament entitled "Support Protecting Everyone" (Liberty, 2021). While this Bill looks to curb pandemic related government emergency powers, it also seems to be using the coronavirus as a smokescreen to address issues that would have existed even if the pandemic had never happened. Moreover, in my opinion, some of Liberty's demands are in direct conflict with a number of measures put in place to help keep people safer.

But organisations like Liberty should remember that in a democracy, a government is elected to run the country and they should be allowed to do so in whichever way they see fit. It will ultimately be the electorate that are subsequently allowed to decide, via the ballot box, whether they have or have not done a good job. It was Winston Churchill who reminded us that "no one pretends that democracy is perfect", but it is the best thing we have.

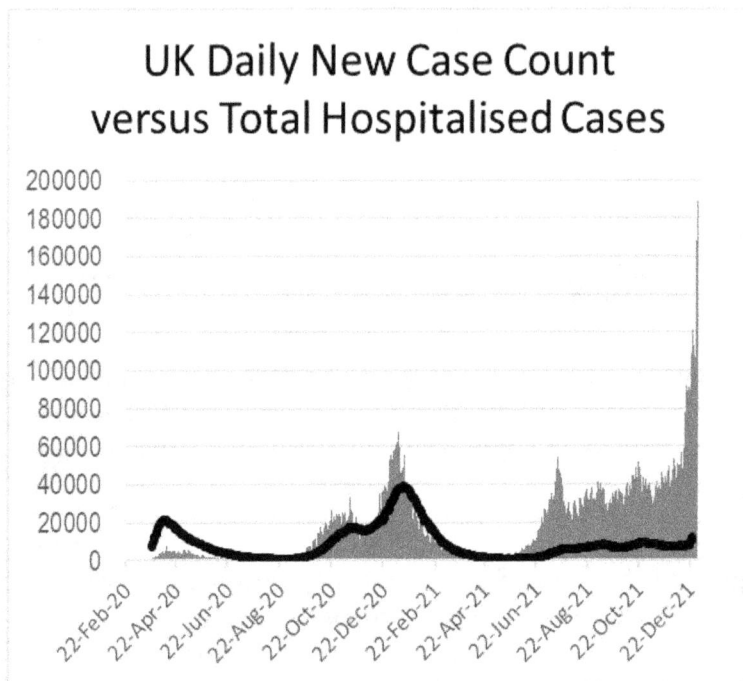

Figure 21: UK – Daily new case count versus total hospitalised

Figure 21 shows the UK's DNCC with the black line indicating the number admitted to hospital with COVID-19.

What is very noticeable is the UK's daily new case count on 25 December 2020 was 32,705, although 11 days later on 6 January 2021, this had almost doubled to 62,322. Although the Christmas holiday break undoubtedly played a part in this surge, so too did the new coronavirus variant discovered in the UK, which spread at an alarming rate.

Running alongside the 2020 post-Christmas DNCC surge was the UK's vaccination programme. In Figure 21, it is noticeable that as the third wave commenced in July 2021, while hospital cases rose, they did not rise anywhere near as sharply as they had done during the second wave. This was attributed to the extensive vaccine take-up by the population. The alarming increase in daily new cases caused by the Omicron variant is clearly visible.

7.4 Running a business during lockdown

There will be some businesses that by their very nature will not be able to operate during a lockdown regardless of its severity. Whether they survive a pandemic could depend upon a number of factors. The scope and conditions attached to any economic stimulus packages that their respective governments may choose to introduce will be a major influence. Almost undoubtedly, the economic consequences of COVID-19 will be shrinking economies and potentially a major global recession, synonymous with business failures and mass unemployment.

UK Chancellor Rishi Sunak's 'Eat Out to Help Out' incentive designed to help the struggling hospitality sector was used more than 150 million times in 84,000 restaurants during August 2020.

During a Downing Street press conference, 26 March 2020, UK Chancellor of the Exchequer, Rishi Sunak announced the country's unprecedented furlough scheme. This was designed to support workers whose jobs were at risk due to the pandemic. Initially 80% of salaries of circa 10 million UK workers would be paid by the government. However, Sunak added the caveat:

"We will not be able to protect every single job or save every single business."

(Sunak,2020)

> ## Employee with Type-1 diabetes dismissed for self-isolating
>
> Following her doctor's advice, the plaintiff, Mrs Jackie Reid, self-isolated at the beginning of the pandemic as her condition made her more vulnerable to the virus. Her employer claimed that by self-isolating she was in breach of her contract.
>
> An industrial tribunal found in favour of the plaintiff awarding her substantial damages. Although the law will obviously vary from country to country, employers should familiarise themselves with the rights of both themselves and their employees under their local employment law (Shaw, 2020).

Sadly, each month since the pandemic was declared, we have seen companies collapse while others have shed employees in an effort to survive. For many organisations we have seen 'business-as-usual' become 'business-as-survival', and many simply have not made it. Some were already struggling economically before the pandemic. One early victim was the UK airline Flybe that found the pandemic to be the proverbial straw that broke the camel's back. It collapsed to the detriment of its supply chain, while leaving a substantial hole in UK and European intercity travel options.

There have been outcries on both sides of the Atlantic because a UK government agency used a photo of a dancer by the name of Desire. The appended caption read "Fatima's next job could be in cyber (she just doesn't know it yet) –

Rethink. Reskill. Reboot". US photographer Krys Alex said she was 'devasted' that her work was used in this way, suggesting that the dancer should retrain. Although the UK Culture Secretary, Oliver Dowden, had the picture pulled, describing it as 'crass', the damage had been done and the post had already gone viral on social media (Djudjic, 2020).

But let's step back and look at the reality of the bigger picture. Firstly, if someone loves their chosen career, it is tragic if circumstances, such as this pandemic, mean they can no longer follow their dream. But this stretches far beyond the performing arts, which I will talk about later in the book. The reality is that there are many people around the world who have trained for a specific profession and now find themselves out of work, some with little or no prospect of finding similar opportunities. Today we are pointing fingers at the pandemic as being the root cause, but we have seen some professions all but disappear in the past simply because society no longer needed them, or automation has made vocations obsolete. We have witnessed blacksmiths largely replaced by motor mechanics, and chimney sweeps by central heating specialists. Others have virtually vanished, such as thatchers, switchboard operators, hot metal typesetters, typists, railway signalmen and elevator operators. Even before the arrival of the twentieth-century, powder monkeys and climbing boys had long since disappeared and the days of the lamplighters were numbered, too. In fact, the World Economic Forum believes that:

"The Forum estimates that by 2025, 85 million jobs may be displaced by a shift in the division of labour between humans and machines."

(Whiting, 2020)

We also see businesses change because of technological advances and improvements in our ability to communicate. For example, news of the 1805 British naval victory at the Battle of Trafalgar took more than two weeks to reach London, a distance of 1,500 miles (2,350 km). It would have taken around three months for that same message to have travelled to Australia, but 100 years later in 1905, it would have taken less than seven hours. Today, it is virtually instantaneous. More recently, enhanced technology has facilitated the increased popularity of online banking, resulting in the closure of some high street bank branches, along with the redundancy of their staff.

On a personal level, had I wanted an appointment to see my doctor in 2019, I would have phoned the surgery and turned up for a face-to-face appointment at the agreed date and time. In the early days of the pandemic, a number of doctors' surgeries were contaminated with COVID-19. So, now in 2021, although I still phone for an appointment, my initial consultation may well be via video call. In the UK, it was always the intent to embrace technology in this manner, but the arrival of coronavirus has certainly expedited the project.

As mentioned in section 7.1.5, the Chinese Prime Minister Li Keqiang has been encouraging the unemployed in Wuhan to become street vendors. You could argue that this would be insulting to anyone who is highly skilled and qualified for a specific career. While there are of course others, one group of professionals who have had to endure some serious culling have been airline pilots. For the foreseeable future, the ever-growing yoke of redundant pilots will be chasing a rapidly shrinking list of opportunities.

According to CNBC, US airlines alone ended the year 2020 with 90,000 fewer workers due to pandemic related redundancies. However, twelve months later, pilot hiring numbers are surpassing pre-coronavirus pandemic levels.

Another group that seems to have become an endangered species in certain parts of the world are English Language teachers. Students have not been travelling to destinations that specialise in offering English as a Foreign Language, primarily to millennials (see section 13.4).

But, invariably, it will be hospitality, events, leisure, entertainment, gymnasiums and tourism that will be among those to suffer most, along with non-essential retail outlets. Other businesses that depend upon offering clients a close contact face-to-face service, such as hairdressers, beauticians and massage parlours are also likely to suffer a similar fate. Moreover, those organisations that expect any business interruption insurance (BII) policy to cover losses may be in for some serious disappointment (refer to section 11).

Each country dictates its own lockdown regulations, and as you will have read in chapter 7, some have been extremely draconian, while others were comparatively relaxed.

Furthermore, every business, large or small, should realise that when a crisis occurs, there will be no moratorium on other crises occurring simultaneously. For instance, we only need look to Australia. During the 2019-2020 southern hemisphere summer period referred to locally as 'Black Summer', Australian emergency services had to deal with unusually intense bushfires, flooding and COVID-19. When breaking the impact down from national level to an individual business viewpoint, there will have been some organisations that may have been adversely affected by two if not all three of these crises. Similarly, at the time that COVID-19 began its rampage across the US, several severe outbreaks of wildfires started far earlier than usual in California, while outbreaks in Oregon were unprecedented. Moreover, the Southern States have had to contend with the consequences of hurricane damage, starting with Laura, which made land fall in August.

As we have seen in chapter 7, lockdowns came in a variety of shapes and sizes from the harsh draconian measures enforced in China to something like the more relaxed Swedish version. Or, as in the case of Taiwan where they have avoided the need to lock down all together. So, which approach is right, and which is wrong?

Let's just recap for a moment and remind ourselves why we really need to have these lockdowns. Simplistically put, if everyone is isolating at home, then the virus cannot spread. This is how SARS was contained in 2002-2003. But, the consequence of everyone isolating at home for long periods is that the global economy will go into meltdown.

"Virus is like a huge sink hole in global economy. No one (not even anyone on this chat!) knows how big/deep it is. And every day world in lockdown it gets bigger and deeper."

(Paumgarten, 2020)

Getting the balance right between saving lives and protecting the economy is a major challenge that I believe is a potential oxymoron. There are also some 'politicians' around the world who have been behaving as though their primary concern is avoiding doing anything unpopular, which could result in them not being re-elected. Time for them to wake up and smell the coffee, although for some, maybe it's too late already!

Until such time as the WHO declares the pandemic is over, exiting a lockdown does not mean that the virus has gone away. Nor is it safe just to pick up life where it was left off before coronavirus arrived on the scene. Sadly, I have seen evidence that certain sections of society in several countries are behaving as though it is all over. Others seem in denial that the pandemic has actually happened. The number of people that can gather together in social groups is dictated by individual countries.

International Labour Organisation – 23 September 2020

The devastating losses in working hours caused by the COVID-19 pandemic have brought a massive drop in labour income for workers around the world.

Excluding any income support provided by respective government measures, the first three quarters of 2020 have witnessed a 3.5 trillion USD drop in income compared with the same period in 2019 (ILO, 2020).

Even so, there are those individuals, primarily, although not exclusively, in the 18 to 30 age range, the millennials, who act as though these restrictions do not apply to them and it's 'party time'. They will pose a constant societal COVID-19 proliferation threat all the while they choose to ignore what is their social responsibility. Such situations are far less likely to occur in countries such as China where the government is completely intolerant of dissent.

There have been many references to the 'new normal', but what exactly does that mean? Is it real or some kind of illusion, like a mirage in a desert that we think we can see but never actually get to? I believe we will not be able to accurately describe what it looks like until we have actually arrived, which in itself begs the question:

"Will the new normal be our final destination or just a transient state?"

What we can safely assume about this 'new normal' is that it could necessitate changes to the way we conduct both our personal and professional lives. Moreover, it probably means that every time the 'R' number swings in the wrong direction, locally or nationally, some kind of lockdown measures may well follow. How often will the economy need to be closed down, partially or totally, necessitating that we run for cover, seeking the sanctuary of our homes. For the time being, that is the 'new normal' and what we need to learn to manage both societally and professionally.

There are, of course, some serious issues that will need addressing before we can finally reach that harmonious destination of *Shangri-La* when we can genuinely believe that the worst is behind us. They will invariably include some key questions such as:

- **Will scientists have discovered a vaccine or a cure?** There was certainly some very encouraging news since Q4 2020. with several vaccines being approved. But, will those vaccinated still be capable of carrying COVID-19 droplets in their nose? Although they are far less likely to be infected by COVID-19, they could still be infectious to others who have not been vaccinated. Will any immunity provided by vaccination continue to be effective if the virus mutates, or will annual COVID vaccinations become a feature of the future, just like seasonal flu vaccinations?

- **Is there some kind of treatment** that may allow us to downgrade COVID-19 from a potentially fatal disease to a chronic but treatable illness? HIV/AIDS is a classic example.

- **Has just about everyone on the planet been exposed to COVID-19 and the virus has nowhere else to go?** Although, hang on! Reports have been appearing about people being re-infected. Are these just isolated cases or, given time, will any post-COVID acquired immunity gradually dissipate?

What we do know is that COVID-19 has already proved to be a massive agent of change. But haven't we been here before? Didn't we have to come to terms with a 'new normal' after World War I, then again after the Spanish flu, not to mention the Great Depression, World War II, the Cold War, the 2007-2008 financial crisis, the ever-growing cyber threat and, in the European Union, Brexit? I believe that, in reality, while the availability of a vaccine, cure or treatment will be key factors, we will pick ourselves up, dust ourselves off and just get on with whatever personal and professional parameters that life presents us.

One of the effects of the pandemic has been on town and city centres, which have, in some cases, been likened to ghost towns. Shops and hospitality outlets depend upon passing trade, but the footfall has been so low, especially with so many workers becoming home based. It is true to say that the traditional 'high street' has been slowly disappearing in recent years, threatened by the ever-growing presence of online alternatives. This has certainly accelerated since

March 2020 because of pandemic lockdowns. Those independent shops and chain stores without an online side to their business have been particularly disadvantaged. Even when lockdown regimes have been relaxed, there has not been an automatic restoring of the 'status quo', and it is already apparent that some businesses will not be reopening. In the UK, the head of the Confederation of British Industry (CBI), Dame Carolyn Fairbairn, pointed out that local businesses from dry cleaners to sandwich bars depend upon the country's offices.

Reports from Japan indicate that Fujitsu will halve its office footprint within three years, as WFH will become a standard option that employees can choose. I worked for Fujitsu Consulting for a number of years, and along with many of my colleagues, I was home based as far back as 1997. Using a hot-desk system, I only went into a Fujitsu office if I had to attend a meeting or needed to replenish my home office supplies. Today, with the multitude of online conferencing platforms, maybe going into the office for meetings will also become a thing of the past.

Meanwhile, Twitter has told employees that, if their role permits, they can WFH 'forever' if they wish, as it reassesses its post-pandemic corporate estate requirements.

7.4.1 Dealing with extensive absenteeism

Consider for a moment that your organisation might look something like the one portrayed in Figure 22, which in this example has 45 employees. Could you manage if it was decimated[16] by a pandemic and looked more like the line-up in Figure 23? Furthermore, absenteeism will invariably be decided at random, possibly robbing you of key employees.

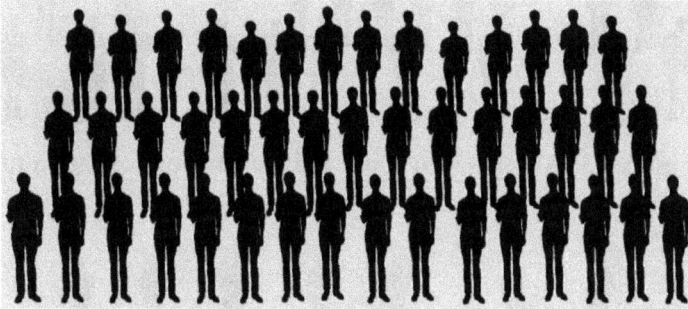

Figure 22: Your organisation might normally look like this

Figure 23 would see your workforce reduced by 35%, from the original hypothetical number of 45 down to 29 employees. The figure of 35% absenteeism could rise or fall depending on the severity of the pandemic. However, the potential effects of social distancing may well be contingent on the nature of your business and your working environment. You may find that these regulations may decimate your workforce still further taking it down to 23 (see figure 24), almost one half of its original size. Moreover, if your premises are open to your customers, you may find you have to restrict the number that can enter at any one time.

---

[16] As we enter 2022, we are certainly witnessing the Omicron variant robbing both public and private sectors of substantial numbers of their employees while they self-isolate.

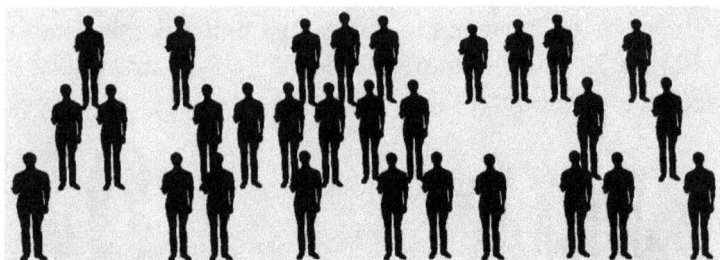

Figure 23: Absenteeism could reduce your organisation to this

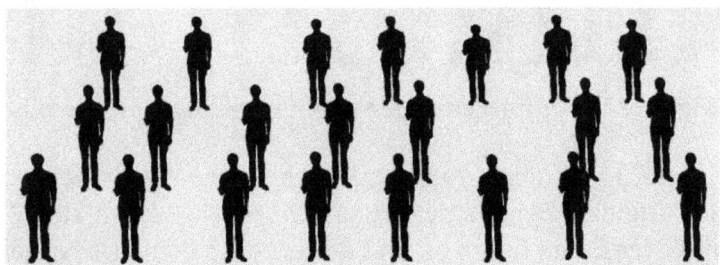

Figure 24: Social distancing could cripple your organisation

By the summer of 2021 here in the UK, we were seeing businesses suffering from staff shortages especially in the hospitality, transport and food industries. This situation was further compounded by year end as both public and private sectors began to suffer significantly from COVID-19 related absenteeism.

OK, so the number of employees that your organisations have will very likely differ from the examples I have used. Even so, you still need to be able to react to staff shortages, the reasons for which will be varied. As soon as COVID-19 became a quantifiable threat, some countries advised the more vulnerable in society to self-isolate. As far as the workforce goes, this would have included people with underlying health conditions, such as asthma or diabetes. This is when gaps could start appearing among the ranks of most if not all organisations. Some of the reasons for absenteeism can include:

Reason	Potential impact
Clinically extremely vulnerable people	Governments may advise people to shield if they have serious underlying health issues such as COPD, asthma, diabetes, heart conditions and pregnancy. Others may also be advised to shield if they are receiving treatment, such as chemotherapy, radiotherapy or immunosuppressant medication.
Sickness	Those individuals who have tested positive for COVID-19, even if they are not presenting any symptoms. Sickness can also be non-pandemic related.
Self-isolation	Anyone who believes they may have been exposed to COVID-19.
Transport disruption	Those who genuinely cannot get to work because of public transport disruption. In some

	countries, public transport was suspended.
Parents or carers	They may need to remain at home to look after sick or elderly relatives or look after children if schools are closed.
Fear	You may have staff who are genuinely scared to come to work.
Lockdowns	Worst case scenario would be, except for essential workers, only those employees capable of being home based could continue to work.

7.4.2 How versatile is your workforce?

In 1996, I initiated and ran the Maltese government's Y2K programme. Although most of the IT systems used relatively modern programming languages, there were still legacy systems to consider. Most were COBOL, plus a language called Massachusetts General Hospital Utility Multi-Programming System (MUMPS). The latter were very large, monolithic and unstructured – a categorical nightmare for the uninitiated.

Using MS-Excel, a skills matrix was constructed, which profiled everyone in the organisation, from top to bottom, demonstrating who was experienced in which programming languages, their competency level and their last hands-on experience.

There was no shortage of resources available for the more modern languages. However, for COBOL the news was not good. The code had hardly been touched in years and the one recognised COBOL programmer still in the organisation was now a senior manager. The news about MUMPS wasn't much better. There was only one MUMPS programmer and he was about to depart on a lengthy round-the-world trip. But the matrix had certainly served us well in demonstrating our strengths and weaknesses.

I also used this skills matrix concept when I became resourcing director for Fujitsu Consulting – Northern Europe. I was responsible for a pool of around 1,500 consultants across five countries. But some significant improvements to the skills matrix were needed from the original Maltese model:

1. The raw data was contained in an Oracle database,[17] although MS-Excel was still used as the front end.
2. It listed far more skills going well beyond just ICT. Additional inclusions were academic and professional qualifications, management consulting, soft skills, project management, programme management, security, data and document management, relevant industry experience, etc. In truth, it could contain any skill that is relevant to your organisation.
3. By also capturing the last time that the consultants had hands-on experience with the various topics, we were able to apply an algorithm to estimate what we called a skills fade factor. Was their knowledge current and

---

[17] Almost any relational database could be used, such as MS Access, which accompanies MS Excel in the Microsoft Office suite of programmes.

would it be a practical option to 'freshen up' the skills if required, etc.

4. It also provided us with a valuable insight into the tacit knowledge capability within the organisation. For example, it revealed that one consultant had worked as a coal miner – not exactly regarded as a core skill at Fujitsu Consulting. Even so, this proved to be invaluable when we were bidding for some consultancy work with a mining corporation.

Originally, across the pool of 1,500 consultants, it could sometimes take two or three labour-intensive days to identify all the appropriate resources that might be available for specific assignments. With the introduction of the skills matrix, this was reduced to between one and two hours, and being parameter driven, it was largely automated.

In addition to facilitating tactical resource management, this approach provided a strategic top-down view of the organisational capability. This further supported recruiting, training and succession planning initiatives. Ideally, succession planning should extend well beyond the C-Suite and identify everyone who is in a key role. For example, the only Maltese government programmer familiar with MUMPS, or perhaps the one person in your organisation who knows how the payroll process works.

Figures 25 and 26 illustrate an example of a skills database enquiry for IT service management capability ITIL®.

For each of the skills you are enquiring against, the management summary reports on the number of consultants that fit each of five competency levels. So if we are looking for information about 'ITIL configuration management', we can see that there are a total of 61 consultants who have some level of experience, of which there are:

- 3 at 'Level 5 – Subject Matter Expert';
- 6 at 'Level 4 – Mastery';
- 24 at 'Level 3 – Application';
- 15 at 'Level 2 – Familiarisation'; and
- 13 at 'Level 1 – Awareness'.

Obviously the higher up the 1-5 scale, the more competent the consultant would be, whereas the lower down the scale, the more training and hand-holding would be required for those employees. This may also be a consideration if your workforce is largely WFH, as this could make hand-holding and on-the-job training more problematical to achieve.

Capability Study - IT Service Management (Summary)

	Total	Level '5' (Expert)	Level '4' (Mastery)	Level '3' (Application)	Level '2' (Familiarisation)	Level '1' (Awareness)
ITIL Service Continuity	45	0	6	14	10	15
ITIL - Service Desk Mgt	58	3	11	15	15	14
ITIL - Release Mgt	62	1	10	19	18	14
ITIL - Problem Mgt	66	2	16	20	13	15
ITIL - IT Library	43	0	8	8	11	16
ITIL - Incident Mgt	61	3	13	24	8	13
ITIL - Financial Mgt	46	0	2	10	17	17
ITIL - Configuration Mgt	61	3	6	24	15	13
ITIL - Change Mgt	66	1	11	28	8	18
ITIL - Capability Mgt	41	1	3	9	15	13
ITIL - Availability Mgt	47	1	6	13	16	11
IT Strategy	135	7	14	34	48	32
IT Services Mgt (ITSM)	128	3	27	36	33	29
IT Architecture	154	8	25	49	49	23

Figure 25: IT service management enquiry – Summary

The previous image provides the organisation with a summary view of its information technology infrastructure library (ITIL) capability, a framework that provides guidance on how to establish an IT service management (ITSM). It lists the disciplines within ITSM and matches this with the number of people with Level '5' – Mastery through to Level '1' – Awareness.

Capability Study - IT Service Management

Name	Location	IT Architecture	IT Services Mgt (ITSM)	IT Strategy	ITIL - Availability Mgt	ITIL - Capability Mgt	ITIL - Change Mgt	ITIL - Configuration Mgt	ITIL - Financial Mgt	ITIL - Incident Mgt	ITIL - IT Library	ITIL - Problem Mgt	ITIL - Release Mgt	ITIL - Service Desk Mgt	ITIL Service Continuity
Brown, Graham	HOME		4 / 2017		4 / 2017	2 / 2000	3 / 2017	3 / 2017		4 / 2017		4 / 2017	2 / ND	3 / ND	4 / 2017
Grey, Rob	HOME		3 / 1996	4 / 2001											
Blue, Tim	EGHAM	4 / 2017	4 / 2017	4 / 2017	4 / 2017	3 / 2017	4 / 2017	5 / 2017	3 / 2001	4 / 2017	4 / 2017	4 / 2017	4 / 2017	4 / 2017	4 / 2017
Scarlet, David	HOME		5 / 2017		5 / 2017	5 / 2017	5 / 2017	5 / 2017	3 / 2017	5 / 2017		5 / 2017	5 / 2017	5 / 2017	4 / 2017
Green, Carol	HOME		3 / ND	3 / ND											
White, Mark	BRACKNELL			2 / 2017											
Purple, Graham	HOME	3 / 2017	4 / 2017		3 / 2017	3 / 2017	4 / 2017	3 / 2017	2 / 2017	4 / 2017	4 / 2017	4 / 2017	2 / 2017	4 / 2017	3 / 2017
Maroon, Alison	HOME	3 / ND	5 / 2017	5 / ND	3 / ND	3 / ND	4 / ND	3 / ND	3 / ND	3 / ND	4 / ND	4 / ND	3 / ND	4 / ND	3 / ND
Verde, Jacqueline	EGHAM			3 / 2016											
Nero, Mona	EGHAM		2 / ND	2 / 2017	2 / ND	2 / ND	2 / ND	2 / ND	2 / ND	2 / ND	2 / ND	2 / ND	2 / ND	2 / ND	2 / ND
Jones, Rhys B.	SOLIHULL			2 / 2018											

Figure 26: IT service management capability – Breakdown

The illustration in Figure 25 provides the organisation with a summary view of its Information Technology Infrastructure Library (ITIL) capability also known as IT Service Management (ITSM). It lists the disciplines within ITSM and the matches this will the number of people with Level '5' – Mastery through to Level '1' – Awareness.

The second 'Detailed Breakdown' report, Figure 26, provides a sample analysis by consultant in relation to the skills enquiry criterion you have selected.

So, if the pandemic randomly decimated your available workforce, would you know who you could call upon to step into potentially exposed roles and responsibilities?

7.4.3 Everyone can work from home, can't they?

Unfortunately, the answer to this question is 'No'. I would suggest that not much thought is required to create a list of all those roles that simply cannot be carried out from home. You would expect such a list to include frontline health workers, first responders, the military, utility providers, the various forms of transport that we depend upon, postal workers, garbage collectors, food store and pharmacy workers. Given due consideration, this list would be extensive.

That said, some of us, in principle, can definitely WFH. It certainly makes sense that organisations have contingency plans in place to facilitate WFH where and when it is practical. This may not necessarily be in response to a pandemic, but it could, for example, be your contingency plan if you are faced with a crisis that causes a potentially lengthy denial of access to one of your key premises. Even so, WFH has already been becoming a way of life for so many of us over recent years. It can certainly help promote a better personal-professional life balance, perhaps something that has slowly been eroded over time.

There are those who may find WFH actually improves their productivity, especially if they are avoiding a long commute before starting work each day. Moreover, working alone will invariably mean less interruptions and distractions. And I am sure it will only be a matter of time before organisations start to question the need to base themselves in expensive real estate, especially if their employees can be home based.

WFH, the UK Office of National Statistics reported that:
- In April 2020, 46.6% of people in employment did some WFH.
- Of those who did some WFH, 86.0% did so as a result of the coronavirus pandemic.

(ONS, 2020)

But, there is not a one-size-fits-all solution to homeworking, and for some people, although their companies may choose to encourage WFH, it is just not practical for any one of a number of reasons. Consider first, someone living in a large house in a quiet, leafy suburb is likely to find this a far more conducive environment for effective WFH than perhaps someone who lives in a house share or a tiny bedsit. They may have no suitable space for working and could be physically uncomfortable just sitting on the end of their bed. These contrasting situations do not present your employees with a level playing field. As one person confided: *"Going to work every day used to get me away from my depressing home."*

All that said, if you spend much of your working day fettered to a computer or smart device, then it is possible that you could WFH, as many national governments are encouraging their citizens to do. That can apply to individuals and even be applied to distributed contingency strategies covering business functions such as call centres, where staff could be home based, too. Even the National Health Service, the UK's biggest employer, has had back office staff WFH.

Socially distanced postmen

Before the pandemic broke, every morning a post office van would arrive and park opposite my house. Two postmen would get out sort the letters and packages for my road, at which point one would head up the road, while the other would go down. They would meet back at the van and carry on to the next drop-off point together.

Now, with social distancing in mind, one arrives driving the post office van, while his mate arrives in a private vehicle. The van driver removes a set of letters and packages and heads off to deliver them. The second postman waits at a safe distance until his colleague has left and then he repeats the process for the remainder of my road. They rendezvous back at the van, but then head off separately to their next drop-off point.

Regardless of size, for companies realising WFH is a serious option for some or even all of their employees, it needs careful planning. Deciding one day that everyone is going to WFH as of the following day is potentially courting disaster unless the groundwork preparations have been done. For example:

- You will need an effective communication strategy for your entire business.
  - This needs to define how your employees are going to be able to communicate with each other, both on a one-to-one and a one-to-many basis. The information flow needs to be bi-directional.
  - You also need to have your communication strategy clearly defined for your stakeholders (again bi-directional), what channels you will use, including backups to provide contingencies against channel failures.
  - Who will be responsible for communicating with who (and when).
- If your employees are going to be home based without any physical supervision, how will you determine their level of productivity. Do they have tangible targets that can be measured remotely?
- Managers may need training on how to manage remote workers.
- Each employee will have their specific WFH requirements. This may include IT equipment, software, desks, Internet link and telephone (especially if they live in a bad reception area for mobile/cell phones). An appropriate level of cyber security measures is crucial to reduce the risk of the company infrastructure being breached. Keep in mind that your ICT team may need time to configure equipment, address any cyber security issues and resolve any other technical problems that WFH personnel may experience.
- Provision may need to be made for employees who may require some ongoing training, continuous professional development or who may need regular support from a colleague. We should not forget that working as a team,

employees can learn so much from each other. Without due consideration and careful planning, this valuable benefit could be lost with WFH.

- If your communication strategy requires the use of an online communication platform (e.g. Zoom, Microsoft Teams, etc.), you may need to consider top-down training for all employees not familiar with your platform of choice. I have facilitated pandemic plan validation exercises that have wasted time because not every participant knew how to sign on and use the online platform.

When the coronavirus pandemic started, laptops and office equipment suppliers were reporting that they were selling out, such was the demand. A just in time procurement approach to any WFH strategy may consequently prove to be disastrous.

- Don't forget if someone has the misfortune of being a new starter with your organisation as a pandemic has kicked-off, you will need to decide how to deal with the situation.
- You will need to validate all aspects of your home working plan to verify it functions correctly (see section 8.2 case study).

7.4.4 Being home based can be tough for first timers

About a month into the pandemic, somebody asked me how I was coping with WFH. I told them the first 20 years had probably been the worst, but I'm getting the hang of it now.

In reality, I have been home based for around 25 years, so having to WFH because of COVID-19 is really no hardship for me. However, if homeworking is new to you, here are some ideas that might help make it easier on yourself:

- If you don't live alone, ideally work in a room where you can shut the door and keep clear of whatever else might be going on at home. That could even mean working in a garden shed if it has everything you need (e.g. heat, power, Internet, etc.). One friend of mine has a motorhome (recreational vehicle) parked in his driveway that doubles up as his office when he is in WFH mode.

- If making conference calls is part of your routine, then you really need to avoid interruptions, especially from small children. The classic example on YouTube is entitled "Kids crash their parent's teleconference call". If you have had a tough day, take a look at it, I'm sure it will bring a smile to your face.

- I use the Pomodoro Technique® (aka the Tomato Timer *https://tomato-timer.com/*) to manage my work intervals. So, I opt to work for 25 minutes slots then take a short break, usually around five minutes. During the break I might make a coffee, do some exercises or perhaps sit in the garden if it is a nice day. I break for lunch and usually take a walk. This helps me to keep my mind fresh throughout the day. Find what works for you.

- I will often listen to music, but nothing intrusive. Many years ago, I was working in Rome for the Italian Ministry of Finance (Dipartimento del Tesoro), while endeavouring to improve my Italian during my spare time. The method I used involved listening to the language lessons that were accompanied by music (primarily Vivaldi's Four Seasons). This was amazingly successful for me. So, when I can I tend to work with background classical adagio music. In fact, as I write this section of the book, I am listening to Pachelbel's Canon – one of my all-time favourites.

But, let us not forget that for people used to being based in a busy environment, WFH can be a very lonely place. I was invited by the US management consulting company, Excelicon, to join a 'town hall' meeting to talk about pandemics. Now, town hall in this context was not an expression I had come across before. I have since learned it has its origins in North America. From a business perspective, it is a way for companies to communicate with their employees regardless of where they are based. In the meeting I was invited to join, I believe there were around 40 participants, and they all had been WFH since the start of the pandemic. This was the company's way of regularly reaching out to them all and keeping them up to date on what was going on. It also gave employees a chance to ask questions of the management and perhaps for the management to say, 'Hey, we haven't forgotten about you guys'.

7.4.5 Isn't this a business continuity issue rather than an IT issue?

How many times have people said just the opposite – isn't business continuity just an IT problem? The pandemic has created a crisis for the vast majority of organisations across the planet. Whatever their business, public or private sector, and not forgetting non-governmental organisations, IT is definitely an integral part of their operations.

So, yes, it is a business continuity issue but with unquestionably IT implications, especially enabling any WFH strategies. But is WFH a new and untried concept? As I previously mentioned, personally I have been home based for around 25 years. The more employees who WFH, the more it offers companies a potential cost saving. Dedicated desks for every employee will likely be superseded by a hot-desk approach.

Some 36 years ago, an IBM UK Senior Operations Analyst, Jeff Grady, was one of my team members who was nominated to pioneer the concept of home working. An IBM 3270 terminal, modem and a leased telephone line were installed at Jeff's house. He was regularly on call outside normal business hours, and this facility meant avoiding a 25-mile (40 km) round trip when called-out, especially at night.

This was shortly after the release of the Hollywood blockbuster *Wargames*. Matthew Broderick played a high school student who unwittingly hacked into the US nuclear missile control system at NORAD, almost starting World War III.

Wargames was a massive wake-up call for the IT industry, and certainly raised the profile of the largely under-estimated and ignored cyber threat. Perhaps it was also influential in IBM insisting that the link to Jeff's home terminal was always activated from the data centre. Maybe this was the origin of the expression "don't call us, we'll call you"?

They say one man's meat is another man's poison. Although some people may be happy to WFH, it is having a detrimental effect on the hospitality sector. Town centre sandwich shops, restaurants, cafes and bars were accustomed to enjoying the patronage of workers taking their lunchtime breaks or maybe stopping off on the way home. They have become victims of reduced footfall resulting from the WFH strategy.

How things have evolved since those early days of home working. Some organisations may already have made provision for staff WFH. They will have provided appropriate IT equipment, in addition to validating that it functions correctly in the home location. This may be an arrangement similar to the 1984 IBM initiative or even as part of a work area recovery plan, typically developed to address a denial of access threat scenario.

Once upon a time ...

When lockdowns became an essential part of everyday life in many countries, the delight that accompanied grandparents and their grandchildren spending quality time together was often no longer possible. While it certainly was not a substitute for being apart, the apparent instant embracing and growth in popularity of online conferencing platforms and chat services perhaps went some way towards reducing the heartache of separation.

Figure 27: Granny Hilary reads a bedtime story to George

Alternatively, others may choose to adopt bring your own device (BYOD) as a cost saving *'panacea',* but they should remember that BYOD does have its pros and cons. While it can offer a relatively quick and inexpensive solution, it is also capable of creating serious longer-term issues. Consequently, if BYOD is mismanaged, it may not so much stand for 'bring your own device' as 'bring your own disaster'.

7.4.6 Is it time to diversify?

While many traditional high street shops were forced to close during lockdowns, there has been a massive growth in online shopping. Leading UK supermarket, Tesco, saw its online sales and grocery deliveries grow by 48%, which, over a three-month period, amounted to £13.4 billion (Burns, 2020). In 1996, Tesco was the first UK supermarket to launch its online shopping business. By the end of 2019, it represented 9% of its turnover. This grew to 16% over a six-week period during lockdown, giving the company the confidence to recruit 16,000 staff to support and sustain this growth. Tesco expects most of the roles to be filled by staff who joined the company on a temporary basis at the start of the pandemic lockdown.

COVID has accelerated trends that were already happening in the marketplace, and you couldn't get a better example than the online grocery business. It had taken Tesco 20 years to get from 0- 9%, and six weeks to go from 9-16% (Jack, 2020).

Many companies of various sizes and across a variety of market sectors have found their order books taking a hammering. A point in case is the fashion industry, which, like tourism and hospitality, has all but died during lockdowns. Those outlets without an online presence are particularly suffering the consequences of being forced to close their doors. This has had a detrimental effect in the upstream supply chain. According to the Bangladesh Garment Manufacturers and Exporters Association (BGMEA), by 1 May 2020, there had been $3.18 billion in cancelled or suspended orders, which is equivalent to 982 million garments (BGMEA, 2020). The potential knock-on effect from global fashion emporiums closing their doors is the loss of two million Bangladeshi jobs (Hossain, 2020).

Others have found their supply chains severely disrupted with countries going into lockdown. Many countries also sourced their medical supplies and PPE for frontline hospital staff from China. With the rapid spread of coronavirus, the demand quickly outstripped the supply, causing countries to scramble to grab whatever resources they could. The demand for ventilators for hospital intensive care units soared, and some companies were able to retool their manufacturing capability to start making them. The Mercedes Formula One team worked with University College London, and within

100 hours was producing a breathing aid. Meanwhile, James Dyson's organisation, famed for its vacuum cleaner manufacture, designed and commenced production of ventilators within ten days. The BBC TV hospital drama, 'Holby City', donated its two ventilators to the NHS.

With the pandemic gaining momentum, countries around the world joined the scramble for sourcing PPE. Like other countries in the developed world, although the UK had sufficient PPE in stock to meet the expected influenza pandemic, this proved to be inadequate for dealing with the more stringent requirements for COVID-19 (Cain, 2020).

Manufacturing companies around the world have re-tooled and started turning out PPE. In response to the WHO's estimated monthly medical face mask requirement of 89 million, Italian companies, Gucci and Fiat Chrysler, led by example, as both helped meet the demand (Parker, T. 2020).

Companies, both large and small, have been using their 3D printers to manufacture face shields. A New Jersey based high school teacher printed and distributed 200 face shields to medical institutions across the country. Even people with 3D printers at home, and who have been laid off, have been making their own contribution (Frandino, 2020).

Australia is one of a number of countries that have reached out to local industries to establish which companies can help address the shortfall in PPE. More than 130 companies came forward offering to manufacture masks, gowns and gloves (Knaus, 2020).

But, what else has been needed, although sometimes in short supply during the pandemic? One commodity that has been difficult to get hold of is hand sanitising gel. Some unbelievably selfish people had even taken to stealing the gel from hospitals, health clinics and doctors' surgeries.

With the WHO posting guidelines on its website for making the product, some distilleries have not been slow in rising to the challenge. With their traditional outlets of pubs, restaurants and shops falling foul of lockdowns, artisan alcohol makers had everything they needed to successfully make the switch.

In section 7.4.2, I talked about the benefit of organisations knowing the full capability of their workforces. Similarly, in preparation for future pandemics and any corresponding surge in product demand, such as PPE, it would make considerable sense for countries to map their industrial capability for switching production in response to this type of demand.

7.4.7 If you must work from the 'office'

For those individuals who must work from the 'office', whether on an occasional basis or full time, your employer has a duty of care. I would recommend you refer to section 5.1.2.2, which talks about making the workplace safe.

7.5 Who gets to pay the bill?

Here in the UK, I find the answer to the question of "Who will have to pay for the pandemic?" a little bit of a paradox. By 1945, the massive debt that the UK had accrued to finance World War I and II was in excess of $21 billion. Adjusting for inflation, that equates to approximately $300 billion today. Through taxation, my generation, who were not even born when the Second World War ended, finally finished paying off that debt in 2006. Eight months after the pandemic declaration, the UK Office for Budget Responsibility estimated that borrowing for the financial year ending April 2021 would be £394 billion sterling (circa $529 billion) although the final figure for that period was £299 billion sterling.

Back in October 2020, I watched a television report about millennials partying in the street in the city of Liverpool, although it could have been any city, almost anywhere in the world. Many were not wearing face masks and social distancing niceties seemed so very far from their minds. At that time, Liverpool had the highest COVID-19 case count for any location in England. So, it is highly likely that some of these revellers had been previously infected and probably passed it on to other revellers. They, in turn, would have shared the virus with siblings and parents at home, and maybe even grandparents, too.

The selfish and thoughtless actions of these individuals are exacerbating the situation, and it is highly likely that there will be fatalities that can be directly linked to this street partying. The cost of pandemic countermeasures rises by the day, and the final global cost will be astronomical. The *Financial Times* reported that even as far back as May 2020, the UK government's debt already exceeded the UK economy for the first time in more than 50 years (Giles & Samson, 2020).

So, who gets to pay? Ironically, as my generation has done its bit before, most have headed off into retirement. It will be those individuals so hellbent on enjoying themselves and others like them. I hope they find that their partying was worth the price they will have to pay, which for some will be far more than just a financial one. While I do have a degree of sympathy for those many individuals not prone to acting irresponsibly in this way, whoever said that life is fair?

CHAPTER 8: VALIDATING YOUR PANDEMIC PLAN

It may seem strange to want to validate a pandemic plan when there is already one out there doing its worst. But depending on where you are located in the world, you could, for example, still be in the first wave, into the second wave, in between the two or even waiting on the arrival of a third wave. I trust you get the picture – it's the old story of 'one size does not fit all'. As you will have seen with Figure 20, despite both being in the US, as New York was coming out of the first wave, Florida was just going in. Even if you believe that validating your plan is too late for COVID-19, pandemics are just like buses – there will be another one along before you know it. While that remark may seem flippant, regretfully, this is a case of 'never a truer word said in jest'.

To help you get some ideas on what to test and how to test it, here are some case studies that are based upon real pandemic validation exercises.

When you validate a plan, whether it is a BCP, an IT disaster recovery plan or a pandemic plan, generally the process you would expect to follow is very similar. My book *Validating Your Business Continuity Plan: Ensuring your BCP actually works* explains the process in detail. For more information, please visit:

www.itgovernancepublishing.co.uk/product/validating-your-business-continuity-plan.

You would usually start with a desktop discussion about the plan, maybe with two or three people. A logical next step might be a workshop environment, and in fact, the 'Wave one: Pandemic exercise' in section 8 is an example of this. Ultimately, you would look to undertake an exercise in a live environment as characterised by section 8.2. In addition to planning and executing your exercise, you would also hold a post-exercise debrief, which is intended to capture the lessons learned. This enables you to effectively facilitate a cycle of continuous plan improvements.

The exercise in section 8.3 took place in a live environment, insofar as it was monitoring how effectively a company's employees were coping with new pandemic procedures. Unlike many live exercises, it was low risk, inexpensive and inobtrusive.

8.1 Wave one: Pandemic exercise

The original version of this case study was published in 2015 in my book *Validating Your Business Continuity Plan: Ensuring your BCP actually works*. It was based upon an actual exercise that I facilitated on behalf of a client. I have decided to include the exercise in this book, as I have received such positive feedback about its usefulness.

While the scenario is an avian influenza pandemic, many of the lessons learned in the exercise apply equally to COVID-19.

One of the benefits of running a simulation of this nature is that you can advance the clock by a few hours or days to suit the scenario. For this exercise, the clock was advanced over a period of weeks, as we dealt with the first wave of a pandemic that had a 12-week duration.

Although this exercise does cover many of the government regulations as decreed by various countries, it does not deal with total lockdowns. However, in most countries, providing other mandatory protective measures can be met, including social distancing, although non-essential shops may be forced to close, online retailers have been permitted to continue operating.

Since 2015, there have been significant advances in the availability and effectiveness of online conferencing platforms, such as Microsoft Teams, GoToMeeting, Cisco Webex and Zoom. In the event of a pandemic, it was always the intent of my client to switch to video conferencing, rather than meet in a traditional conference room, although, at the time of the exercise, a conferring platform had not been selected. Consequently, I have assumed that Zoom would be the platform of choice and I modified the text of this case study accordingly.

Introduction

Organisations preparing to face a pandemic need to appreciate that they are dealing with a threat to their staff, and their HR department should be primed to play a leading role. Moreover, it also presents a potential threat to both their customers and suppliers, and could have significant implications on all aspects of an organisation's supply chain. Within the UK, pandemics have been classified by the government as a Tier 1 threat to its security, and it is ranked alongside terrorism, cyber attacks, natural hazards and military conflicts.

Scenario

The first wave of a life threatening and highly infectious mutant version of avian flu is rapidly proliferating around the globe. 77 countries have already reported infections to date. With the infection count rising at an alarming rate, and the death toll mounting, the WHO has declared that the outbreak has reached its highest classification level – 'Phase 6' – indicating that a global pandemic is officially underway. A number of countries have already declared public health emergencies.

This validation case study looks at a London-based mail order company that runs a 24/7 operation. It receives around 70% of its orders via the Internet, with the remainder procured via telesales. Its CMT has been convened and its pandemic plan has been activated. Although the exercise lasted only a few hours, the simulated duration covered several weeks. To add a degree of realism, the organisation's doctor was invited to join the CMT to act as a pandemic subject matter expert.

This section includes only a subset of some of the activities that occurred during this exercise. In one instance, the 'clock' was advanced by up to four weeks. Even so, the study provides a substantial amount of data to reflect upon for organisations looking at their own pandemic planning arrangements.

Simulated duration: 12 weeks

Detail

Week one

The majority of the CMT joined the meeting via Zoom while isolated in their respective offices, plus two from home and the company doctor from his surgery. However, before the exercise could begin, a number of technical issues had to be resolved. These were primarily caused by most of the CMT having never used Zoom before, and no training had been arranged. The nominated minute taker also needed instructions regarding how to make a recording of the proceedings.

Once the Zoom issues had been resolved, the first observation made by the CMT was that the pandemic plan remained in a draft format, and it had never been signed off. Even so, after checking that everyone had the same version and had prepared for the exercise using the identical version, it was decided to proceed with the exercise and validate what was in front of them.

The HR department informed the CMT that they believed that absenteeism was higher than normal for the time of year. However, as several members of the HR team had reported feeling unwell and had been sent home, it was not possible to provide a precise number at this time.

The company doctor briefed the CMT on how the pandemic was likely to develop, basing his comments upon both what was known already about the current pandemic, along with historical information about previous pandemics. He warned that a pandemic can follow a wave-like pattern, with the potential of several months respite between waves.

At this time, the average recovery time that could be expected from the disease was unclear. Even so, people may well suffer with post-viral fatigue,[18] causing total exhaustion, leaving victims not fit enough to work for several weeks after they are no longer infectious. Even though many associated deaths had already been reported globally, no statistical data was yet available regarding the case fatality ratio (CFR). This indicates the proportion of symptomatic cases that result in fatalities. Estimations of the CFR are particularly difficult to

---

[18] In the case of COVID-19, this would be referred to as 'long COVID'.

calculate during the early stages of a pandemic. The doctor warned the CMT that based on the table of historical data provided by the WHO (The WHO, 2013, p 19), fatalities within the company were a distinct possibility.

The doctor reminded the CMT that the sick bay facilities were very basic and only had one bed. It would be sensible to temporarily expand these to accommodate employees taken ill at work while arrangements were made to transport them home or to hospital. He also suggested that the company may like to look at ways of allowing staff to WFH if they have a pre-existing condition, such as asthma, which makes them particularly vulnerable to influenza. He added that there are more than four million adult asthma suffers in the UK alone. He also reminded the CMT that it was possible that to slow down the spread of the virus, the government could impose a lockdown on all non-essential services.

He concluded his briefing by emphasising the importance of total compliance with all recommendations from the Ministry of Health, particularly with respect to preventing the spread of the disease. These are likely to include, although are not necessarily limited to, social distancing at work, hand and respiratory hygiene, along with the avoidance of all unnecessary travel. Moreover, employees that use public transport have a greater probability of being exposed to the disease.

The organisation should also be prepared to accept that the government may encourage people to stay at home and self-isolate if they have come into contact with the disease, but are not necessarily presenting any symptoms (e.g. one of their close family members has been diagnosed with influenza, etc.).

8: Validating your pandemic plan

The pandemic plan had anticipated much of what the doctor covered, and it included actions to identify which employees travelled to the London office using public transport, along with the creation of a list of employees who could WFH.[19]

It was not clear how long HR would take to respond to this action, as they were already short staffed. However, the HR director anticipated that absenteeism could rise during the pandemic for any one of a number of reasons, including no access to transportation, fear of infection and illness. If the government decides to close schools, some employees may be absent while they are taking care of young dependants. Moreover, employees with infected elderly parents may also feel duty-bound to provide care for them. The director also acknowledged the doctor's warning regarding potential fatalities among employees, and advised the CMT that a counselling service had already been arranged for dealing with any resultant trauma among staff.

The administration director was asked to check if the company's BII included pandemics or was there some small print that meant they were not covered (see section 12.1 Business interruption insurance).

The CMT next turned its attention to identifying critical and non-critical business activities, and each member of the

---

[19] There is no reason why lists of this nature cannot be prepared in advance of an incident or crisis as part of business continuity planning, and then periodically reviewed. With the possibility of absenteeism rising, this is an additional task that could be avoided once a crisis has kicked-off. This is also something of importance, not just for dealing with a pandemic threat, but for addressing other potential threats, such as transport strikes or terrorist attacks that might affect the transport network.

CMT was tasked with drawing up a list for their respective sections. They were also charged with creating a list of those employees who were in non-critical roles but had the skills and experience to undertake a key role if required.[20]

The final three decisions made by the CMT were that:

1. The company would immediately:
   o Replace the hand towels in the toilets with paper towels.
   o Sanitising hand gel dispensers were to be situated throughout the company's premises and employees would be encouraged to use them regularly.
   o Face masks, visors and disposable gloves were to be made available for all employees, along with instructions for their use. A replacement supply was also to be kept on site for use when needed. All telemarketing staff were to be allocated their own personal headsets and they would be positively discouraged from lending their headset or using anyone else's.
   o A rigorous programme of sanitising stair handrails, lift buttons, door handles, telephones, computer keyboards, cafeteria chairs and tables, plus any other potential source of infection in the company's premises, was to be introduced with immediate effect. However, the building services director reminded the CMT that while he appreciated the

---

[20] This information should already be available as a deliverable from the business impact analysis process.

importance of these additional measures, more staff would be required to undertake these extra duties.

2. All future CMT sessions were to be held using the Zoom teleconferencing facility, to reduce the risk of cross infection among the team.

3. CMT deputy members were to be kept appraised of all decisions and actions in case any of them needed to replace the primary CMT members.

Week two

The building services director reported that he was having difficulty in sourcing sanitising gel dispensers and face masks because of the demand.[21]

The CMT concluded that the critical aspects of the business that had to be kept running were the:

- Warehouse operation, including upstream supply chain management, order picking and shipping;
- Customer services;
- In-bound telemarketing calls;
- The payroll process; and
- The position on statutory reporting obligations was unclear and should continue unless the company was advised to the contrary.

All other activities would be performed on a best efforts basis, and even though it would be disruptive, in a worst-case

---

[21] During the 2015 MERS outbreak in South Korea, demand for PPE and sanitising hand gel quickly outstripped supplies. Equally, when COVID-19 started, there was a worldwide shortage of PPE.

scenario, these other departments could be temporarily suspended.

Preliminary figures were now available, and it was estimated that around 79% of the workforce travelled to work using public transport. Some 12% either walked or cycled, and with the limited number of car parking spaces only allocated to disabled employees and the management team, very few used their own vehicles.

The ICT director said that the technology was already in place to enable customer services and telemarketing staff to work remotely, and, providing they had an Internet connection, they could WFH. However, some CMT members expressed concern that there could be employees who try and exploit the situation if they are not being constantly monitored by their supervisors. The director reassured the CMT that individual performance measuring software was now available, so each employee's productivity could be remotely monitored. He suggested that they should be made fully aware that if they did WFH, 'Big Brother' would be watching.

Absenteeism was estimated to be 5% of the workforce. Randomised absenteeism modelling (RAM) was used to establish which employees were not at work and which departments were affected, although the reasons for each absent employee were not recorded.[22]

---

[22] While clearly needing to observe employment law, each organisation may well choose to adopt a different approach to absenteeism. While some may allow unpaid leave of absence (assuming employees are not actually sick), others may opt to keep them on full pay. For this, establishing the reasons of absenteeism could be important.

The HR director agreed to communicate with staff on how working practices would be affected by the pandemic. Section heads would be briefed on the specific changes to their respective areas, which they would disseminate to their staff.

Week four

Absenteeism was now at 22% and the RAM approach dictated that two members of the CMT had been infected and had to be replaced by their deputies.

In response to a rise in customers enquiring about the status of order deliveries, the communications and media department are asked to prepare a statement that was to be issued via the company website and social media. When placing new orders, customers should also be advised of potential delays. While apologising for any hold up in order processing resulting from the effects of the pandemic on the workforce, the statement should assure clients that the company will strive to ensure that orders will be delivered as quickly as possible. It should also reassure the clients of the company's continuing commitment to customer service.

The CMT decided to ease overtime constraints, and section managers would be instructed to encourage staff to volunteer. But there was to be categorically no attempt to pressure staff into working extra hours. The HR director warned against the potential health effects of working excessive overtime over a prolonged period. He proposed that a cap of 16 hours per week should be applied.

The outsourced ICT supplier contacted the company to say that staff shortages caused by the pandemic meant that they were obliged to activate the *force majeure* clause in the contract. They could no longer guarantee to meet the agreed service levels for incident resolution for the foreseeable future. This meant that any vital maintenance required to address failures in the company's online services, regardless of severity, could remain unresolved indefinitely.

In light of this, the CMT asked the ICT director whether they should invoke the disaster recovery plan and transfer the ICT operation to the fall-back site. The director advised against this because at this time there would be no benefit, as the service was still functioning. In fact, activating the disaster recovery plan could create unnecessary problems, particularly with the number of absent staff growing by the week. Moreover, if an outsourcing failure did occur, such as a software failure or a cyber attack, then it was possible that it could be replicated at the disaster recovery site.

The CMT learned that the RAM had also dictated that a member of the accounts department had died in hospital and a number of her colleagues were in a state of panic. The HR director contacted the pre-arranged counselling service but was told that, at best, it would be several days before they could attend, because of their current case load.

The deceased was a young mother with two small children, and the director was asked if he would be visiting the family on behalf of the company to pay his respects. He felt that as it was possible that her family could also be infected, he was not prepared to put himself or any other member of his team in a situation where they could be unnecessarily exposed to the disease. Instead, he would write a personal letter to the family and offer both his and the company's condolences. At this point discussions became very heated, and the director's intentions were challenged. He was accused of being totally heartless by one of his colleagues. But when asked if he was prepared to go instead and put himself, and possibly his work colleagues and his family at risk, the irate colleague apologised and backed down.[23] On checking, it also transpired that no next of kin contact details had been recorded for the deceased.

Week six

Absenteeism was now at 43%, and the RAM approach dictated that a third member of the CMT had been infected and had to be replaced by her deputy. However, the deputy was also sick, and, with no other suitable candidates available, the CMT agreed to absorb the missing director's responsibilities among the rest of the team.

Trains, buses and London Underground services were being frequently cancelled because of staff sickness. Many employees were arriving noticeably late for work. Warehouse activity was being especially affected.

With staff due to be paid this week, both the payroll clerk and her assistant had gone sick. No one else knew how the payroll process worked, and there were no written procedures for someone else to try and follow – how will staff be paid? The HR director responded by advising the CMT that an agreement sanctioned by the CFO had already been reached with the company's bank. Staff would be paid the same as they were paid last month, and any appropriate reconciliation would be addressed after payroll staff had returned to work. This agreement would remain in place until the bank was asked to discontinue it.

---

[23] Here we face a moral dilemma – do we or do we not? Normally, many companies would want to show a caring side and support the family of a deceased employee. However, in this situation, by so doing they could put the health of other employees and their families in jeopardy.

A number of non-essential staff who were currently WFH had been instructed to report to the warehouse to backfill for absenteeism in that section. Three declined, while four others demanded extra compensation because of the increased risk of infection they believed they would be subjected to, both at work and travelling to and from work. The CMT decided to consider their response.

As the positions requiring backfilling were of a relatively unskilled nature and the ranks of the unemployed workforce was growing rapidly by the day, it was suggested that the company should quickly recruit some temporary staff. However, the HR director explained that the recruiting process was time consuming, as it involved taking character references to reduce the chance of pilfering, which had been a major problem in the past.[24]

The outsourced delivery company had not arrived to collect the orders ready for dispatch. When contacted, its office manager apologised and said they were short staffed. He assured the CMT that a collection would be made tomorrow.

Two more employees have died and the *Evening Standard* has requested an interview about how the pandemic is affecting the company and how it is rising to the challenge. After much debate, the CMT decides not to comment on the deaths and to refer the reporter to the statements already

---

[24] Some companies may find their recruiting process is unnecessarily longer than it needs to be, which can prove to be a major handicap when new resources are urgently needed.

made. It was argued that after all it is only one of many organisations caught up in a common crisis.[25]

Week ten

Absenteeism was down from its week eight peak of 58% and was back to 31%. The CMT opted to monitor the situation and react to any negative changes as and when they occurred.

Week twelve

Absenteeism is now down to 9% and the effects of the pandemic's first wave appear to be drawing to a close. As with week ten, the CMT opted to continue monitoring the situation and react as necessary.

Key lessons learned:

- Ensure that your plan has been completed, signed off and is regularly reviewed.
- Much of the work, such as creating lists and identifying critical parts of the organisation, should have been done in advance of this exercise as part of the BCM process. This is information that could be needed in a number of different scenarios, not just restricted to a pandemic.
- Items, such as sanitising gel dispensers, and PPE, such as face masks and gloves, need to be procured before a pandemic starts, to ensure an adequate supply is secured.

---

[25] Normally, I would expect a company to have a media plan in place and be able to issue meaningful statements and respond effectively to media questions. However, a pandemic is something that is likely to have a serious effect on many thousands of organisations around the globe, and each could choose to react differently if they find themselves in the glare of the media spotlight.

- Sick bay facilities should be reviewed for suitability for temporarily accommodating staff who are taken ill on the premises.

- Both your upstream and downstream supply chain will invariably be affected by a pandemic, as will your customers. Employees of this particular company are also heavily dependent on public transport to get to work, so any disruption to the transport network will have a detrimental effect on their ability to get to work.

- HR policies need to be carefully thought through. Due consideration needs to be given to how to deal with situations, such as requests for paid or unpaid leave, employees demanding extra compensation[26] or employees refusing to undertake certain tasks as it may increase their exposure to the disease.

- Having a set of documented procedures available could make the difference as to whether an organisation survives or not, especially if you need to bring in untrained staff. In the case of payroll, although there were contingency measures in place, there could be a substantial amount of reconciliation work waiting for the payroll team to return to, work that could take some time to clear.

- Do not assume that because you have BII you are covered for pandemics – read the small print.

---

[26] If you make allowances for one employee and grant extra compensation, you may find it generates similar demands from other employees, so try and avoid creating precedents of this nature.

- Have a communications and media response plan in place, as they will be required for many of the situations that organisations find themselves facing. Ensure you keep your stakeholders informed of what is happening.

- Considering the delay for trauma counselling, unless you have an agreement in place for the provision of a dedicated service, you will have to accept that you will be competing with other companies for resources. Even then, counsellors can also become victims of the pandemic.

- Although this was a pandemic scenario, employees' next of kin details should be on record. Other incidents, such as fires or explosions that result in injuries or fatalities, even a simple accident at work, could necessitate the need to contact them.

- If you intend to use an online conferencing platform, such as Zoom, it would be very sensible to ensure that everyone who would need to use it is trained. Hold regular Zoom meetings to provide an opportunity for staff to become more familiar with the product you have selected.

Remember, this was only an exercise, and yet the situation became very tense, especially over the HR director's intentions on how to deal with workforce bereavements. Be warned, being in a real crisis situation can feel like being in a pressure cooker.

8.2 Teaching children by remote learning

Some people believe that it doesn't matter how old we are, we can always learn something new, which gives credence to the expression that 'every day is a school day'. So, while this case study relates to a school, it could just as equally apply to a business. In line with the UK government lockdown directive, the Royal Hospital School (RHS) closed on Friday 20 March, but remote learning for the 750 pupils commenced the following Monday. This didn't just happen by accident – the school was prepared. Even in China, a country that seemed better prepared than most to respond to the pandemic, it took around three weeks to get its online teaching programmes up and running.

As a matter of course, all pupils up to age 16 use a school-provided iPad as part of their school equipment, while 17-18 year olds are more likely to opt for a laptop. These are used in the classroom under the guidance of experienced teachers, as part of a careful blend of progressive educational technology and traditional teaching methods. Those pupils with their own iPads are allowed to bring them to the school, but they are not sanctioned for any school-related activity. So, for any learning events, BYOD was not permitted.

iPads are embedded in the teaching and learning at RHS, which is totally committed to this approach. The school has been recognised as a beacon school for technology, as an Apple Regional Training Centre, Edtech 50 School and through 360 degree Online Safety Mark accreditation.

There is full Wi-Fi access across the school site. Its systems and firewall have been configured so that pupils can safely and securely use their iPad to communicate through authorised online channels, such as email and task manager, manage their time effectively and have full access to document files and resources.

Through significant advances in both software and hardware, the teachers and pastoral staff are able to take a greater level of control over pupils' school devices. In the classroom, this is through the use of Apple's Classroom app and using Bluetooth technology, which enables teachers to control the use of apps and the network. This reduces the level of *digital distraction*,[27] thereby increasing the emphasis on the iPad as a tool for learning.

Preparations for the arrival of the pandemic had started a full month before the UK lockdown. In addition to continuity of education, this also included the logistical challenge of organising homeward journeys for the boarding pupils, close to 20% of the pupils, many of whom live overseas.

Once the lockdown commenced, teachers had to be able to change their *modus operandi* from the customary teaching within the classroom to teaching online.

With the initial warning signs coming out of China in January 2020, the possibility of a pandemic was seen at RHS as highly likely. By way of preparation, and using the Microsoft Teams platform, teachers spent a two-week period WFH while they taught the pupils who were located in their respective classrooms. WFH in this way is not dissimilar to setting aside an area in a company's premises to emulate remote working. This gave both teachers and pupils the

---

[27] Whenever I am training, I am always conscious that some 'students' seem more focused on their smartphones than they are in participating in the lesson. By removing the opportunity of 'digital distraction', RHS has harnessed technology without allowing students to become a slave to its darker side.

opportunity to become fully conversant with the technology and the remote teaching concept, while resolving any technical issues that arose.

On Monday 23 March 2020, with the majority of children now at home, the school's remote teaching programme hit the ground running.

"We use Microsoft Teams and OneNote to enable pupils accessing learning remotely to see their teacher, the class whiteboard, textbooks, tasks and work sheets. Pupils are able to participate in lessons through asking and answer questions, being involved in class discussions and activities, and receive high quality feedback on their work. This sector leading approach is the closest we could get to the pupil being physically in the classroom. Lessons are also recorded to enable all pupils to revisit content, or access lessons at a more suitable time for their time zone." (RHS, 2020)

Being prepared to face a pandemic in this way is commendable, and the school should be rightly proud of its achievement. It also offers those unprepared businesses with some serious food for thought vis-à-vis their own pandemic planning preparations.

8.3 Is your work environment safe?

In times gone by, I can remember people walking around the work environment with a clipboard and a stopwatch just observing – often a good indication that a time and motion study was in progress. Now, since COVID-19 arrived, maybe minus the stopwatch, clipboard carrying individuals could well be verifying that pandemic safety plans are functioning efficiently in the workplace.

8: Validating your pandemic plan

This exercise was part of a programme of activities looking at 'high traffic areas', where bottlenecks could potentially cause social distancing issues. In this simple but important example, instead of someone armed with that infamous clipboard just stood there watching, it was possible to observe peoples' behaviour via CCTV. This company operated a high level of perimeter security, and cameras were already in situ as part of its security arrangements. They had been in position so long that most employees seemed to have forgotten they were there. However, it was concluded that had they been conscious of someone stood at the gate watching their every move, they may not have behaved so naturally.

The object of this exercise was threefold:

- To observe what employees did and didn't do when entering or leaving the company's premises via a security gate which, although it had a small gatekeeper hut, was generally unmanned.
- Did they follow COVID-19 protocols and procedures?
- Did this ingress/egress present any risk of cross-infection?

The gate in question was a turnstile gate (also known as a baffle gate) and was approximately 2 metres in height. It could operate in both directions, and so could work as either an exit or an entrance, or both. However, during the pandemic, it had been designated as an ingress at the start of the day and an egress at going home time. The gate was monitored and controlled from the centralised security office, and a two-way communication system was available if required.

Approximately 100 employees used this side gate, and they would normally all arrive during a 15-minute window and leave in the evening over a 10-minute period. The gate was sanitised twice every day, once before employees arrived and once afterward. Entry and exit was dependent on the employee having a valid security swipe card and a keypad entry code. Visitors were directed to the main gate. In addition to the normal entry and exit procedure, they had been instructed to adhere to the following simple four-step process:

1. Employees to wear a face mask before approaching the gate. If they were exiting at the end of the day, it was assumed they would already be wearing one, as this was compulsory inside the company's premises.
2. If more than one employee was waiting to pass through the gate, a queue was to be formed, ensuring social distancing was observed using the two-metre markers placed on the pavement.
3. Before passing through the gate, employees were to thoroughly sanitise their hands with gel from the dispenser (dispensers are situated approximately four metres either side of the gate).
4. Once through the gate, sanitise hands again before proceeding.

After studying one week's worth of CCTV footage, the following points had been noted:

- Every day, the gate was punctually and thoroughly cleaned before the morning arrival and then again later in the morning in preparation for the end of day departures. The gel dispensers were replenished on each occasion.

- All employees were seen wearing masks, although six habitually did not cover their noses.

- Most, although not all, employees used the sanitising gel before passing through the gate, although it appeared random vis-à-vis who did not. However, it was noticed that offenders who seemed more focused on their smartphones tended to be the miscreants.

- At least two only seemed to work the gel into the palms of their hands, but omitted to cover their fingertips and the backs of their hands, which could have left them possibly contaminated.

- One individual was seen to thoroughly apply gel to his hands and then, before passing through the gate, he used a handkerchief to blow his nose.

- It was noticed that three particular employees were always bunched up together, ignoring social distancing, and were usually deep in conversation as they approached the gate. It was later established that they had formed a bubble and were in a car share, travelling to work together.

- On the third morning it was raining heavily and a group of seven employees arriving simultaneously, disregarded social distancing instructions and were huddled together to get what shelter they could from the gate portico before passing through. Once through, they rushed towards the building with none performing the second sanitising step. However, even when the weather was not inclement, around only 50% remembered to apply more gel after passing through the gate.

- One employee, having already entered through the gate, was seen leaving in a hurry, not only disregarding the hand sanitising instructions but also against the flow of the inbound traffic. Approximately two minutes later he returned and, once again, rushed through the gate without hand sanitising. It was assumed he had returned to his vehicle to collect something he had earlier forgotten.

So, what was learnt from this exercise? Clearly, the content of the training programme had been largely absorbed by most of the employees using this particular gate. However, there was still more work to be done. So what recommendations were made?

1. Put up posters as a reminder of what is expected of everyone.
2. For the morning arrival and the evening departure periods, from the central security office, assign a security officer to proactively monitor the comings and goings of the employees through the gate. Should anyone be observed passing the gel dispenser without sanitising their hands, or not appearing to thoroughly cover their hands with gel, the duty guard can:

   a. Remotely lock the gate to prevent entry;
   b. Communicate over the two-way communication system to remind the employee to properly sanitise their hands; and
   c. Release the gate only when they have complied.

   Furthermore, if they are not wearing a mask or their mask isn't covering both mouth and nose, a similar approach can be adopted.

3. The company had already budgeted for a covered walkway to be constructed from the car park to the gate. To avoid repetitions of the crowding under the gate portico during inclement weather, this project should be actioned as early as possible. Staff waiting to leave in

the evening could still socially distance and shelter under the overhang of the building's roof when necessary.

4. Anyone passing through the main gate was having their temperature taken, but not through this unmanned side gate. The final recommendation was that the company assigns a member of staff to check temperatures at the gate. Alternatively, implement an automated temperature scanning solution, similar to those used in airports, which can be monitored from the central security office.

CHAPTER 9: VACCINATIONS – A SILVER BULLET?

Vaccinations are nothing new. Edward Jenner (1749-1823) is recognised as being the founder of vaccinology, and he is credited with creating the smallpox vaccine in 1798.

Winding forward 200 years or so, 8 December 2020 was a 'Red Letter' day – a day of special significance – for all of humanity. The first approved COVID vaccination was administered outside of a controlled trial, heralding the start of the UK's COVID vaccine roll-out programme. Other countries were swift to follow. But this does not present us with a panacea or licence to revert to pre-COVID practices either in our personal or professional lives. Indeed, the virus continues to spread, and new variants have been detected, too. However, while the arrival of the vaccine is certainly a massive step in the right direction, for the time being social distancing, wearing a face mask and regular hand washing should continue.

With a number of different vaccines now approved, it was the Pfizer-BioNTech COVID-19 vaccine that was first to receive approval in the UK. The Oxford/AstraZeneca and Moderna vaccines also received approval before the month was out, with around 40 other vaccines in various stages of development around the world. Speaking at a Downing Street coronavirus briefing about the speed of vaccine development and deployment, UK Chief Scientific Advisor, Sir Patrick Vallance, said:

"Ten years ago, we would not have been able to do this. That is the extraordinary thing about this. The new vaccine technologies have allowed us to do this. Had the

pandemic occurred ten years ago, we would not have been in this position now."

(Vallance, 2021)

But the person who made history on that 'Red Letter' day was Margaret Keenan. She was just a few days short of her 91st birthday, and received the first injection to be dispensed at 06:31 GMT at University Hospital Coventry. She remarked that it was the "best early birthday present". Margaret Keenan was soon joined by health workers, care home staff, vulnerable people and many others, as the UK rolls out its vaccination programme.

"Broadly, vaccines are being given to the most vulnerable first, as set out in a list of nine high-priority groups, covering around 30 million people. They are thought to represent 90-99% of those at risk of dying from Covid-19."

(BBC News, 2020)

Developing a vaccine inside a year is nothing short of miraculous, as it is not unusual for the process to take decades if indeed a vaccine is ever found. Around 40 years has been spent, so far unsuccessfully, in searching for a vaccine for HIV/AIDS, and yet a vaccine for COVID-19 was developed, tested and approved inside 12 months.

In the twelve months since the first vaccines were approved, many of the wealthier nations have been quick to drive their vaccination programmes forward. In fact:

- Over 58% of the world population had been vaccinated by year end 2021
- In excess of 9 billion doses have been administered

- Only 8.5% of people in low-income countries have received just a single dose with the African continent lagging noticeably behind the more affluent countries of the world (Our World Data, 2021)

  "Rich countries have a critical responsibility not just to safeguard their own populations but to support the distribution of vaccines to developing countries."

  (Stern & Ward, 2021)

So that was the good news. Now here's the bad news!

With many nation vaccination programmes making good progress, perhaps it is an appropriate moment to borrow some famous wartime words from the late Sir Winston Churchill. Speaking after the Allied victory at the battle of El Alamein, Egypt, in 1942, he said:

"This is not the end; it is not even the beginning of the end. But it is, perhaps, the end of the beginning."

And so it is with the pandemic. We should certainly take some comfort and encouragement from the positive news of vaccine development, but we also should mark well the words of warning from UK Prime Minister, Boris Johnson. While he was clearly very excited to observe the first vaccination session conducted at St Guy's Hospital, London, he added the caveat that: *"We can't afford to relax now"* (ITV, 2020). To relax would be to invite the virus to make the most of its window of opportunity before vaccinations become widely distributed throughout the global population. But exactly how long will that take?

By 8 December 2020, the vaccine roll-out programme had started in the UK. But when will it reach the rest of the world? One thing that is certain is that, initially, the supply of vaccine cannot possibly meet the initial demand. Moreover, Airfinity CEO, Rasmus Bech Hansen, told Bloomberg TV that since it needs to be stored at a temperature of -70°C, the Pfizer vaccine is not a suitable solution for much of the world (Hansen, 2020).

Meanwhile, as BBC journalist David Shukman reports, pharmaceutical companies have had to face challenges in scaling up the vaccine production. Furthermore, with global supply chains having not yet returned to their pre-pandemic capacity, some raw materials required for vaccine production may be in short supply. With the global population standing at 7.8 billion, although not everyone needs to be vaccinated, an estimated 70% would need to be in order to achieve 'herd immunity'. This leaves the world needing roughly 5.4 billion people to be vaccinated. Manufacturers were looking to deliver 2.6 billion doses by year-end 2021, but they over-achieved by producing over 9 billion. Even so, with vaccine recipients often requiring multiple doses to maximise effectiveness, less than 60% of the global population were fully vaccinated. Consequently, a global roll-out targeting 5.4 million is unlikely to be completed until possibly well into 2023. Moreover, when the poorest nations receive the vaccines, in some cases there will be the immense logistical task of distribution (Shukman, 2020).

In some parts of the world, it may simply not be safe to initiate a vaccination programme. In recent years, health workers in Pakistan supporting polio vaccinations have been attacked and killed forcing the suspension of the programme. Similarly, the Democratic Republic of the Congo (DRC) has been the scene of several Ebola outbreaks in recent years, and health workers have been confronted by abuse and violence.

9: Vaccinations – A silver bullet?

"Doctors and nurses who work in the heart of the Ebola outbreak zone in Democratic Republic of the Congo say they've had enough. For weeks they've been subjected to threats of violence and even actual assaults."

(Aizenman, 2019)

Health workers threatened to strike after two hospitals were attacked and a Cameroonian WHO epidemiologist, Dr Richard Valery Mouzoko, was gunned down in the DRC city of Butembo. Other conflict zones, such as Syria and Yemen, may also prove to be problematical for the vaccine rollout.

Like the virus, there are still things that we need to learn about the vaccines such as:

- How long will it protect us for? As with other countries, the UK started its vaccine booster programme in the autumn of 2021 with many people receiving their third dose.
- For the most vulnerable in society, will it change a potentially fatal disease into a chronic but treatable illness?
- Will we need regular vaccinations, like seasonal influenza?
- Will the vaccine still work against the new virus variants that are being detected?
- Will it prevent transmission of the virus? Although it should stop us getting sick from COVID-19, will it stop us from passing it on to other people? Like other diseases, such as typhoid, HIV, C. difficile, influenzas, cholera and tuberculosis, we know that COVID-19 can be spread by asymptomatic carriers of the virus. So, in essence, could we be creating more asymptomatic carriers with every vaccination?

With these points in mind, for the time being, we cannot afford to prematurely do away with social distancing, face masks and hand washing.

But are some countries cutting corners and taking risks with their vaccine development? China and Russia have apparently approved vaccines without waiting for their efficacy results, and experts agree that the rushed process has serious risks (Zimmer, et al., 2020). The Russian approached prompted John Moore, a virologist at Weill Cornell Medical College, to state:

> *"This is all beyond stupid ... Putin doesn't have a vaccine, he's just making a political statement."*

(Zimmer, 2020)

During 2020, there were credible reports circulating of cyber attacks on COVID-19 vaccine research and development (R&D) organisations. A proliferation of anti-vaccine propaganda has also been witnessed. The UK's National Cyber Security Centre (NCSC), part of GCHQ, has identified Russia as the origin of the majority of these cyber attacks. The NSCS conclusions are also supported by the Canadian Communications Security Establishment (CSE), the US Department for Homeland Security Cybersecurity Infrastructure Security Agency (CISA) and the National Security Agency (NSA) (NSCS, 2020).

In the UK, a government source said that a hacking attempt by the Russian state had been anticipated from the beginning of the pandemic, adding:

> *"It's entirely in keeping with how they operate."*

(Fisher et al., 2020).

GCHQ proactively placed a protective cyber shield around the vaccine research facilities at Oxford University in the very early stages of the pandemic (Fisher, et al., 2020).

The apparent actions by the Russian hackers does beg some interesting questions:

1. Were the Russians trying to steal information to advance their own vaccine R&D?
2. Were the Russians trying to disrupt the R&D using Advanced Persistent Threat (APT) techniques?[28]
3. Perhaps, both 1 and 2 above.

As previously mentioned in chapter 3, anti-vaccine propaganda has been rampant, and most noticeably on social media, causing untold damage to the integrity and confidence in the vaccines. In fact, fake news circulated that one of the first two volunteers in the Oxford AstraZeneca vaccine trial, Elisa Granato, had died two days after she received the injection. BBC journalist Fergus Walsh was following the progress of this vaccine trial. He spoke to Granato on a regular basis and was able to confirm that the story of her death was simply untrue (Fullfact, 2020).

When vaccines began to come online, countries were looking to sensible and well respected celebrities for support and endorsement of the vaccine products. This is by no means a new concept:

- George Washington evidently encouraged his troops to receive the variolation against smallpox during the

---

[28] Although not an APT, the Stuxnet worm, which was believed to have been active sometime between 2005 and 2010, was designed to disrupt the Iranian nuclear programme.

American War of Independence. But, as one comic recently pointed out, none of these early vaccination pioneers are still alive today!

- Elvis Presley made a very public endorsement of polio vaccines in 1956, and was recorded on camera receiving the 'Salk' vaccination.

- In the 1980s, the children's author, Roald Dahl, strongly promoted measles vaccination after his daughter died from the illness.

Writing in *The Guardian*, Denis Campbell refers to research published in *The Lancet*:

> *"Public trust in vaccines has risen in most of Europe in the past five years, with the largest survey of global attitudes to vaccinations suggesting that just 7% of Britons would not accept a Covid-19 vaccine in March. According to the findings in the Lancet, this rose to 11% in June and 14% in July, however."*

(Campbell, 2020)

Certainly, in the UK, the NHS has been making plans to enlist the support of celebrities and influencers to encourage that growing band of doubters among the population to reconsider as detailed in *The Lancet*. In fact, on 16 December 2020, @NHSEnglandLDN was able to Tweet that actor Sir Ian McKellen (famed for playing the part of Gandalf in the *Lord of the Rings* film trilogy) had been vaccinated. Speaking on camera after his COVID-19 vaccination, the 81-year-old said he felt "euphoric."(COVID-19 vaccine, 2020).

Meanwhile, setting a good example in December 2020 in the US, the President-elect, Joe Bidden, and the outgoing Vice President, Mike Pence, were also vaccinated live on camera.

9: Vaccinations – A silver bullet?

I have one final thought about vaccines that I would like to share with you. Thinking back to my first trip in the 1980s to The Gambia in West Africa, on arrival I had to prove that I had had a Yellow Fever vaccination. Without a valid vaccination certificate, I would have been denied entry into the country. One Australian airline (Qantas) was quick to state that as COVID-19 vaccines began rolling out, it will only accept passengers who can prove they have been vaccinated. Other airlines and some countries have chosen to follow a similar line. It is even possible that some employers may insist on a vaccine being a pre-requisite, too. For example, this might include:

- Armed forces;
- Airlines for flight and cabin crew, in addition to passengers;
- Cruise ships for both crew and passengers. In fact, as the cruise industry started to make its first tentative steps towards reopening in 2021, several operators were insisting that passengers were fully vaccinated before boarding;
- Health services and care homes;
- Food processing plants, some of which have proved to be major concentrations of risk vis-à-vis COVID infection; and
- Austria became the first western country to announce every citizen must be vaccinated by February 2022. Others may follow.

So, should governments consider issuing some sort of universal vaccine passport?[29]

One final observation I feel worth mentioning concerns the behaviour of the European Union and its attempt to impose vaccine export controls. Its issue was primarily with AstraZeneca and the company's apparent failure to keep to the agreed vaccine delivery schedule. AstraZeneca has cited production problems in its Belgium and Netherlands plants as the cause of the delay. Although the EU later backtracked on a threat to restrict the flow of contracted vaccines to Northern Ireland, this was not before the WHO chief, Dr Tedros Adhanom Ghebreyesus, criticised the EU for what he called "vaccine nationalism". He believes this could lead to a "protracted pandemic recovery".

Speaking on BBC Radio 4 about potential confrontations between states and multinational drugs companies, Director of the Global Health Program at Georgetown University, Thomas Bollyky, said:

"This was not inevitable, but it was predictable."

On the Andrew Marr show, Irish Prime Minister Michael Martin acknowledged that the EU had a genuine grievance with AstraZeneca. However, he went on to say that threatening to impose controls on vaccines crossing the Irish border crossing was not an appropriate way of resolving the issue (Martin, 2021).

---

[29] Christmas 2020, Spain announced that it would keep a register of those citizens who refused the COVID vaccine. It has indicated that it will share this list with other European Union nations. Is this the tip of a potentially very large COVID passport iceberg?

9: Vaccinations – A silver bullet?

We have already seen several mutations of coronavirus, although it appears the initial batch of approved vaccines can cope with the new variants. But, we need to remember that although the richer nations may be more focused on vaccinating their citizens against the virus, we overlook the developing and poorer nations at our peril. If they are left unprotected, it will provide a massive opportunity for the SARS-CoV-2 virus to continue mutating. The consequence may be to ultimately render any developed world vaccination programmes as ineffectual.

CHAPTER 10: TESTING AND TRACING

Within a week of declaring the coronavirus outbreak to be a pandemic, WHO head Tedros Adhanom Ghebreyesus broadcast an urgent message to the world:

> *"We have a simple message to all countries - test, test, test," WHO Director General Tedros Adhanom Ghebreyesus told a news conference in Geneva, calling the pandemic "the defining global health crisis of our time.*
>
> *All countries should be able to test all suspected cases, they cannot fight this pandemic blindfolded.*
>
> *Without testing, cases cannot be isolated and the chain of infection will not be broken, he said."* (Farge and Revill, 2020)

At the start of 2020, as the SARS-CoV-2 virus had been previously unknown, there were no specific tests available to positively identify it within a potential victim. However, a few countries already had a process in place to trace people who had been potentially infected.

10.1 Testing

There are two different kinds of tests for COVID-19, one of which is an antibody test and the second is a viral test. The first indicates whether you have previously been infected by the virus, even if you were asymptomatic. The second establishes if you are currently infected.

Those individuals who know or suspect they had COVID-19, may be able to help others currently suffering from the virus by donating plasma containing antibodies. The **antibody test** will identify suitable donors whose plasma can be transfused into patients with immune systems that are struggling to create their own antibodies in response to COVID-19. This test can also be used to help estimate what percentage of a country's population may have been asymptomatic, which I talked about in section 7.

As we headed towards year-end 2020, it was clear that some countries were performing more viral testing per capita than others. As reported in section 7.1.3, China successfully undertook a very impressive logistical challenge by performing more than 10 million tests across the city of Wuhan inside two weeks.

In the UK, the government has been severely criticised for being slow to get its testing programme up and running. It had been regularly making performance commitments that it subsequently failed to achieve. Yet, by Christmas 2020, the UK was outperforming every other country in ratio of test to population count. The US was not far behind in second position, considerably ahead of Russia in third.

Country	Population	Total Tests	Ratio
US	331,922,012	236,655,914	0.71
India	1,386,331,362	163,170,557	0.12
China	1,447,783,333	160,000,000	0.11
Russia	145,967,407	86,704,613	0.59
UK	**68,055,370**	**50,851,151**	**0.75**
Germany	83,911,630	31,974,158	0.38
France	65,342,268	31,237,270	0.48

Figure 28: COVID testing by year-end 2020

We must remember that the figures in the preceding table do not represent the number of people tested in each country, as some, such as frontline heath workers, would be tested on a regular basis.

Rather than leave it to the plethora of official testing sites, a few organisations are now regularly testing their employees. The most obvious ones are the health services and care services, plus the larger food stores. The UK educational sector was gearing up to go down this route before the January 2021 lockdown was imposed. This was intended to cover staff teaching across all age ranges, plus tertiary level students. Elite sportspeople who are permitted to continue plying their trade, even in lockdown, are also being tested regularly.

Many countries insist on arriving travellers presenting a COVID-19 test certificate, which declares that the holder has received a negative test result within the previous two or three days. However, the European Union's law enforcement agency, Europol, reported that fraudsters selling very authentic-looking certificates to travellers had already been apprehended in the UK, France and Spain (Europol, 2021). Almost certainly, fraudsters will be offering similar certificates in other parts of the world, too.

10.2 Could medical detection dogs help?

Dogs are amazing animals or, more to the point, they have an astonishing sense of smell. It is estimated that it is between 10,000 and 100,000 times more effective than humans. They can be trained to detect a variety of things, including explosives, munitions, drugs, money and cancer in humans, and now they are being trained to detect COVID-19 in people even if they are asymptomatic.

In the UK, NHS staff are taking part in trials to ascertain the effectiveness of this initiative. If successful, dogs could be deployed at, among other places, airports, to assist with non-invasive COVID screening of arriving passengers. The trial is being led in the UK by the London School of Hygiene & Tropical Medicine in conjunction with Durham University and the Medical Detection Dogs charity based in Milton Keynes.

More than 100 NHS staff from Kettering General Hospital, plus 17 other hospitals across the UK, have signed up to help (NHS England, 2020). By May 2021, the London School of Hygiene and Tropical Medicine reported that 'bio-detection' dogs can identify COVID-19 with up to 94% accuracy (LSHTM, 2021).

A good friend of mine, who works in aviation security, once told me that whatever illicit items people are trying to smuggle undetected through airports (e.g. drugs, explosives, ordinance, money, etc.), a dog can invariably be trained to detect it. Maybe we will see COVID-19 added to that prohibited list of items. That said, what became apparent as we entered 2021 was that COVID-trained dogs were being deployed by a number of countries across the world.

10.3 Contact tracing

With every country deciding on how it was going to manage the pandemic, including its criteria for reporting on new cases and fatalities, etc., it is hardly surprising that countries decided to 'do their own thing' with regard to contact tracing. I have concluded that it would be possible to write a separate sizeable tome just covering the pros and cons plus the successes and failures in and around testing, tracing and isolating (TTI). So, in the pages of this book, I will restrict my thoughts to an overview.

10: Testing and tracing

Some countries already had tracing processes in place, notably South Korea and Japan, although their chosen approaches were digital and analogue, respectively. This led to some questions being raised about the scalability of the Japanese method. Even so, both countries appeared to have made a good start to managing the pandemic. However, by year-end 2020, they were both experiencing a third pandemic wave, with each wave worse than its predecessor, resulting in the loss of some of that well deserved early kudos. The UK already had a contact tracing process in situ. However, when the pandemic was declared, it was quickly realised that there were scalability issues, and it was not considered fit to meet the challenge from coronavirus. The country has since developed a replacement system, although this has not been without its teething problems.

It has been commonplace for large 'armies' of tracers to be recruited. Referred to as disease detectives, their primary objective had been to interview individuals who have tested positive and establish who they may have infected. Some countries have done this centrally, while others have embraced a localised approach. Some have used telephony, others have adopted a boots-on-the-ground approach, knocking on doors in their quest for information. But the common theme has been to identify who may have been infected. One notable difference has been the timelines the tracers are using, which can vary from 2 days to 14 days. Moreover, their contacts have occasionally proved unwilling to give up information regarding who they may have infected. Stories are also abound of people instructed to self-isolate that have simply ignored the directive.

We have seen China using smartphones and the Alipay health code app very effectively to perform contact tracing (see section 7.1.4). It also seems that if a Chinese citizen's smartphone has 'pinged', they have little option but to follow whatever regulations are in force at the time. This is an excellent example of how a totalitarian government can easily score over the democracies of the world.

Tracking the movement of a mobile (cell) phone has been possible for some time now, although there are those countries where constitutional constraints forbid the collection and use of such data. Monitoring of social media posts can also help verify or challenge information collected via interviews by tracing operatives. Whether it is a phone being tracked, or social media being monitored, it smacks of 'Big Brother' tactics, something that citizens of the democracies are likely to find unacceptable. Perhaps they have failed to realise, but there are those democratically elected governments that have already gone down this route, in the name of counter-terrorism, and law and order, long before coronavirus appeared (Clark, 2018, p 121). Moreover, the proliferation of smartphones across the planet, especially among 'senior citizens', can only facilitate the future effectiveness of TTI. In the UK alone, ownership of smartphones in the age range 55-64 has risen from 9% in 2012 to 80% in 2019 (Statista, 2021).

There is no doubt in my mind that an effective TTI process can make a substantial difference to how effectively a country manages its pandemic response. In preparing for future pandemics, I believe that the democracies of the world have some tough and potentially unpopular decisions to make. Without enforced isolation of the infected, and quarantine of the exposed, plus unrestrained digital monitoring of smartphones and social media, any future pandemics may prove to be just a rerun of SARS-CoV-2.

CHAPTER 11: IT'S AN ILL WIND …

As the proverb from the Middle Ages goes, "It's an ill wind that blows nobody any good". It is strange that the proverb's actual meaning seems to contradict itself – when things have gone wrong, some good may come out of it. In the case of the coronavirus pandemic, we have seen an ever-growing list of victims, both from a personal and a business perspective, but there have also most definitely been some beneficiaries. Here are some of their stories.

"Investors are a strange bunch, inoculating themselves from emotions and training themselves to look for investment opportunities during hard times."

(Haill, 2020)

The pandemic has not been bad news for everyone, and some have clearly prospered. Anyone who invested in companies manufacturing PPE or COVID-19 testing kits may well have been on to a winner. Virus killing cleaning products have also seen demands soar. Conversely, anyone who shorted oil on the stock markets at the outset of the pandemic will have been delighted when the price plummeted in line with the fall in demand.

I have already spoken about some businesses that, in many cases, changed direction and started making something or providing a service that was suddenly in demand. In PwC's Global Crisis Survey 2021, around 20% of responders said that the crisis had had a positive overall impact on their organisation (PwC, 2021).

Three of the organisations featured in this section, Amazon, Netflix and Zoom saw their share prices rocket. Quoted in $US, the Nasdaq shows that each of these three has now fallen back from the peaks they had enjoyed during the year. Even so, at year-end 2020, Amazon and Netflix prices were more or less double their respective March values, while Zoom had trebled.

	March	Peak	Dec 31
Amazon	1,785	3,531	3,258
Netflix	298	562	540
Zoom	105	568	337

Figure 29: Share price behaviour comparison[30]

Twelve months on, both Netflix and Amazon were up on their 31 December 2020 close, trading at $602.44 and $3,334.34 respectively. Zoom, however, had substantially dropped backed to $183.91 (Nasdaq).

Amazon

The *Financial Times* reported that online retail behemoth Amazon doubled its quarterly profits, while it also hired 175,000 new employees during the pandemic.

> *"Locked down shoppers drove sales 40 per cent higher, year-on-year, to $88.9bn, helping the company record $5.2bn in net income for the three months to the end of June."*

(Lee, 2020)

---

[30] The figures quoted above for Amazon, Netflix and Zoom were derived from a Nasdaq snapshot.

This surge in profits came despite Amazon's COVID-19 related expenses, which amounted to $4 billion over the same period. Although representing a small proportion of these costs, the world also witnessed a charitable side of the organisation. Having long since been accused of being the nemesis of high street book retailers, Amazon stunned the industry by donating £250,000 to a fund in aid of bookshops hit by COVID-19 (BBC News, 2020).

Netflix

CBS reported that Netflix had added 16 million subscribers during 1Q2020 when the pandemic had barely taken off. This was double the company's own forecast for the period. Deprived of entertainment from theatres, cinemas and concerts, many turned to online streaming services as an alternative. This represented the largest three-month leap in the company's 13-year history.

Zoom

Google is much more than just a search engine, despite rival products, it has long since become a word that has entered the English language meaning 'go and search online' for information. This is a little bit like 'hoover' becoming synonymous with vacuum cleaners decades ago. I can also tell you that when I first joined IBM it was not appreciated if you referred to making a Xerox photocopy of something, especially as IBM made photocopiers, too. Today, we have another word that has entered the language, 'Zoom' or 'Zooming', and it has quickly become commonplace for people to say: "let's Zoom next week".

"If you go back to December 2019, we had a north of 10 million daily participants on the platform. In March

it went to 200 million and in April it shot up to over 300 million daily participants on the platform."

Harry Mosely, CIO, Zoom (Mosely, 2020)

Hospitality

Although industries, such as hospitality, tourism, events and much of the retail sector have taken a serious hit under the weight of lockdowns, there have been some success stories to tell. Fine-dining restaurants are unlikely to be patronised by individuals who would be prepared to pay $50-100 for a meal delivered in a polystyrene container. Moreover, in better days, these restaurants would usually place an exceptionally large mark-up on alcoholic beverages, especially wine and cocktails. All that said, any business falling into this category may learn something from the case study in section 12.10, Louis' Steak House – Hong Kong, that survived six crises, including the economic devastation that Hong Kong experienced from SARS.

At the less expensive end of the restaurant sector, low end and fast food restaurants with the ability to provide a take-away option have certainly won out over the fine-dining brigade. Not only can customers click and collect, but they can also simply wait for food to be delivered to their door by the growing army of specialist companies, such as Uber Eats, DoorDash, Grubhub and Deliveroo. The restaurant food delivery business has certainly been booming during the pandemic as demand has soared. So too have standalone kitchens, not attached to restaurants, whose sole purpose is supporting the cooked food delivery business.

Supermarkets

Immense pressure was put on supermarkets when pre-lockdown panic buying came to town, but this had a very positive effect on their bottom lines. We have also seen how supermarkets with an online presence have experienced a massive and rapid increase in demand for this service. But, supermarkets have also benefitted from two other changes in our eating habits:

1. Serial restaurant eaters who were unable to visit their preferred venues needed to change their dining habits. Eating-in saw a rise in demand on supermarkets, especially those that offered easy-to-prepare meal deals, which generally included a starter, main, side dish and a sweet. Oh, and some even offered a bottle of wine, too.
2. Then there were those individuals who usually ate midday at work and suddenly found themselves at home. It seems that many decided to spend time baking bread and cakes, and preparing meals, and they would naturally need ingredients from their local supermarket.

Online retailing

Amazon aside, any retail business without an online presence would find it nigh on impossible to trade during lockdowns. In the UK, the Arcadia fashion empire is the umbrella name for several well-known high street brands. The organisation failed to modify its business model in response to a changing marketplace. Continuing to rely solely on high street footfall, especially in a pandemic, sounded the death knell for Arcadia.

Many of Arcadia's competitors with online platforms, although they haven't necessarily excelled with their high street route to market closed off, have so far survived. By comparison, there are other fashion retailers that only trade online and have certainly benefitted from the pandemic. Without the overheads of a high street store, online fashion group, ASOS (As Seen On Screen), has seen its customer base jump by three million to around 23 million in the UK alone. This represents 35% of the UK population, while its worldwide sales were up 19%. However, ASOS is concerned that its younger customers may become victims of the pandemic and lose their jobs, which will ultimately affect its sales numbers (BBC News, 2020).

Moreover, writing in Forbes, Chris Furnari reported that:

> *"As the coronavirus began spreading across the U.S. earlier this year, total e-commerce penetration experienced 10 years of growth in just three months' time (March-May)."*

(Furnari, 2020)

Sale of laptops and tablets

With so many people being encouraged to WFH, the demand for laptops and tablets rocketed. Many schools were also on the hunt for equipment to support their pupils' home schooling needs. *The Wall Street Journal* reported that shelves were being stripped of laptops, while monitors were also in short supply.

> *"Equipment makers were already grappling with supply-chain bottlenecks before demand in U.S. spiked."*

(Neddleman & Tilley, 2020)

Hardly surprising was the associated increased sales of PC chips experienced by Advanced Micro Devices (AMD). Reporting for the *Financial Times*, Richard Waters commented:

> *"If anything, the crisis has only lifted its [AMD's] prospects by fuelling sales of home PCs and bringing*

more demand for data centre capacity from big internet companies that use its chips."

(Waters, 2020)

Online gaming

With millions at home looking for something to entertain themselves with, many turned to online gaming. This has provided many of the gaming industry players with a golden opportunity, and they have flourished in the conditions generated by the pandemic.

"Overall, video game sales in March approached $1.6 billion, representing a 35-percent year over year increase."

(Smith, 2020)

While industry experts believe that sales will dip when the pandemic finally recedes, they are also hopeful that they can at the very least retain the patronage of online gaming newbies that they have acquired.

Gymnasiums

Many gyms in different parts of the world found themselves being the victims of lockdown closure orders from their respective governments. Some defied these lockdown regulations and remained open, but ultimately found themselves on the wrong side of the law.

The vast majority of gyms can offer substantial arrays of fitness equipment and serve their clientele usually by opening early and closing late. When they have been allowed to operate, they are expected to adhere to social distancing requirements across their entire premises, including the locker room. Moreover, if they do not have sufficient staff, can they depend upon every member to properly wipe off the equipment when they finish using it? This must take account of those doubting Thomas's out there who remain in denial about the existence of the pandemic, or don't believe it will affect them. To compound the issue, I have not come across any gyms, save one (see section 12.5) that was in any way prepared to face the pandemic.

On a personal note

It must have been towards the end of March 2020 that the world began to discover my book *Business Continuity and the Pandemic Threat*. I cannot remember a time in my career when I have been so much in demand for consultancy, training and webinars. I have had enquires from as far afield as Hong Kong and Singapore, India, the Middle East, Europe, UK and the US. And of course, my publisher wanted me to write this sequel, too.

With the subtitle of *Potentially the Biggest Survival Challenge Facing Organisations*, I still find it surreal that when the book was published back in 2016, people laughed at me.

CHAPTER 12: CASE STUDIES

Millions of people around the world were forced into lockdown and they suddenly found themselves at home with time on their hands. They reacted in so many different ways. Some faced this situation with fear and trepidation, for any one of a number of reasons. Conversely, there are those I know personally who looked upon this free time as a heaven-sent opportunity to undertake some personal projects they had been meaning to do in some cases for years. Two learned new languages, one learned to play the guitar, while several cleaned out their garages and sold surplus items on websites, such as eBay. As for me, in what free time I found, I set about writing this book.

It was Napoleon Bonaparte who attempted to deride the British when he is alleged to have said:

"Britain is just a nation of shopkeepers."

Winding forward two centuries and we find that, from an employee headcount perspective, 95% of all British businesses are classified as 'micro-businesses', each employing between one and nine staff. Numerically, this would more or less fit into the typical headcount of a shop as envisaged by Bonaparte back in the late eighteenth and early nineteenth century. But, so many of these micro-businesses are simply not part of the retail sector. Even so, collectively they are the engine room of the British economy.

If I consider my own situation, I have been working as a freelance consultant since 2013, and late into my career I have developed what I would call a portfolio career:

- I provide consultancy on business continuity, IT disaster recovery, crisis management and of course pandemic planning.
- I offer commercial training around my area of expertise.
- Occasionally, I lecture to both undergraduate and postgraduate students at universities.
- Finally, I discovered late in my career that I enjoy writing and I have become a successful published author. My first book, *In Hindsight: A compendium of Business Continuity case studies*, topped the Amazon bestsellers lists, while my third publication, the prequel to this book, became a world bestseller.

So, how did the pandemic affect my own business? The university lecturing all but stopped. But, the world discovered the prequel to this book, and I was being regularly contacted about consultancy primarily around contingency planning for pandemics. I received enquiries from as far afield as Australia to the east and the US to the west. The demand for my classroom training courses dropped off, and those courses that I did continue to run turned into an online alternative (see section 13.7). But, what has also kept me busy during the pandemic has been writing. In addition to this book, I have three other books partially written. So, in putting together this chapter of case studies, rather than focus on how the bigger organisations have weathered the pandemic storm, I chose to primarily look at examples from that 95% of the British economy made up of micro-businesses.

12: Case studies

"You   have   to   adapt   to   survive."
Nicola Bradshaw, Little Brown Fairy Cake shop
owner, Westgate-on-Sea

Survival can depend upon a business' versatility and whether
it can find legal and safe workarounds to any lockdown
constraints. I have previously mentioned those businesses,
both large and small, that switched to making PPE to meet
the soaring demand. In this chapter, I look at a number of
SMEs whose resourcefulness and resilience helped them to
survive. For example:

- Some businesses believed that business interruption
  insurance (BII) would cover their pandemic-related
  losses. But did it?
- The nutritionist who worked face-to-face with clients
  pre-COVID found that she could still work with her
  clients by switching to an online approach.
- The restaurant that survived and flourished by
  switching to offering a take-out service, only to find it
  was in danger of becoming a victim of its own success.
- The hairdresser who started selling ladies lingerie
  online during lockdown.
- The entrepreneur with the cancelled gin festival
  switched to jam making.
- The gymnasium that had actually done some pandemic
  preparation.
- The business that survived not just one but six severe
  crises, including a pandemic.

I nearly didn't include the final case study in this section as
it is not about COVID-19. That said, it was located in a

British-controlled colony for the first 23 years that it traded – until Hong Kong was decolonised. However, I included it because it makes the point that any business can expect to have to deal with different types of crises. In the case of Louis' Steak House (refer to section 12.4), it survived several, including the 2002-2003 SARS outbreak that economically decimated Hong Kong. By including this study, I particularly wanted businesses, especially small and micro enterprises, to realise that they should be prepared to face different types of crises.

12.1 Business interruption insurance

Author's note:

This section was written in collaboration with Catherine Feeney, Overseas Lecturer at Edinburgh Napier University.

During my career I have worked for several insurance companies, albeit in information technology roles. This included four years at Zurich Insurance Group. In times of crises that disrupt business operations, organisations will invariably turn to their insurers and make a claim on their BII policies. This section examines what amounts to a conflict between businesses and insurers, specifically in the UK and the US. Similar situations are likely to exist within the insurance industry across the globe, especially as many of the major insurers within the UK and the US are themselves multinational organisations. That said, differences in the interpretation and application of BII are likely to be affected by variations in local legislation and regulation.

I would also imagine that many businesses believed that their cover would include something disruptive, such as a pandemic. But the UK's Association of British Insurers has warned claimants that:

12: Case studies

"No country in the world is able to provide widespread pandemic insurance."

(ABI, 2020)

The reality is that the insurance industry just cannot afford it. Laura Hay, Global Head of Insurance at KPMG International, also remarked that

"Most insurers learned the lessons from the SARS outbreak of 2003 and introduced exclusion clauses for communicable diseases and epidemics/pandemics into most non-life products such as business interruption."

(Hay, 2020)

So, who is more likely to be going bankrupt over BII – the insurers or the businesses that believed they were protected from COVID-19? Firstly, BII is not a compulsory insurance product that legislation stipulates organisations must have. But, for those that do have a BII policy, unless they have scrutinised the small print thoroughly, they may find that it is far from being the catch-all that perhaps they believed it was.

But let's take a step back and consider the origins of BII. It was introduced mainly as a product to leverage as much benefit out of a business contract as possible. It's not compulsory and it comes with its own pitfalls. Currently with COVID-19 being applied to the mix, it's the insurance industry that businesses feel is not meeting its obligations. Whichever party wins, be it the businesses or the insurers, the other will be hardest hit and met with considerable challenges in their financial viability. This could detrimentally affect the efficiency of their situations and probably progress for many companies towards bankruptcy on the losing side.

The battle is on, already resistance to paying out by the insurance industry is occurring. In the UK, Ramnath identified that:

> *"Business interruption insurance, which is often bundled with property insurance, covers income losses and other expenses for a specified period if a business is forced to close due to physical loss or damage from a covered peril."*

(Ramnath, 2020)

Among other determinants of BII as identified here were, *"Most business interruption policies historically derive from Victorian concerns about factories and the link to physical damage,"* said Roger Franklin, a partner at law firm Edwin Coe. *"Over the years, they have extended it to issues that arise from non-physical damage."* (Ralph & Vincent, 2020).

Interviewed by the BBC, Nigel Manton, owner of Fresh Skin Clinic in the UK county of Cheshire, said he had paid out £10,000 for BII, which now appears not to be valid vis-à-vis COVID cover.

Fresh Skin Clinic is one of hundreds of companies that have been denied cover from coronavirus, and the consequential result is likely to be bankruptcy. Manton told the BBC that:

> *"All businesses thought they'd inoculated themselves by buying this insurance and they have found that this financial vaccine doesn't work."*

(Thomas, 2020)

As it has become such an important feature of the COVID-19 lockdown situation, the UK's financial services regulating body, the Financial Conduct Authority (FCA), has established a test case and taken it to the High Court for judges to decide on the outcomes. Ralph & Vincent maintain that:

> *"The fate of thousands of small UK businesses affected by the coronavirus will be at stake ... when regulators take on the insurance industry ... in a legal battle worth potentially billions of pounds."*

(Ralph & Vincent, 2020)

They go on to say that the issues have been some of the most controversial to arise from the crisis, recognising that the court's rulings will have ramifications well beyond just the specific policies under discussion.

The intervention of the FCA will enable a relatively speedy resolution through the courts. The test case looks at 17 policy wordings from eight different insurers, and asks whether COVID-19 triggers a pay-out. As the regulator has studied other policies, it expects the court's ruling to apply to nearly 50 insurers that sold cover to 370,000 customers (Ralph & Vincent, 2020).

The court is looking at four questions in relation to the claims:

1. What does denial of access mean?
2. Does COVID count as an 'incident' or an 'emergency'?
3. Was COVID on or near the premises?
4. How much should the insurer pay?

There are expectations that whatever the judgment that is made, there will be appeals by the defeated parties, probably to the Supreme Court (again to facilitate speedy conclusion for the benefits of those appealing). All things considered, the process is still likely to take months, and in the meantime, some businesses are in great difficulty and bankruptcy is imminent. In reality, some businesses may not survive long enough to hear the court's final ruling.

The test case is based on the premise of uncertainty in comprehending the terminology in the writings of the insurance policies and their effect in paying out to insurance policyholders. The FCA also added that:

> *"The issues surrounding BI policies are complex and have the potential to create ongoing uncertainty for both customers and firms ... The variation in the types of cover provided and wordings used mean it can be difficult to determine whether customers have cover and can make a valid claim."*

(Pinsent Masons, 2020)

The FCA continues by stating that whatever ruling the court hands down regarding the test case, will be legally binding on insurers. In assessing whether insurers are handling claims fairly, the FCA will also address any BII-related contractual uncertainties and 'causation' issues, thereby providing clarity for policyholders and insurers.

The judges further pointed out that in considering a case of this complexity, and the possible prospect of a nuanced judgement, they noted that judgment may be a more onerous task to write than anticipated and cannot be rushed, given the importance that this case will have on many different parties and individuals. The FCA's test case called upon the court to consider the application of a representative sample of multiple policy wordings, underwritten by 8 insurers, to a set of illustrative assumed facts. It was hoped by the FCA that the court's judgment will go on to resolve various issues in dispute between insurers and policyholders whose policies are relevantly similar.

Eight insurance companies each voluntarily agreed to act as defendants in the test case:

1. Arch Insurance (UK) Ltd.
2. Argenta Syndicate Management Ltd.
3. Ecclesiastical Insurance Office Plc.
4. MS Amlin Underwriting Ltd.
5. Hiscox Insurance Company Ltd.
6. QBE UK Ltd.
7. Royal & Sun Alliance Insurance Plc.
8. Zurich Insurance Plc.

High Court ruling – 15 September 2020

The UK High Court handed down its judgment, which runs to more than 150 pages. It ruled that small businesses that have a 'disease' clause in their business interruption policies were entitled to compensation, as they were covered for COVID-19.

Meanwhile in the US, the equivalent of the FCA, the Securities & Exchange Commission, has not followed a similar route as the UK. Consequently, a 'Business Interruption Group' (_werbig.org_) has been activated and mobilised representing thousands of businesses, and employing millions of Americans across every sector of the economy. It states that:

> "*As businesses struggle to survive amid the COVID-19 pandemic, we continue to fight for fair and equitable solutions that will ensure small and mid-size businesses receive the insurance coverage they need in order to keep their doors open.*"

(Business Interruption Group, 2020)

In line with the Association of British Insurers (ABI), the insurance world observed that:

"Retroactive business interruption measures could bankrupt US insurers in two months.

Global pandemics like COVID-19 have been deemed uninsurable by private insurers. The sheer size and unpredictability of pandemic events makes them nigh on impossible for the industry to apply a standard underwriting practice to.

For that reason, most standard insurance contracts around the world include clear policy wording that excludes coverage for pandemic and communicable diseases."

(Moorcraft, 2020)

Francesco Maruffi is a partner in the Dispute Resolution practice at international law firm, Baker McKenzie. He concluded that:

"The outcome of any such litigation is very much dependent on the possibility to plead the existence of valid insurance coverage for business interruption Covid-19 related. As there is no one-size-fits all approach each claim should be assessed on a case-by-case basis taking into account the policy wording and its construction."

(Maruffi, 2020)

In the US, local states are looking at individual laws regarding managing these situations. The cohesive approach of the FCA will enable the litigation to be as speedy as possible through utilising the test cases through the civil courts processes. As Maruffi also states:

"The outcome of any such litigation is very much dependent on the possibility to plead the existence of valid insurance coverage for business interruption Covid-19 related. As there is no one-size-fits all approach each claim should be assessed on a case-by-case basis taking into account the policy wording and its construction."

Therefore, in the US, many individual cases will have to be resolved with litigation, which could take a considerable amount of time to the detriment of the actual business in sustaining its position as an active company.

12.2 Debbie Gallimore – Nutritionist

Debbie Gallimore is a registered nutritional therapist and well-being coach based in the UK town of Sale in Cheshire.

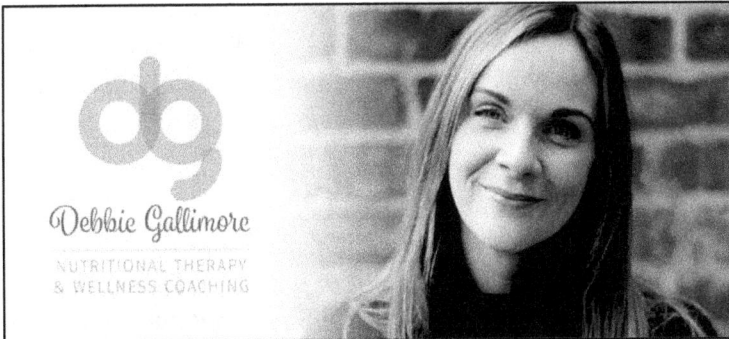

Figure 30: Debbie Gallimore – Nutritional therapy & wellness therapy

She is passionate about food and health, and genuinely believes that we are meant to feel great, stay healthy, and live long and successful lives.

She helps clients to choose the right foods and habits to transform their bodies for optimal health. With a tailored nutrition plan and motivational health coaching, Debbie believes that her clients will be living life to the full again in no time.

This is Debbie's story.

"Before the Pandemic Outbreak

Having built up my nutrition business over a seven year period, I have become well established as a leading Nutritionist in Sale who supports the health and wellbeing-of people in the county of Cheshire, Manchester and further afield across neighbouring towns.

I designed my business model to be primarily face-to-face consultations. My focus is predominantly on weight loss, female hormone issues, digestion, stress and anxiety conditions, and autoimmune dysfunction. Across a broad age group, I see a spectrum of patients with ailments that range from mild discomfort to those experiencing extreme debilitation. In some instances, their conditions can often be having a significant impact on their quality of life.

Generally, via an initial telephone consultation, I would conduct an evaluation of their needs and assess the length of time we will be working together. Building a rapport and trust with patients is paramount in providing an appropriate level of care. It is also vital in gaining patient buy-in and compliance for them to make changes required to support improvements to their wellness. I find face-to-face sessions allow that rapport to develop quickly and providing direction is then almost always carried out with ease.

COVID-19 and the lockdown

Mid-March and the COVID-19 outbreak saw the beginning of a new era, and a scary time for small, independent businesses. Like so many other SMEs, I did not have a pandemic plan in place. It was vital to quickly understand the impact on my operational structure, ability to serve patients effectively and the potential financial impact.

When the lockdown came into force, I realised that all face-to-face contact must stop, and the clinic environment would have to be closed. Some consolation was that at least the initial telephone consultations could continue. Even so, the sense of panic and anxiety I felt was at an all-time high.

How was I to ensure that I could continue supporting clients as well as dealing with the potential threat to my financial situation with the inevitable reduction in patient queries? Looking back, I can see that the first 2 weeks were unproductive as I, like the rest of the world, watched COVID unfold. The UK government's daily news updates at 5pm became essential viewing, as I endeavoured to make sense of it all, but it did little to alleviate my sense of fear.

With two children to home school and ensure their safety, work felt secondary for a brief moment. Throughout the first 2 weeks, I emailed patients assuring them that I will continue to support and coach them throughout the crisis. My thoughts turned to how anxious they might be and how their well-being could be affected by the potentially depressing and ever-growing daily COVID-19 death rate statistics. Moreover, some of my clients would have found themselves categorised as vulnerable, either from an age perspective or underlying health reasons, or even both. Consequently, their welfare had to be a priority.

Patients who were due to start with me on a face-to-face programme the following month, began to advise that they did no longer wish to start. Totally understandable, as financial situations were not quite known at that time. The consequence was I went from a full diary of new starters in April to zero. Scary place to be, but in hindsight, a welcome breather to enable me to build my own resilience and think about the coming months ahead.

- *How could I ensure that I could run a household with two children and home schooling, plus a business at the same time?*
- *How could I ensure my mental health and those of my husband and children would not be affected?*
- *What did I need to do as a business to survive the coming months?*

The switch to online consultations

I quickly moved my current patients over to online resources, such as Zoom, FaceTime and telephone consultations. This was met by little resistance as the rapport already built with my patients allowed this to be a seamless transition. My mistake was allowing myself to being patient driven by their personal preference of which online platform they wanted to use. This resulted in some inefficiency and frustration at my end. In trying to be flexible in terms of accepting each client's platform choice, it actually created more avoidable work for me. Making sure you were using the right one, each platform had to be set up to reflect the relevant data for every client's personal details. Moreover, there were often connection difficulties which needed resolving that could occur at both ends. To compound such difficulties, the solutions required to address connection difficulties with Zoom were invariably different from those required to address similar issues with other platforms. Very frustrating!

I decided three weeks into remote working that in order to improve my working efficiency, I needed to insist that all consultations took place on a single online platform. I concluded that Zoom would be the best solution all round. Those patients unfamiliar with Zoom needed access to the online service along with some basic instructions on its use.

I was very happy and relieved that this change was met with very little resistance from clients. But by standardising the platform I used, it helped me enormously in streamlining the services I could offer, while greatly improving my own time management.

Online working became the norm, resulting in no perceivable detrimental effect to patients' support and growth. Some even preferred the online consultations. For working mums who were also home schooling, it allowed them to continue on their health journeys without delay.

COVID-19 presented a new set of issues in clinic. This included heightened anxiety and stress, leading to unhealthy eating habits and increase in alcohol consumption. A high percentage of women have emotional connections with food, alcohol and other stimulants, and therefore my coaching skills had to adapt to the current situation. I am pleased to say that every patient I was able to coach felt supported with very little negative effect of stress and anxiety at that time.

As with all crises, we humans adapt as we become accustomed to a new sense of normality. The 'experts' have led us to believe that COVID-19 could be with us for some considerable time to come. Even so, I saw an increase in new patient queries in May and June. It seems that a pandemic brings a sense of 'I need to prioritise my health', so I'm happy to report that I am back to working at full capacity.

With the current relaxing of lockdown measures, I am now physically seeing patients in clinic two days a week. Wearing full PPE has become essential for face-to-face consultations. As important is the scheduling of a 15-minute interval between each session for cleaning the clinic to ensure the safety of both patients and myself.

Looking forward

COVID-19, I feel, has led all small independent businesses to seriously scrutinise their working model. Online working in both one to one and group settings may be a more future proof and economical way to work going forward. It could also be a welcome option for busy people who have difficulty in finding the time to attend the clinic.

Online group programmes have been a success for me for over two years, and it continues to be a valuable aspect of my business model in supporting more people in achieving good health. Developing more online material, as well as supporting one-to-one clients, both remotely and in clinic, is the ideal.

COVID-19 has taught us all a valuable lesson in business: insofar as we need to be resilient, while ready to adapt to change. With my own business, it has become obvious that it is vital to be flexible in the way I work with my clients."

12.3 A taste of 'Mustard'

Owned by husband and wife team, Gavin and Jane, 'Mustard' is a popular American-themed diner based in the town of Sale, Cheshire, UK. Normally one would be managing the diner while the other was at home with their children.

In the early evenings you would normally have found it absolutely packed out. Tables couldn't be reserved as the diner operated a first come, first served policy. One disappointed customer found herself faced with the prospect of an hours' wait for a table. She walked out and left a derogatory '1-star' rated comment on TripAdvisor because the restaurant was full, even though she never actually ate there (Clark, 2018, p 71). If nothing else, in her frustration she was actually telling the world how popular the restaurant was, for which Mustard's management team very much appreciated the great publicity.

Then came the pandemic, and with it the inevitable lockdown being enforced across the UK. Like all other restaurants, Mustard was forced to close its doors.

After two days of sitting at home considering their apparent very limited options, came that 'lightbulb' moment. The front of the diner had windows that could be opened like a serving hatch. Switching to take-out and, in addition to offering a delivery service via specialist companies such as Deliveroo and Uber Eats, the 'hatch' enabled customers to collect their orders without needing to go into the restaurant. Moreover, by only taking orders on the phone, along with just a card payment option, handling of potentially contaminated cash was unnecessary. Social distancing was observed, the local populace fed, Mustard survived, and the risk of any COVID-19 cross infection was minimised.

Figure 31: Mustard diner switched to take-outs during lockdown

As the coronavirus gloom briefly receded between pandemic waves, the diner found itself once again a popular eating venue. Despite the resurrected desire for eating at a table, the demand for take-away food continued more or less undiminished. The husband and wife team found it impossible for just one person to manage the logistical challenge of acting as Maître D', plus overseeing the take-away orders. Moreover, few of the restaurant staff seemed able to step up and deal with the demands of the take-away orders, leaving the business in danger of becoming a victim of its own success. A solution was ultimately found. One of the diner's staff would be asked to babysit the couple's children, leaving Jane and Gavin free to share the extra load between them.

Mustard's popularity was not limited to the food it served, it extended to its hot punch and the craft beers on offer, too. Then came the night the police came to call, necessitating the management to appeal to customers via its Facebook page:

Mustard

MUSTARD

31 December 2020 at 10:41 ·

"TIER 4 & THE HATCH

In the light of a recent visit from the police, we need to make you all aware of the following ...

Trafford has a no drinking in the street policy and our popular craft beers & hot punches are attracting quite the crowd! Which is great for us! But the police are checking that we are making you aware (which we are) to consume them indoors.

Also the police are visiting us nightly to remind us to remind you that alcohol should be pre ordered, you can do so on 0161 973 0927 ahead of your visit to the hatch.

They would also like us to disperse any crowds quickly. Please help us to keep it moving.

As always, we are forever grateful for your support and we thank you in advance for helping us to follow the guidelines & remain operating."

The local community response was an immediate outpouring of support and gratitude for the Mustard team. Positive customer feedback became a regular feature as they queued in an orderly and socially distanced fashion outside the diner while their orders were prepared.

12.4 From a cancelled gin festival to jam making

May 2020 was to be the month that entrepreneurs Mark Scarborough, his son Jack and friend Dave MacAskill had planned to hold their chilli and gin festival. The venue was to be Fort Purbrook, which is one of several fortifications built in the mid-nineteenth century to protect the naval city of Portsmouth from an attack by the French.

But like so many others, the festival became a victim of COVID-19 and was cancelled, leaving the trio awash with 100 different varieties of chilli plants, amounting to around 3,000 in total.

Over the years, Mark had enjoyed making a variety of jams and chutneys. Rather than waste them, he decided to try out the chillies as ingredients for his preserves. Local farms and health shops quickly showed interest in the products and so, from their base at Widley, just north of Portsmouth, the trio have set up a business called *Chillies from Widley* (Barber, 2020).[31]

Not to be deterred by the pandemic, as I write, the 'boys' have confirmed the dates for their next chilli and gin festival – 21st and 22nd May 2022.

---

[31] As I write, there is no website yet, but *Chillies from Widley* does have a Facebook page if you would like more information.

12.5 RESULTS inc Gymnasium

Figure 32: RESULTS inc Gymnasium

This is the only gymnasium I have come across that had given any thought to pandemic planning. As we welcomed the New Year 2020, it was operating from locations at Cheadle, Didsbury and Sale in Cheshire, UK. The company has never traded on space or equipment but has focused on building relationships with its members. For many years, its motto was 'Exercise that works, delivered by people who care', although as part of its recent rebranding exercise, its tagline has become 'Fit Together'.

With warning signs that a pandemic seemed imminent, based on events in other countries, it was assumed that it was just a matter of time before the UK went into lockdown. Owner, Joe Lightfoot takes up the story.

"We had planned to be in the position that in the event of a lockdown, we could flick a switch and continue to deliver a fitness service to members, even when the gyms were barred from opening. As part of that preparation several initiatives were taken:

- *A Private Members Only Facebook Group was created.*
- *An email announcement was prepared informing members of what contingency measures had been put in place for lockdown.*
- *The RESULTS inc University page was created on the gyms website and includes well over one-hundred resources, of which around half are workout videos. At the point of lockdown starting, these resources were by no means finished. However, there was sufficient material there to provide a programme for members that would last around two weeks, enough time to complete the remaining components when details of lockdown measures had been finalised by the UK government.*
- *When outdoor workouts were permitted again, gym car parks were pressed into service allowing portable equipment (e.g. weights, etc.) to feature as part of these programmes. Social distancing was keenly observed as was sanitising equipment after its use."*

Frequent podcasts were prepared and each of the coaches would be regularly reaching out to members to ensure they were OK. Joe was determined that members would be getting good value for their monthly membership.

While some sensible cuts were made on the expenditure side, none of the staff were furloughed or made redundant. Even the cleaner was still paid, even though for a time she had no gyms to clean. But from a business perspective, with some members having to or wanting to cancel their memberships, revenue did suffer. However, the revenue slide was bolstered when the company picked up a corporate client. With the newfound responsibility of looking after the new client's nine-hundred home-based employees, Joe found himself producing livestreamed workouts every day from his own home.

As the pandemic kicked-off, the lease for the Cheadle gym's premises had 18 months to run and, at that time, the intent was to renew the lease. However, during the first lockdown, the percentage of Cheadle members cancelling their memberships was far higher than the other two gyms. Moreover, when the lockdown restrictions were eased, while there was quite a nice surge of returning and new members at the Didsbury and Sale gyms, the corresponding numbers at Cheadle were disappointingly low.

By September 2020, with less than a year left on the lease, two of the company's team members opted to move on. As this coincided with the fall off of membership, it was decided after much thought to close Cheadle. While the gym could have recruited and trained new staff, Joe always felt that there would be another pandemic wave just over the horizon. The final catalyst in the decision-making process was another business being prepared to take over the lease for the Cheadle premises.

Being only two miles (3.2 km) from the Didsbury gym, with the decision being made to close Cheadle, attempts were made to persuade the now 'homeless' members to transfer to Didsbury – some did, others didn't. In hindsight, it is quite possible that the decision to close Cheadle may have happened anyway. However, what is clear is that COVID-19 most definitely both expedited and influenced the decision-making process.

In considering the challenge that his business has had to face from the pandemic crisis, Joe believes that it has taught him a lot about himself and his team. He concluded by saying:

> *"It's been a really tough and challenging time, but from a purely entrepreneurial point of view, I don't think I have had this much fun for a long time. I am not a peacetime General; I am a war time General."*

12.6 From The London Kitchen to COVID testing centre

Figure 33: The London Kitchen

Entrepreneur Damian Clarkson is the founder and Managing Director of the award-winning The London Kitchen, which was specially created in 2009 as an event catering business. Damian and his small but talented team have catered for some ground-breaking and highly prestigious events, including London Fashion Week and BMW's Rolls Royce UK Centenary celebrations. With the arrival of the pandemic, the events industry all but closed down. Damian offered to work at one of three new COVID testing centres in London's Fulham area. With his application accepted, he expected to be working in a high visibility vest or in a windy car park, but he found himself in a brand-new, yet to be opened, community centre. Writing on his Facebook page, Damian takes up the story:

> *"I'm now managing a team of 20-25 people from a wide range of backgrounds including actors, West End sound engineers and event rigging crew. We set up before Christmas, changed direction from walk in to prebooked as tiers escalated and opened a week ago, now testing 400 people a day. It helps right now, has a huge social benefit and it's great being in a team again. Hopefully this need will taper off as COVID retreats and we can get back to what we enjoy doing. Stay safe everyone and try and find a positive use for this unplanned time."*

12.7 From hairdressing to ladies' lingerie

Like some of the businesses featured in this book, hairdressing salons became a victim of the lockdown. It has come to my notice that some hairdressers resumed working by visiting clients in their homes to continue the service. That said, I believe that this was strictly under the radar, especially as in the UK at least they would have been under the government's furlough compensation scheme. Furthermore, by going into their clients' homes, in certain instances they would have been breaking lockdown regulations. There are, of course, those members of the public that observed lockdown restrictions by opting for the 'coronacut' – i.e. a haircut at home in desperation, often using nail scissors.

One hairdresser, who has requested anonymity, decided not to beat a path to her clients' front doors, but chose to diversify her business interests instead. While looking for inspiration in terms of what exactly she could do, when that '*eureka*' moment came, it took her in the direction of selling ladies lingerie online.

This could have been heavy on the setup costs. However, her initial business model involved offering a niche range of products on Amazon and eBay, while using a drop shipping company to dispatch the products to the customers. So, she did not need to set up an eCommerce website along with potentially expensive Search Engine Optimisation (SEO) to drive customers to her site. Moreover, by using a drop shipper, she never actually had to buy stock or handle the products. Consequently, the initial outlay was very low.

After three months of lockdown, she was able to reopen her salon. The first week witnessed unusually long-haired customers queuing up six-deep while waiting in line for their much overdue coiffuring. Since then, business has gone very quiet. It has been said that the coronavirus has acted as a massive agent of change, and just maybe that has encompassed hairdressing. It seems that many customers have taken a liking to having their hair cut at home, rather than at the traditional hairdressing salon. Although it seems her diversified business activities are initially showing much promise, if the demand for hairdressing continues to disappoint, 'our girl' may have to rethink her business strategy in that respect.

On a slightly different ladies lingerie tack, several years ago, one of my work colleagues, Barbara was explaining that she had been looking into the business of selling women's used underwear. I must admit that my initial response was that 'she was having a laugh' – except she wasn't. She was being incredibly serious about it.

Here my naivety came to the fore as I never realised that there was a demand for such products. But, apparently there is money to be made from such a venture, and there are even online marketplaces where you can buy and sell such items. I also learned that even the US provider of stock photography, Shutterstock, has a section of pictures entitled 'used underwear images'. But despite of all her research and preparation, she never took the plunge – that was until now.

Moving on to January 2020, in a situation completely unrelated to the pandemic, she was made redundant from her role in marketing. With the pandemic bearing down on us, it was not a good time to be job hunting. So, having already done all the research and initial preparation, she opted to launch her business. Even in the middle of a pandemic, I am pleased to report that her business is booming.

12.8 The Seed Co-operative, Spalding, Lincolnshire, UK

From the heart of Lincolnshire in the UK, the community owned Spalding based Seed Co-operative supplies close to 400 different kinds of fruit and vegetable seeds. With the entire country entering lockdown, many individuals chose to pass the time by taking on varying degrees of gardening initiatives. Some were large ambitious projects, while others were just small, window box size ventures. But regardless of size, most had one thing in common – they needed seeds.

One of the beneficiaries was the Seed Co-operative. As the first total lockdown commenced in the UK, orders were around 600% up on normal for the time of year, and the company attempted to deal with hundreds and hundreds of orders every day. By the morning of 24 March 2020, the company had to turn off the till on its website, as they could no longer guarantee to deliver product orders.

A combination of hard work and dedication from the Co-operative's team, along with a good harvest of seeds, enabled it to successfully navigate these challenging times. Peter Brinch, the chairperson, said in his introduction to the Co-operative's 2020 annual report:

> *"Covid-19 has turned life upside down for the whole nation. In the upheaval there has been a silver lining for the Seed Cooperative. Covid has led to a huge increase in seed sales. For a long period of time the web-shop had to reduce its opening hours to two hour windows as this generated enough seed orders to keep staff busy for the rest of the week."*

(Brinch, 2020)

12.9 Pub desks

The hospitality industry was always going to be one of the first to suffer from the negative effects of the pandemic. Having to contend with a variety of business-constraining pandemic countermeasures, including complete lockdowns, there are many venues that are simply going to struggle to survive.

In the UK, some public houses have started offering desks as an alternative to WFH. With a constant supply of hot or cold beverages, plus food when required, this provides the customer with an often much needed change of scenery, and for pub landlords, it generates some much needed alternative income.

Providing local country legislation, social distancing protocols and appropriate COVID-19 related safety measures can be observed, there is no reason why other hospitality outlets could not consider a similar initiative.

12: Case studies

12.10 Louis' Steak House – Hong Kong

This is the tale of six crises, including having to deal with the economic fall-out from SARS. All businesses can expect to periodically have to deal with a serious crisis that may even threaten their existence. Those that have embraced business continuity principles will be more resilient and better positioned to survive such challenges, while other unprepared companies might fail to recover. This study examines the case of Louis' Steak House in Hong Kong, and considers how many major crises is it reasonable to expect a business to encounter and yet survive. Louis' Steak House first opened in 1974, while Hong Kong was still under British colonial rule. History has demonstrated that tourism and hospitality are fragile industries (Feeney, 2014). Even so, in the 40 or so years since its inauguration, Louis' Steak House has arguably experienced more than its fair share of crises, none of which were of its own making.

The Yeung brothers' venture opened in 1974 at a most inopportune moment in time when the world was reeling from a financial crisis and stock market crash. However, the brothers were very creative in meeting this initial challenge, as William Yeung explained:

"We had promotions and lucky draws. We gave away an airline ticket to Bangkok – at the time it was a big thing – and a film camera."

(Carvalho, 2015)

The restaurant prospered and became renowned for its signature dishes of 'Tomahawk Steak' and 'Fish Maw'. On 4 June 1989, Beijing witnessed the Tiananmen Square massacre, which had a big knock-on effect on business in Hong Kong (Carvalho, 2015). Other changes were on the

259

horizon. In 1997, Hong Kong was decolonised and handed back to China by the departing British. Many of Louis' patrons came from the British armed forces, police and civil servants who returned to the UK.

"Many British soldiers, expats and businessmen were frequent visitors to the steakhouse."

(Ejinsight, 2015)

In 2003, Louis' was challenged again when Hong Kong was hit by a novel virus called Severe Acute Respiratory Syndrome (SARS). Although it is now known to have originated in China's Guangdong province, to the world it appeared that Hong Kong was the source. The virus proliferated rapidly from Hong Kong and quickly established footholds in Toronto, Singapore, Vietnam and Taiwan.

On the ground in Hong Kong, most restaurants, bars and cinemas remained empty, while the wearing of protective face masks became the norm. Airlines cancelled flights to and from the territory, as passenger numbers plummeted by as much as 77% in April 2003. Between March and May 2003, hotel occupancy rates dropped from 79% to 18%. Moreover, the World Travel and Tourism Council has estimated that the devastation to Asian tourism from the SARS outbreak resulted in up to three million people in the industry losing their jobs (Feeney, 2014). Reuters' Gary Ling also remarked that:

"It looked like Hong Kong had no more future as it appeared as the epicentre of SARS and people would not want to travel there."

(Clark, 2016)

Despite relatively few human fatalities, SARS was an economic tsunami creating US$30 to $50 billion in losses over a period of just a few months (TASW, 2011).

In the face of a deadly virus that ultimately spread to 26 countries, Louis' managed to survive with an average of only four customers per night. It went on to prosper again and celebrated its 40th anniversary in 2014 with US consul-general Clifford Hart and Cardinal John Tong Hon among the guests who attended the party (Ejinsight, 2015).

It was in the last quarter of 2014, that many businesses, including Louis', were also affected by civil unrest (Cheung, 2015). Sometimes referred to as 'Occupy Central' or the 'Umbrella Revolution', the protesters were demanding universal suffrage and had set up four camps. Three were on Hong Kong Island at Causeway Bay, Admiralty and Central, plus a fourth in the Mong Kok District of Kowloon.

The protesters camps were all blocking major arterial roads and completely disrupting the traffic flow in these areas, a situation that local authorities surprisingly tolerated for over two months. These sites remained permanently manned during the protests, until police forcibly removed them. Those shops and businesses in the affected areas that managed to open, in some cases reported a drop in sales of up to 90%, where customers were deterred by the presence of the demonstrators (Clark, 2016, pp 79-81).

After 41 years, Louis' has now finally closed its doors for the last time. However, any one of the crises it faced during its time in business could have been enough to jeopardise its survival chances along the way:

- Opening in 1974 during a financial crisis and stock market crash.

- Knock-on effect of the Tiananmen Square massacre on Hong Kong businesses.
- Permanent loss of regular clientele when the British handed Hong Kong back to China in 1997.
- The SARS pandemic in 2003, which turned Hong Kong into a pariah location.
- Global financial crisis of 2008 that saw Lehman Brothers file for bankruptcy.
- The 2014 Hong Kong's Occupy Central civil disorder protests.

If nothing else, like Louis', both large and small organisations need to appreciate that they can find themselves facing multiple crises. Apart from choosing to open during a financial crisis and stock market crash, none of the crises were within Louis' control.

Organisations need to appreciate that they can end up suffering from collateral damage from someone else's catastrophe, and their crisis management plans should reflect this. Moreover, it is not beyond the bounds of probability that organisations could find themselves facing multiple crises simultaneously.

The final crisis that sounded the death knell for Louis' in 2015 was rising rents. Like many other companies in Hong Kong. Louis' was being squeezed out by rents that were twice as high as New York.

Albeit two years later, CBRE has established that, as of September 2017, Hong Kong (Central) has the most expensive business rental rates in the world and weighs in at one and half times more expensive than second placed Beijing's Finance Street (Putzier, 2017).

12: Case studies

Yeung explained that *"over the past few years, the rent has gone up 20 percent at every contract renewal ... the landlord also reduced the duration of the contract from three to two years"*. (Cheung, 2015).

Other restaurants and small retail outlets have also fallen foul of massive rent increases. Some may have the flexibility to change their business model and move to cheaper premises or trade online. For example, in the hospitality sector, this might suit a food 'take-away' operation that can deliver food, but for a traditional restaurant this would simply be impractical, especially if it depends upon premises with a high footfall.

Maybe the last word should be given to the BBC's Kate Hunt who reported on the effect of extreme rent rises on small businesses in Hong Kong. She maintains that a two- or three-year lease is the norm in Hong Kong, compared to five- to ten-year tenancies in the UK. Hunt also featured the plight of a shoe shop called Shoegirl, owned by Jennifer Cheung, which was forced to close, again a victim of rising rents. Over a period approaching nine years, the annual rent had risen from HK$360,000 to around HK$1 million. Cheung has since successfully relaunched her business online.

12.11 Concentrations of risk

The first concentrations of risk to hit the headlines were cruise ships, and in particular the Diamond Princess. Likened by some to floating 'petri dishes', one professor of bioethics said on the subject:

12: Case studies

"Boats are notorious places for being incubators for viruses." Arthur Caplan, New York University School of Medicine

(Cheng & Yamaguchi, 2020)

Care homes for the elderly and people with special health needs have found themselves in the frontline in the fight against COVID-19 infections. Likewise, prison communities which, unless locked down before an infection finds its way in, are also an area of serious potential exposure. Food processing plants have not had a good press either, with many proving to be infection hotspots.

12.11.1 Cruise ships

In 2019, the combined gross income generated by the cruise industry was £120 billion (Billion Pound Cruises - All at Sea, 2020), having enjoyed an average annual growth rate of 5.4% since 2009 (Micallef, 2020). By the beginning of 2020, the cruise industry's passenger capacity was around 32 million annually. Close to 300 cruise ships were expected to be in operation, in addition to the anticipated debuts of a further 19 during the year (CLIA, 2020, p 13).

With the pandemic gathering momentum, from the moment the plight of the passengers and crew aboard the Diamond Princess became headline news, any appeal for people to go cruising started fading. But, it was to be another five weeks after the Diamond Princess story first broke before cruising was finally halted, with an initial one-month suspension. A statement from the Cruise Lines International Association (CLIA) read:

12: Case studies

"On the declaration of a pandemic, we voluntarily suspended operations worldwide, one of the first industries to do so."

(Billion Pound Cruises – All at Sea, 2020).

The CDC Director issued a 'No Sail Order' for cruise ships on 14 March 2020, and commended the CLIA for its willingness to voluntary suspend cruise ship operations (CDC, 2020).

Before docking back in Yokohama, passengers were informed that an elderly gentleman who had left the ship in Hong Kong on 25 January 2020, had been hospitalised after being diagnosed with COVID-19. The world looked on as the ship was quarantined in Yokohama, Japan on 4 February 2020, in what initially became the largest concentration of COVID-19 infections outside of China (BBC Our World – Coronavirus Cruising, 2020).

There has been some disagreement over the identity of 'patient zero', the original person who spread the infection throughout the Diamond Princess. Identifying the Hong Kong patient only by his surname 'Wu', the *South China Morning Post* claims that Japanese health authorities have also released data on the number of infections on the ship. This showed there were two confirmed passengers whose symptoms first presented on 20 January, three days earlier than Wu's case (Zhang, 2020).

What is clear is that Mr 'Wu' was not the first case to have been diagnosed in Hong Kong. This was recorded as a 39-year-old man whose COVID-19 infection was confirmed on 23 January 2020 (Hong Kong CHP, 2020), two days before Mr 'Wu' disembarked from the Diamond Princess.

Initial testing by Japanese authorities revealed more than 700 passengers and crew tested positive for COVID-19, of which around half were asymptomatic. Writing in the BMJ, Chris Baraniuk reported that Japanese authority records suggested that infections actually fell among passengers after the introduction of quarantine measures onboard the Diamond Princess. This leads us to conclude that the majority of cross infection occurred before the ship returned to Yokohama. Unfortunately, infection among the crew who were having regular contact with both their colleagues and the passengers continued to rise (Baraniuk, 2020).

The way in which the Japanese authorities handled the quarantining of the ship, plus the subsequent disembarkation and transit of passengers has not been without criticism. Some passengers were permitted to travel who later tested positive for COVID-19. Even so, it should be remembered that what the Japanese were facing was a world-first, and they certainly did not have a proven set of procedures to follow.

In addition to the Diamond Princess, other ships have been caught up in the coronavirus outbreak. The Holland America owned 'MS Westerdam' was refused entry by Taiwan, Guam, the Philippines and Japan, before finally being granted permission to dock and disembark passengers by Cambodia (McCurry, 2020). The ship had also attempted to dock in Bangkok, but was denied permission. It was subsequently escorted out of Thailand's territorial waters by a Thai Navy frigate HTMS Bhumibol (*Bangkok Post*, 2020).

It was claimed by cruise company, Holland America, that no one aboard the Westerdam had tested positive for COVID-19 before the ship docked in Cambodia (Holland America, 2020). However, one 83-year-old woman left the ship and flew to Malaysia, where she was subsequently diagnosed with COVID-19 (BBC News, 2020).

Another cruise ship from the Holland America fleet, the 'MS Zaandam' had a similar experience with South American ports. Although the voyage was planned to end in Buenos Aires, Argentina, the cruise was cancelled, and it returned to its home port of Miami (Billion Pound Cruises – All at Sea, 2020).

The Grand Princess, which was known to have COVID-19 patients onboard, was initially refused permission to dock in Oakland, California, although the authorities relented four days later. Even so, strict procedures were enforced before passengers were permitted to disembark and enter local quarantine, but crew had to remain onboard (Luscombe, 2020).

Managing the norovirus threat

Cruise ships are well rehearsed in dealing with common viruses, such as norovirus, which can proliferate rapidly through a tightly packed vessel. I have witnessed first-hand how efficiently and effectively crews manage such eventualities. For example:

- Conducting considerable extra cleaning throughout the ships.
- Closing the self-service buffets.
- Encouraging passengers to regularly wash their hands and make frequent use of the hand cleaning sanitising gels found around the ships. This is also standard practice when passengers are urged to use the sanitising hand gel as they enter restaurants.

- Persuading passengers to use the toilets in their cabins rather than public facilities.

- Quarantining infected passengers in the cabins for at least 48 hours after they have stopped presenting symptoms.

Now, while this highly infectious norovirus stomach bug that causes vomiting and diarrhoea is very unpleasant, it cannot be realistically compared with coronavirus, which of course can be fatal. In effect, what the cruise ships were facing with COVID-19 was unprecedented. Speaking about coronavirus in relation to cruise ships, former Public Health England Infectious Diseases expert, Dr Bharat Pankhania, expressed his concern when he observed:

> *"In the confined space in a ship, you have people moving around, air flows, sewage systems, air condition all in a very confined place. It spreads like wildfire through that cruise liner."*

(Billion Pound Cruises – All at Sea, 2020)

By contrast, in his BMJ article, Baraniuk reported that no evidence was found to suggest that the air conditioning or wastewater systems played any part in the spread of COVID-19 onboard the Diamond Princess (Baraniuk, 2020).

Taylor Dolven of the *Miami Herald* claimed the publication had created a database that shows that as of 2 May 2020, at least 2,700 cruise ship passengers across the global fleet had caught COVID-19, of whom 74 had died.

With countries around the world banning cruising in their territorial waters, there are hundreds of ships at a standstill. Some are moored in their home ports, while others are moored at various safe anchorage points around the world.

Most cruise ships have left skeleton crews on board, which include officers and deck hands. The logistical problem of crew getting home initially proved challenging, especially with many countries closing their borders. This caused psychological issues among some crew members, often around the uncertainty of how long they would be stuck for.

A hotly debated issue has considered whether the cruising industry was just a victim of the pandemic, or even part of the cause of its rapid proliferation. One estimate calculated that one in every five cruise ships were known to have passengers or crew infected by COVID-19. Moreover, as former cruise ship doctor, Kate Bunyan, remarked:

> *"In the UK we have a large part of the population who enjoy cruising that are over 70. So the risk aboard a cruise ship is that you have people loving their holiday but are actually more vulnerable and that is a pretty toxic combination."*

(Billion Pound Cruises – All at Sea, 2020)

With cruises calling into ports that, in retrospect, we now know that the coronavirus was already doing its worst, and it was perhaps almost inevitable that passengers who went ashore would carry the virus back onboard the ships.

Australia conducted a criminal enquiry into the spread of COVID-19 around the country, which was believed to have originated from the Ruby Princess. New South Wales Police Commissioner Mike Fuller announced the launching of a criminal investigation into the Ruby Princess cruise ship (Ship Technology, 2020). However, state officials have since apologised following the conclusion of that investigation. The findings ruled that the local authorities made 'serious errors' in allowing the 2,650 passengers to disembark in

Sydney. The ship was ultimately linked to at least 900 cases of COVID-9 and 28 deaths (BBC News, 2020).

What is clear is that much anger has been expressed after authorities permitted the Ruby Princess's passengers to disembark on 19 March 2020, before COVID-19 test results were returned. One rather weak reason given was that it was permitted out of concern for passengers and their flights – both internal and international (Noyes, 2020). Hundreds of passengers later tested positive and 15 died, which represented more than a quarter of the fatalities recorded in Australia at the time. Police also boarded the ship and seized its 'black box' as part of the ongoing investigation (Sky News, 2020).

As the pandemic gathered momentum, this was reflected by a sharp fall in the cruise industry's share prices. In fact, market confidence in the cruise industry was already falling in the five weeks leading up to the WHO's declaration of a pandemic on 11 March 2020. The following table compares the effect on the share values of the three largest cruising corporations.

In May 2020, Royal Caribbean revealed that the pandemic was costing it around $150 million per month (Parker, B. 2020). while Carnival's monthly loss was closer to $1 billion (Hancock, 2020). Norwegian announced an average monthly loss of $633 million for the first quarter of 2020 (Sharpe, 2020), although these figures do not cover an entire month since the suspension of cruising.

The stand-out statistic is the share values of each dropped more than 80% in the two months from 17 January to 18 March 2020.

Name	Price Jan 17, 2020	Price Mar 18, 2020	Percentage drop in price	Monthly Lost Revenue
Carnival	$51.90	$9.30	82%	$1 Billion
Royal Caribbean	$135.05	$22.33	83%	$150 Million
Norwegian	$59.65	$7.77	87%	$570 Million[32]

**Figure 34: Top three cruise corporations share price comparison
(Source: NYSE, 2020)**

The cruise industry got a lot of bad press in the early days of the pandemic, and passenger confidence will have been damaged. Consequently, some 'fences will need to be mended' with regard to health and safety. So, where does the industry go from here? Several things need to come together before passengers can confidently start boarding cruise ships again. Going forward, cruising operators can be sure that they will be under scrutiny from the public, the media and health authorities. Even if just one ship has one single case of COVID-19, it will almost undoubtedly become a big story that could have ramifications across the entire cruise industry.

Some cruise operators relaunched their offerings by adopting the model of catering for single fully vaccinated nationalists. In the outset, these were short cruises of three to five days, without an itinerary, so there would be no port visits. This avoided the problem experienced by several cruise ships

---

[32] Norwegian's posted figures for January to March 2020 include the two months leading up to the pandemic shutdown in March.

with various countries closing their borders and banning ships from docking. So, for example, Aida would take Germans, Costa would focus on Italians and P&O would be for Brits, while Carnival would be for the US market. A final word of optimism for the cruise industry comes from Lucy Huxley, Editor of *Travel Weekly* who told the BBC:

> *"The cruise industry has probably done more than any other travel sector of travel, more than hotels or airlines, to make sure it really is safe from health and safety, hygiene and testing passengers before they board a ship making them ready to restart as soon as Governments allow."*

(Thomson, 2021)

In fact, my own pandemic cruising experience is also worth recording here as cruising operators took their first tentative new steps. In August 2021, my wife and I embarked on the P&O cruise ship Britannia for what was described as a 4-night 'seacation'. The ship sailed from Southampton for a cruise along the English Channel and Irish Sea before returning to its home port.

Every passenger had to be a UK resident and prove that they had been double vaccinated. Furthermore, they each had to have a negative result from a COVID-19 lateral flow test taken immediately before boarding. Anyone failing to meet this no-nonsense criteria simply were not permitted to sail.

The Britannia has a capacity of circa 3,600 passengers but sailed only 60% full. Regular sanitising, social distancing and face mask wearing protocols, especially in public areas, were pro-actively encouraged. Frequent cleaning of common touch points (e.g. handrails and elevator buttons etc.) were conducted by the crew. In what would normally be the self-service restaurant, passengers were served by crew members to reduce the risk of cross contamination.

For contingency purposes, an area of the ship was off limits where a number of cabins had been allocated for passenger isolation purposes should they be needed. It wasn't.

We have since embarked on two back-to-back cruises aboard the Regal Princess spending a total of 14 days at sea. While the first stayed in UK waters, the second visited ports in France and Spain.

In my opinion, both P&O and Princess Cruises had made every effort to protect both passengers and crew from the coronavirus. As passengers, we felt completely safe.

Yet, year end 2021 witnessed a significant rise in the number of COVID-19 cases associated with cruising. The CDC issued a warning to avoid cruise ship travel regardless of vaccination status but stopped short of issuing an outright banning order (Lee, 2021).

12.11.2 Care homes

While there are a few notable exceptions, in many countries, the residents of care homes proved to be particularly vulnerable to COVID-19. Some because of their age, while others because of underlying health conditions. There were those unfortunate individuals that ticked both boxes. When countries declared their new COVID-19 case and fatality rates each day, sadly care home residents often featured in these statistics for the wrong reasons. Once it had gained a foothold in a home, the virus would invariably spread quickly and do its worst.

"In care homes across Europe, at the beginning of the pandemic staff were left without PPE, testing regimes

were poor, and care home residents who needed hospital treatment didn't get it."

(Professor Kontopantelis, 2020, University of Manchester)

It would be easy to say that countries had no plan in place regarding the managing of these homes in a pandemic. However, although I believe there may be some truth in that statement, I feel that saying that would be just too 'black and white'.

But, to begin with, we need to acknowledge the missed learning opportunities that the Diamond Princess presented the world. With the ship in quarantine in Yokohama, Japan, passengers were confined to their cabins while crew members moved freely about the ship carrying out their duties. This included not only working alongside their fellow crew members, but at the very least, also visiting cabins to deliver food to passengers, although in some instances they would have taken the virus with them, too.

Many experts considered the Diamond Princess situation to be similar to an apparent common practice of care staff working across multiple homes. If they were infected, even if they were asymptomatic, they would take the virus with them wherever they went. Certainly in the UK, where there are in excess of 15,000 care homes, some are affiliated to a branded chains of providers where it is not uncommon for staff to work in more than one place.

As previously mentioned, PPE was initially in very short supply globally, and primary hospitals and, in particular, critical care unit staff were seen as the priority. Consequently, care home workers were often being asked to work without the PPE they really needed.

Not every care home was infected, and there were those that took drastic measures to protect the residents in their care. Initially, some homes banned visitors and allowed only 'window' visits. Others reduced visitor numbers and looked for creative ways to enable safe visits with relatives. Instead of going home themselves at the end of each shift, some staff even elected to move into their care homes and live with their elderly patients, often in fairly rudimentary conditions. There are reports of dedicated staff leaving their own families and doing this in some cases for several weeks at a time. Very commendable.

Eventually, repeat testing for COVID-19 for both staff and residents was widely introduced, although one cannot help thinking that this was tantamount to shutting the stable door after the horse had bolted.

But, let us consider a couple of success stories – Germany and Hong Kong.

12.11.2.1 The German approach

Upon realising that the pandemic was heading in its direction, the UK's NHS activated its pandemic plan and cleared as many hospitals' beds as possible in preparation for receiving COVID-19 patients. This required discharging most fit, elderly patients and seeing them placed into care homes. In hindsight, while no evidence has yet been presented, it is possible that some of these discharged patients had already been infected by the virus and thus took it with them to care homes.

The UK was not alone in this respect, and Germany followed a similar path, but with one very notable difference. Care homes were legally not permitted to receive patients from hospitals unless they could quarantine them for at least two weeks.

A survey conducted by the International Long-Term Care Policy Network had responses from 824 German care homes. They represented 64,772 residents between them (approximately 8% of the total number of German care home residents). The survey reported that 80% of all homes had remained COVID-19 free (Rothgang, et al., 2020).

12.11.2.2 Hong Kong took a lesson from SARS

Around 16% of Hong Kong's 7.5 million population are 65 years and above. In fact, it has one of the highest percentages per capita of elderly citizens in the world who are 80 years old and over and living in care homes.

During the 2002-2003 SARS outbreak, more than 70% of all care home residents who became infected actually died, compared to an average global mortality rate of around 6%. Preparations for the next epidemic had started in 2004 with the creation of the Centre for Health Protection and a three-tier emergency response system was developed the following year. Two opportunities to gain experience in using this system afforded themselves in 2009 and 2010 with outbreaks of swine and avian influenza. Second level emergencies also presented themselves in 2012 and 2013 by way of further avian influenza outbreaks, and then again in 2015 for MERS.

Whenever there is an outbreak of influenza, all care home staff are expected routinely to wear face masks, something not widely practiced in the west. This naturally applies to emerging infectious diseases, such as COVID-19. Should any staff become asymptomatic, the face mask wearing culture substantially reduces the risk to residents. This risk is further reduced when residents wear face masks, too.

Hospitals were also responsible for not discharging elderly patients into care homes until they were virus free. At least two tests had to be returned negative before such a transfer could be actioned.

With the virus beginning to spread globally, in line with its emergency response protocols, Hong Kong care homes went into lockdown. Visitors were banned from entering care homes in early February 2020. Contact with family members was maintained by the use of video calls and 'window' visits, a practice followed in many other countries. However, it was noted that these lockdown measures did cause loneliness among the residents and psychological suffering for both them and their families.

Six months into the pandemic and Hong Kong's COVID-19 case count was approaching a comparatively modest 5,000 infections and 99 deaths. Of that 5,000, only 132 were care home residents who were located across 16 homes. Compared with the number of care home residents infected in other countries, Hong Kong's approached has clearly been a success.

12.11.3 Prisons

In early July 2020, Ghislaine Maxwell was apprehended by the FBI and arraigned on charges relating to the late disgraced financier Jeffrey Epstein. She was detained in the Metropolitan Detention Centre, a Brooklyn jail. On 10 July 2020, appearing before the US District Court in Manhattan, she requested bail. She cited her justification as being the high risk of being infected by COVID-19 while in the detention centre. The month before her arrest, some 55 inmates and staff had tested positive for COVID-19 (Stempel, 2020). Her request was denied.

Shortly after the pandemic was declared in March 2020, one high-profile prisoner to have tested positive for COVID-19 was convict Harvey Weinstein, although he has since recovered (Freifield, 2020). Out of a total population in excess of 6 million prisoners (US Department of Justice, 2021), by the end of June 2020, throughout the US, more than 68,000 cases of COVID-19 had been diagnosed throughout the country's correction institutions. *The New York Times* reported that deaths in prisons attributed to COVID-19 had risen by 73% in the six weeks ending 30 June 2020.

12.11.4 *Food processing plants*

So, what pandemic-linked dubious record do the US, the UK, Germany, France, Spain and Portugal, among others, all have in common? With respect to this section, it relates to the high number of COVID-19 infections detected in some of their food processing plants and abattoirs. In some cases, the discovery of hundreds of infected workers has been followed by the closure of the plants, although others have controversially remained open. There are also instances where local communities have registered new COVID-19 case spikes, which were subsequently traced back to the plants.

Although some unions have pointed the finger at poor working conditions, there does not seem to be one single confirmed factor identified as the cause. However, some theories have been presented:

- In some plants, the very nature of their design makes it difficult to observe social distancing. It is also entirely possible that the maximisation of production output of some plants depends upon not introducing social distancing measures. In other words, the economic aspect of the business is in direct conflict with the health and safety of the workers.

- The wearing of face masks and goggles is mandatory in some food processing premises, in others it has not been enforced. Recommendations have been made by various health bodies, including the CDC, that indoor food production line workers should wear full protective PPE.

- Employees are working indoors, which we now know is more conducive to cross-infection than being outdoors. Moreover, the circulation of fresh air by leaving doors and windows open is not always possible. This is especially true during warmer months, as these plants need to be maintained at low temperatures in the interest of food hygiene.

- It has been suggested that cold and damp indoor environments are akin to petri dishes, as the coronavirus can survive and spread.

- Work in the plants can be physically demanding, and some might consider it as being similar to having a workout. But, this can result in people breathing more heavily, which can facilitate the spread of the disease.

- It is known that the virus can be transmitted when people talk. In the plants, there is noisy machinery that necessitates workers having to shout to be heard. This can intensify the spread of infected droplets.

- Migrant workers, who may not be entitled to sick pay, are often used in plants. Some have been reluctant to report any COVID-19 symptoms in case they lose money.

- There are those workers who do not live locally, and some plants provide accommodation in dormitories. But, such conditions are also favourable for the spread of the virus. Ironically, some market gardeners who employ seasonal workers have also had cases of COVID-19 infections believed to have stemmed from the accommodation provided for the workers.

Although this section focuses on the food production industry because it has had a bad press, many of the points raised above could just as equally apply to other factory environments outside of the food industry.

CHAPTER 13: IMPACT ON EDUCATION

Should education be classified as a business or an industry? There are arguments both for and against. Whatever you own personal opinion happens to be, there are certainly lessons (both positive and negative) that the more traditional business sectors can learn from the educational response to the pandemic. This chapter considers the effects of these lockdown restrictions and responses, by looking at educational examples primarily from the UK and China.

Many universities, schools, kindergartens and even commercial training organisations around the world have been closed down to restrict the spread of COVID-19. The formal classroom teaching approach was one of the early victims of the pandemic. In the UK, some schools remained open for the children of essential workers (e.g. emergency services, health and care workers, etc.) who would not be able provide home schooling support.

There have been many encouraging accounts of children being effectively home schooled, although this has invariably depended upon the appropriate technology being available to support this. As previously mentioned, supply chain issues for tablets and laptops quickly manifested themselves as the business world also scrambled to procure equipment to support their staff WFH.

Conversely, disturbing reports have also surfaced of children, often in their teen years, locking themselves away in their bedrooms for hours on end much to the consternation of their parents. Concern grows for the longer term psychological impact that this could cause.

13: Impact on education

"In 1665, following an outbreak of the bubonic plague in England, Cambridge University closed its doors, forcing Newton to return home to Woolsthorpe Manor. While sitting in the garden there one day, he saw an apple fall from a tree, providing him with the inspiration to eventually formulate his law of universal gravitation".

(Nix, 2020)

One must wonder whether anyone forced to work at home during the pandemic, may, like Isaac Newton, also experience an '*Annus Mirabilis*'.

What is unsurprisingly apparent is that schools and universities are just as vulnerable to both staff and pupils being infected with COVID-19 as any other sector of the community. In the UK, schools reopened at the end of August 2020. However, within a just few days, incidents of infected staff and pupils were being reported. On one day alone in Greater Manchester, COVID cases were confirmed at more than 40 schools, necessitating children being sent home (Gill, 2020).

Concern had also been expressed in the UK regarding universities reopening their doors again in September. There had already been incidents reported vis-à-vis students blatantly ignoring social gathering rules and partying. In response, some universities issued tough warnings that any miscreants caught engaging in such activities faced expulsion. Even so, universities throughout the UK have had to insist that students testing positive, plus those who are known to have been exposed to COVID-19, must isolate. The consequence has been thousands of students isolated in halls of residence and shared accommodation.

Although the vast majority of students who almost inevitably become infected with COVID-19 may well be asymptomatic, the concern surrounds the potential impact when they return home, taking the infection into the wider community. US universities reopened two months earlier, from which there were certainly lessons to have been learned, although they seem to have been largely ignored. Writing in *The BMJ*, Gavin Yarney, Professor of Global Health and Public Policy and Rochelle Walensky, Chief of Division of Infectious Diseases observed:

"The national reopening experiment already looks to have been a disaster."

(Yamey & Walensky, 2020)

Major campus outbreaks have resulted in universities being shut down. The University of North Carolina (UNC) is an example where, from a 30,000 student population, 130 new student cases plus five staff were detected in the first week. This prompted UNC to switch to online classes. Across the country, at least 26,000 cases have been reported in 750 colleges and universities, an average of 35 cases per institution.

Yamey and Walensky identify three specific lessons that can be taken from the US experience:

1. Curbing community transmission of COVID before reopening. They cite the positive example of Taiwan in reopening its universities only after achieving virtual elimination of community transmission.
2. The value of quarantining students before arrival.
3. Transmission of the infection between asymptomatic students can be rapid. Congregate situations, especially

residential halls and shared off-campus accommodation, can create high-risk locations.

Any testing programmes should include both students and staff, and every effort should be made to shield the older and more vulnerable, particular those with underlying health conditions.

13.1 The Royal Hospital School, Ipswich, UK

The RHS is an independent co-educational boarding and day school for 11-18 year olds. It provides an outstanding, full and broad education, fit for the modern world, and enriched by a unique naval heritage. Having spent five years there myself, I can tell you it is an amazing place.

Figure 35: The RHS, Ipswich

Founded in 1712 in Greenwich, London, it moved to its spectacular site, set in 200 acres of Suffolk countryside overlooking the River Stour, in 1933. The school has continued to develop its stunning purpose-built site and has grown in size and reputation to become one of the UK's leading independent schools (RHS, 2020).

From a very early stage of the pandemic, RHS had an evolving set of risk assessments and plans. But, as in any crisis, plans need to be flexible, although they were based upon its guiding three principles of:

1. Protecting the health and well-being of pupils, staff and the wider community by minimising any risk of transmitting the virus.
2. Prioritising the learning and academic progress of pupils, regardless of whether they can be physically in school.
3. Maintaining effective communications with both the pupils and staff community.

Like every other school in the UK, RHS went into lockdown on 20 March 2020. But, unlike so many other schools, and in fact many businesses too, the following Monday, lessons seamlessly recommenced, offering its entire academic timetable, albeit online (see section 8.2 – Teaching children by remote learning). Boarders were cared for at the school until it was safe to return home.

When the school reopened as the UK lockdown was relaxed, over 720 pupils returned. With 400 boarders included in the mix, RHS has adopted the Boarding School's Association COVID Safe Charter. All pupils and staff are constantly reminded to observe social distancing guidelines.

"There is genuine recognition that to be back in class is a positive step but as both a parent and a headteacher, there is also a concern about what lies ahead. Further disruption to our children's education could be much harder a second time around. The initial novelty that was associated with a national lockdown may be replaced with a sense of frustration and helplessness for

pupils who are already concerned about the implications for their future in the workplace."

(Simon Lockyer, Headmaster, RHS, September 2020)

As it proved necessary to lock down again in January 2021, the school immediately reverted to live, online teaching.

"After the COVID-19 forced closure on Friday 20th March, with iPads the school had provided pupils, and using Microsoft Teams, 108 teachers began teaching 750 pupils, in 38 countries, 28 subjects the following Monday. By the time the school reopened, over 22,000 online lessons had been delivered."

(Independent School Parent, 2020)

"The moment the schools closed RHS were providing a full online timetable for all of their pupils. We were so impressed that our children didn't miss a single lesson and still had such regular meetings with their tutors. Our kids also loved all the fun sports challenges to help them stay fit and have some fun! Thank you RHS for supporting our children through such a tough time."

(RHS parent)

Many people around the world, especially the elderly, may well have felt isolated and lonely whenever they found themselves in lockdown. As part of a joint initiative run by the RHS Compass Programme, which teaches citizenship, and the school's alumni association, pupils were encouraged to write to around 800 of the older alumni to help combat loneliness, (Sandalls, 2020).

Some pupils went even further. Three Year 11 RHS students also wrote letters on behalf of the Rural Coffee Caravan which were delivered to those isolated, elderly, or vulnerable during the pandemic. Their efforts did not go unnoticed. They were among a number of teenagers recognised by the inaugural Suffolk Hope awards whose judges included representatives from Suffolk police, Suffolk County Council and Suffolk Hate Crime Network (Earth, 2021).

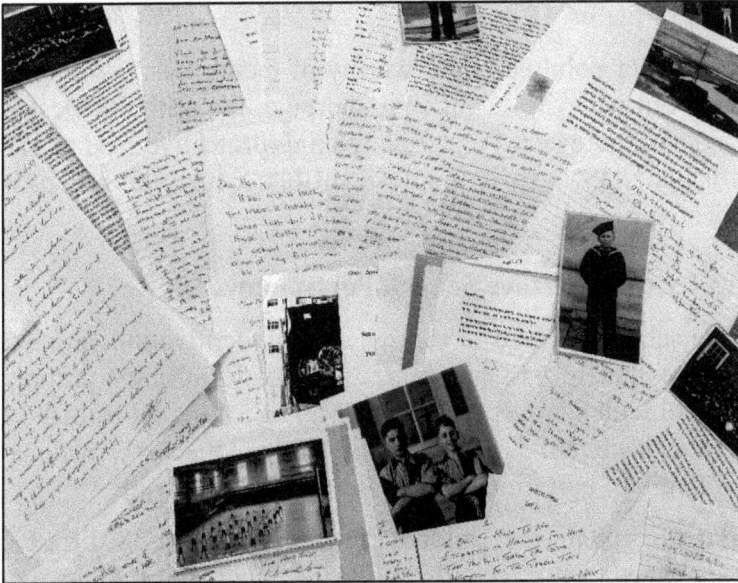

Figure 36: Just a few of the letters written by RHS pupils

Back at school, pupils have been expected to use alcohol-based hand sanitising gel whenever they are entering classrooms. Face mask wearing, plus handwashing etiquette is also rigorously enforced, especially after using the toilet plus before and after meals. Sanitising wipes are provided for pupils to clean their desks before and after every lesson.

Day pupils presenting any COVID-19 type symptoms (see section 4.1.3) should not be sent to school on that day. Pupils presenting any COVID-19 like symptoms while at school will be escorted to the health centre. Day pupils will remain at the centre while awaiting collection by their parents/guardians.

Such was the effectiveness of the measures implemented by the RHS, by the end of term, December 2020, the school had only one case (a day pupil) of COVID-19 reported among staff or pupils.

One other point certainly worthy of mention is, wanting to help out with the initial PPE shortage, the school's Design and Technology team started making protective face masks for the NHS in the county of Suffolk, where the school is located.

13.2 Cottage Grove School, Portsmouth, UK

The school is based in an area of high deprivation, and has approximately 450 pupils. It is a two-form entry primary school with a nursery attached, with ages ranging from 4-11 years. There are 85 staff, of which 28 are teachers, made up of a mix of part time and full time.

Between them, the children can speak around 38 different languages, with only 45% having English as their first language. The other main language groups include Bengali, Kurdish, Farsi, Arabic and Romanian. A number of the parents would normally be studying for doctorates or masters' degrees at the University of Portsmouth, so consequently many of the children are transient.

A large proportion of the local children come from high-rise and low-rise council owned apartments, local authority temporary lodging and Salvation Army supported housing. Occasionally, children will come from local woman's refuge centres. When a child first arrives, staff can never be sure exactly how long they will be attending the school.

Headteacher, Polly Honeychurch, who has been at the school for over 20 years, takes up the story:

"Leading up to the pandemic

In early 2020, the media was full of the images of the coronavirus outbreak in Wuhan, plus the Diamond Princess quarantined in Japan. However, we didn't feel threatened in anyway as that was on the other side of the planet. Then, before anything came through official channels, I was warned of the impending pandemic via the book club I belong to. A fellow member's husband is a consultant at Queen Alexander Hospital, Portsmouth, and he too had been watching the developments in China and Japan. The friend remarked that she had never seen her husband so scared. He simply said, "that is coming here!"

Polly Honeychurch
Headteacher

Figure 37: Cottage Grove Primary

Staying safe in school

In line with the first UK national lockdown directives, we closed the school except for vulnerable children and the children of key workers. This left us with between 40 and 50 children still attending school. Where practical, I instructed staff to work from home but there are some jobs which you can only do on site, such as teaching those children in attendance, however few, cleaning and lunchtime supervision.

What was good to see was the children adapted very quickly to the changes that we had to introduce. More often than not it was the staff that needed reminding, especially about social distancing. I found it necessary to reorganise the staff room by reducing the number of easy chairs from thirty to six and reducing chairs at the staffroom table. Disinfectant spray was left on the table for staff to clean up after they had finished.

While staff were trying to adapt to the cultural changes imposed making references to the 'new norm', for the children joining us in the reception year, to them, this was the norm. Moreover, the children often proved to be far more resilient than adults.

Morning and afternoon school arrivals and departures were staggered, and the year groups were instructed to use separate entry and exit points. However, some parents did prove problematic especially those who would not observe social distancing protocols or wear masks when delivering or collecting their children. I did have parents inform me that they were reluctant to come to the school as they felt threatened by this inconsiderate and anti-social behaviour. Moreover, while parents had previously always been welcomed into the school, we had to insist that they remained outside the parameter and, if they did need to speak to someone, they would have to make an appointment.

Children were split up into year group bubbles. Movement around the school was restricted and we introduced a one-way system. Girls' and boys' toilets were reallocated to year groups to prevent any potential for cross-over infection between the groups. A staggered arrival for lunch with each year group bubble being allocated their own tables. Instead of queuing at the kitchen hatch for their lunch, it was brought to them at their tables. When they had finished, their tables and chairs were cleaned in preparation for the next group.

Prior to the pandemic, assemblies were held daily, this is currently reduced to one assembly each week. This was an online session which children and staff could sign into whether they were in school or at home. We have been using the Google Meet platform, but I quickly learned of its limitations as I managed to crash it when over one hundred tried to logon simultaneously. We now have a Zoom account which allows up to 500 users. It has been very encouraging to see a good level of engagement from those at home.

Between the initial lockdown in March and the end of November 2020, we had just two cases of COVID-19 in school. One pupil and one staff member. However, in December 2020 alone, the case count shot up to 20, which included 10% of all staff.

A number of staff have also been 'pinged' by track and trace and they have self-isolated for the statutory ten days. But staff never knew why they had been pinged and none presented any symptoms. They were either never pinged at all or were pinged on multiple occasions, and some appeared to lose confidence in the system especially when they never presented any symptoms.

In January 2021, self-testing kits arrived at school for use by staff and these were the type sent out for use at home rather than testing centres. The only training I had received was in the form of two one-hour webinars and I then had to instruct staff how to self-test.

Communications

Lines of communications have not always been reliable or coherent. I often learned of policy changes via the media or the daily briefings from Downing Street rather than directly from the Department for Education (DfE). That said, the DfE took to issuing communications often via lengthy documents one day and then continued to regularly reissue the documents with minor changes. But they would not just indicate what had changed, making it necessary to re-read the entire document, thereby causing unnecessary information overload. This wasted valuable time, which could have been avoided.

One mixed message that caused confusion was that politicians were initially making statements that school environments were safe. Then immediately before the January 2021 lockdown came, the contradiction when we were told that schools were vectors of transmission. Which is it?

We have also been receiving confusing and often conflicting messages from the DfE regarding face masks and social distancing.

Online teaching

We have learnt so much since the initial lockdown in March regarding how to go about online learning for children. In hindsight, what the school could offer children at the outset was awful compared to what we are doing now.

13: Impact on education

During that initial lockdown, it gave the school the chance to try out some things and I gave teachers the opportunity to deliver in a way that they wanted to. By September, we had reviewed what everyone had done and how successful or not that had been.

The Key Stage 2 children, that's the 7-11 year olds, use Google Classroom. Every child has their own Google email address which they would use when they logged-in while in the classroom. At home they would go through the same process.

From September 2020, they were able to try using Google Classroom in the school, which was good practice for studying at home. Every day in Google Classroom, work is already set for them and it is easy for them to contact their teacher. It is also easy for teachers to email the whole class at a time or individuals.

Ideally, classes would engage in regular Google Meet sessions. However, the school needed to be mindful that siblings may be sharing a device so they cannot guarantee that all children in a class will be logged on simultaneously.

There are still children who do not have access to a device. Initially, the school was allocated 64 computers from the government scheme and we have since given out 90 devices to families so far. Other families are on a waiting list, although we have no devices physically in school to give them at present. The government is promising more equipment and the school is awaiting the green light to order them as we will be instructed what we can order and when. I do also appreciate that there have been supply chain issues as many businesses have been scrambling to procure laptops and tablets to support their own home workers

Key Stage 1 children, aged from 5 to 7 years, are using a platform called Seesaw. This is easier for them than Google Classroom, especially as it can be used on a phone or tablet making it a lot more accessible.

Some families do not have internet access and the school has obtained SIM cards, each preloaded with 10 Gigabytes of data. When they have used the allocation, they can go back to the school for a replacement card. Routers for families have also been ordered but they have not yet arrived.

There is a big digital divide between families and I consider these children with no home broadband or devices to be vulnerable children. These are the children that would typically be put in school during lockdowns alongside essential worker's children.

While there are still some families that will not engage with online learning, an estimated 70% are taking home schooling seriously. Occasionally, the issue has been the result of parents not knowing what to do, and we have endeavoured to plug the gap by providing tutorials for them. But, on a positive note, there are two families back in Dubai and one in Romania still accessing online lessons.

At the centre of the community

The austerity cuts experienced in the UK since the financial crisis have resulted in many local services disappearing, leaving schools as the only constant. Consequently, the only place people can go to is the school as, in many cases, that is all that is left. Therefore, parents have been turning to the school for a whole range of things such as:

- *Technical support to assist with home schooling;*
- *Emotional support;*
- *Physical support; and*

- *Food to cover school lunches.*

It seems that whatever problem the local community has, the answer will be invariably found at the school.

Communicating with some parents can be challenging when messages can be lost in translation. Explaining what isolation means has sometimes proved difficult. One parent had nine children at the school from two separate families. However, despite counselling to the contrary from the school, he would spend time with both groups. He was also known to have travelled back and forward to Bolton in the north west of the UK, an area that has been flagged for its almost uninterrupted high infection rate. He and his children were all ultimately infected by COVID-19.

A few silver linings ...

Strange as it might seem, there have actually been some benefits from how we have reacted to the pandemic. Firstly, I have noticed a big improvement in the children's behaviour, something that is always appreciated by teachers.

It had always been my intent to empower the management team to make decisions on behalf of the school, thereby delegating some responsibilities. The pandemic rather forced my hand in terms of expediting the implementation. Staff were then encouraged to take any concerns or issues to the management team who were empowered to address them accordingly. There have been occasions when staff have not got the resolution they wanted, and some have subsequently come to me to appeal the decision. However, even if I didn't happen to agree with the ruling handed down, I was not prepared to undermine the team's authority.

I have also noted the positive effect that lunchtime table services have had on the children. I have decided that after the pandemic is over, we will continue with the practice as it is a much nicer experience for them than the way it was done before.

Finally, limiting the contact between children in the school has worked really well. Despite being in the middle of a pandemic, there has been very little evidence of colds and flu.

In conclusion

Since the pandemic started, in the interest of health and safety, we have found ourselves continually having to refine the way things have been done. I have learnt not to take things at face value and never to judge a book by its cover. For example, there have been some people who I have previously underrated and yet they have stepped up and gone above and beyond. Conversely, there have been others that I thought were totally dependable that just could not cope.

It is also important to know what you can control and what you cannot, such as limiting the number of children I have in school. I had made that decision to restrict numbers even before the instruction to close in early January had been sent out by the DfE.

Finally, I recognise that my job has changed beyond all recognition over the last year. On reflection, it makes me wonder whether this much changed role is the 'new norm' for head teachers everywhere."

13.3 Hangzhou Primary Schools, China

With a population of over 10 million, the city of Hangzhou is located in the Chinese province of Zhejiang, some 110 miles (180 kms) south-west of Shanghai. The city's schools were closed for the Chinese New Year holiday on 26 January

2020, three days after the lockdown had been imposed in Wuhan, approximately 470 miles (750 kms) to the west of Hangzhou. However, like other schools across China, they did not reopen when planned on 8 February 2020, as the COVID-19 lockdown measures had been extended across the country.

While schools were still physically closed, online learning for students started on 25 February 2020 using DingTalk, an Alibaba Group product, which is described as an enterprise communication and collaboration platform.

Finally, Hangzhou schools started reopening between 13 and 19 April for staff to be trained in the new COVID-19 regulations. The students had a staggered return over the following week.

The new regulations were strictly enforced as described below:

Campus entry and exit

1. Prior arrival all students and staff must have completed the education board administered health-check survey.
2. All staff and students must be temperature checked upon arrival.
3. Social distancing – spots circa one metre apart placed on the floor for those waiting to enter.
4. Student entry staggered with the oldest students arriving first and then each grade arrives in ten-minute intervals.
5. Staggered exit with grade 1 exiting first and then every ten minutes another grade departs.
6. Health staff present at entry to help anyone with a fever or who are presenting other symptoms.

Classroom

1. No groupwork or shared desks.
2. Staff and students required to wear masks at all times (this was in place for around two weeks).
3. Each classroom has a designated entrance and exit.
4. Anyone entering a classroom must use alcohol gel to wash hands prior to each entry.
5. Initially, the use of air-conditioning was not permitted. However, after three weeks, as the temperature rose, the school had the system disinfected and its use was again allowed.
6. All student and staff are temperature checked twice a day and the results recorded and provided to the school administration and education board.

Dining

1. All students eat in their own classrooms and bring their own sterilised dishes and utensils.
2. For subject teachers who are not homeroom teachers, the dining hall is open, but they can only eat in socially distanced and dedicated spots.

General

1. All classrooms and offices are provided with alcohol gel.
2. All staff and students are required to wear masks.
3. Staff are allocated with one mask every day.
4. Interclass events are prohibited during April, May and June.
5. No contact PE classes or team sports are allowed.

6. Classes receive designated slots for outside play (implemented after mid-May) so each class can use a designated outside space once every two days. (Each block has eight classes and two designated spaces.)

In case of staff or students presenting symptoms

1. If a member of staff or a student has a high temperature and/or other symptoms, they are assessed on site (for the purpose of deciding how strictly to apply classroom quarantine measures) before being sent to hospital.
2. Any classroom in which they have taught in is quarantined until the results of COVID-19 testing are known.
3. In the case of fever, the person in question cannot return to the school until they have been fever free for 48 hours (provided they tested clear of the virus). This regulation was in effect until around the start of June.

13.4 English Language Schools face a bleak future

While countries around the world struggle to keep their education systems running or to restart them as quickly as possible, destinations that specialise in offering English as a Foreign Language are facing lean times.

It is estimated that in 2019 in the Republic of Malta (pop: 493,559), around 14% of the country's GDP came from tourism. Students who travelled to Malta for English Language tuition accounted for just over half of the tourism figures. But, during July 2020, only 1,800 of the expected 18,000 weekly student intake actually travelled to Malta. Consequently, the 1,400 English language teachers were feeling very exposed. Deloitte estimates that even with a best case government rescue package, at least half would still lose their jobs (Arena, 2020).

13.5 Home schooling

With schools closing around the world, many countries are promoting 'home schooling'. There are those schools that can offer their students online support, as in the example of the Hangzhou World Foreign Language school (see section 13.3).

I do feel it must be challenging for many parents expected to take on the role of 'teacher', particularly if they are WFH themselves and they have their own work objectives to meet. When all is said and done, to become a teacher you usually need to undertake several years of training – something that most parents will not have done. It is also possible that children may know more about some academic subjects than their parents.

Even though my sons' schooling days are well behind me, I have tried to put myself in the position of a parent expected to home school their own children. I have a master's degree, I occasionally lecture in universities and I run commercial training courses. Yet, when I look at the school curriculum across the various age groups, I believe that in most subjects I would have most definitely struggled.

Home schooling can also rely upon technical resources, such as laptops or tablets, and for some families this can be an expense too far, especially if there are several children at home all competing for the same resources. Maybe even the same resources that parents need for home working.

While some schools have been able to provide 'online' lessons for their students, in the UK, the BBC had previously set up what they called BBC Bitesize, which certainly proved its worth during the pandemic. This provides daily education options for children from three years old up to the post-16-year-old age group. It also provides tips for parents in supporting their children's home-based learning.

German national Andrea Springmann lives in Hong Kong with her husband and two children. Like many parents, she has endeavoured to home school her children which includes Chinese language lessons. As she reported on her Facebook page, her children are now more proficient at Mandarin than she is.

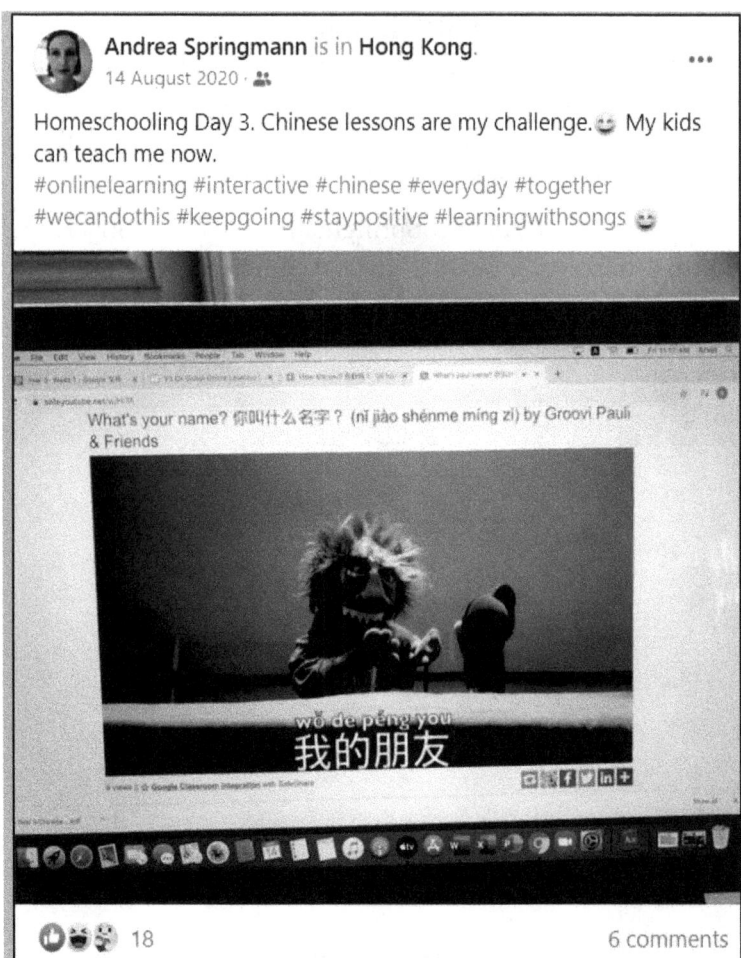

Figure 38: Online Lessons

As for online lessons, these can be pre-recorded lessons or live, interactive sessions. One English as a Foreign Language teacher I know was expected to go down the pre-recorded route, while another had to be available for live tuition. Both had returned to the UK when the pandemic started, and while it may have seemed convenient to be able run online English lessons from the comfort of your own home, time zone differences meant that one teacher, had to start work at 2.00 am.

13.6 Traditional university

Students completing their university studies in the 2019-2020 academic year would not have anticipated the disruption that was about to be caused by the pandemic in their final few weeks. Along with schools, universities were closed as countries went into lockdown. In the UK, this happened just two to three weeks before the Easter holiday break.

Universities, along with other institutions in the UK, are finding it financially very difficult during the COVID-19 crisis. Approximately 2.38 million students attended in the academic year 2018-2019. The Institute of Fiscal Studies [IFS] states:

"The total size of the university sector's losses is highly uncertain: we estimate that long-run losses could come in anywhere between £3 billion and £19 billion, or between 7.5% and nearly half of the sector's overall income in one year."

(Drayton & Waltmann, 2020)

The IFS also estimates that *"The biggest losses will likely stem from falls in international student enrolments (between £1.4 billion and £4.3 billion, with a central estimate of £2.8 billion"*. So, around 33% of expected income would normally come from 25% of students. This is seriously significant for universities and higher education institutes.

In a recent London Economics report it identified that:

13: Impact on education

Combining the impact of the economic downturn with the expected deferral rate due to the uncertainty caused by the pandemic, compared to 2018-219 first year enrolments, approximately 232,000 students will no longer enrol in higher education in 2020-221. Equivalent to a 24% decline compared to the baseline (2018-219) cohort, this will result in heavy economic fallout. With so many of the current universities being financially vulnerable, the threat of bankruptcy for some draws nearer unless support funding from other sources materialises. (Halterbeck, et al., 2020, p 15).

The UK government has since indicated funding is available on application. Education Secretary, Gavin Williamson, sought to reassure the sector when he announced:

"We understand the challenges universities are facing, which is why we have already provided a range of support to ease financial pressures."

(Department for Education, 2020)

The government has indicated that as a condition for taking part in the scheme, universities will be required to make changes that meet wider government objectives, depending on the individual provider's circumstances. Among these are delivery of high-quality courses with strong graduate outcomes, which is already a prerogative. However, they do not wish the focus on resources at the front line to be at the expense of reduced administrative costs. The three main objectives that the government restructuring initiative requires are:

1. Protect the welfare of current students.
2. Supporting the role higher education providers play in regional and local economies through the provision of

high-quality courses aligned with economic and societal need.

3. Preserving the sector's internationally outstanding science base (noting specific support is being made available for research activities).

Consideration will also be given to the 'impact groups' of students, teaching provision, local economy and communities, along with research knowledge and exchange. These requirements have been identified and contained within the document for prospective funding application.

The *New Statesmen* (2020) outlines that universities have already responded to a freeze on hiring new staff, cuts on temporary teaching posts and graduate student teaching jobs, along with restructuring and redundancies being part of the required objectives. They also state that thousands of jobs are already at risk. Worrying announcements have already been made at prestigious universities, including Oxford, Liverpool, York, Birmingham, Manchester, Nottingham, Glasgow, King's College London and Durham, among others.

The unions have already pressurised for redundancies to be limited, with threats of strikes if the voluntary route is not followed first. This academic year has been a difficult one for staff, with issues of pay and pensions coming before the pandemic requirements were established. The next few years will be lean ones especially until a vaccine for COVID-19 is widely available to ensure that overseas students return in the numbers managed previously. Education has been completely turned around, and the future at this moment, until other areas of the economy are resolved, is looking very challenging.

Have universities become a concentration of risk?

Early September 2020, the University of South Carolina reported more than 1,000 of its 35,000 students had tested positive for COVID-19. Students have been urged to remain vigilant regarding social distancing, hand hygiene and mask wearing, while avoiding unnecessary social activities. Similar conditions have been reported by other universities.

13.7 Commercial training

I have been running a variety of training courses for over 20 years, primarily for commercial clients, and occasionally as a visiting university lecturer. During that time, while I have delivered programme management and project management, my preference is most definitely for business continuity, ICT disaster recovery and crisis management. It will probably come as no surprise to you that, more recently, I have added pandemic preparedness training to my repertoire. What is more, I can often dip into my various publications and pull out a relevant case study or two.

But, I do like working in a classroom with the students. To see the whites of their eyes, read their body language, and try and keep them awake during the 'graveyard shift', which tends to come immediately after lunch. And all this time I am pacing up and down the room while endeavouring to find appropriate words of wisdom to shower on the students. Judging by the positive consistency of the feedback I have received, the students largely appreciate my style of delivery.

Then came the pandemic. No one was travelling and classroom-based courses just stopped overnight. Even private in-house training courses for specific clients ceased, especially when countries started to close their borders. In fact, training had slipped way down the list of most companies' priorities in the face of the pandemic. The global education business TES issued a stark warning in April 2020 that "Without support, training providers won't survive" (Parker, K. 2020).

Thank heavens for the variety of online platforms that are now available for conferences and training. Having now worked with several, my own preference is Zoom. I also have to admit that online training does have its benefits. Yes, I have hooked up simultaneously with students in different parts of the world. No, I haven't had to travel to deliver courses, which for some clients can add an extra day at each end of the course. Moreover, due to different time zones, I have been able to deliver two courses alongside each other in the same week – one in the Middle East followed by one in the US. Make no mistake, it's hard work, but it can be done.

But there are downsides to the online approach. Although the feedback I have received has been just as positive as with the classroom delivery, I can't always see the students, especially if they have their videos turned off. I am not always sure if they are even there, unless I ask questions or invite them to go to a syndicate room for an exercise. I guess for those individuals who would prefer to sit in the backrow of a classroom in the interest of remaining inconspicuous, being able to decide whether the course facilitator can see them or not must be very appealing. Moreover, we must not forget the real danger of 'Zoom overload', or the equivalent for other online platforms, which I guess is a variation of 'death by PowerPoint'.

While I have mastered how to mute and unmute the students' microphones, I am yet to discover how to turn on their videos. Perhaps that would be considered too invasive.

But let's be pragmatic about online training. If students and the course facilitator can all work effectively together in an online environment, just the cost savings alone for travel, hotel and the training venue could spell the beginning of the end of classroom training. When you add travel time to and from the training venue, the case for discontinuing classroom training gets ever stronger. I am sure this will not be lost on the army of accountants out there who will invariably be charged with minimising post COVID-19 business expenditure.

Coronavirus has been called a harbinger of change. So, among other things, perhaps that may mean the days of formal classroom training are numbered – RIP.

But then in December 2021, I experienced what was a 'first' for me. I travelled to Dubai where I delivered two courses on behalf of Meirc Plus – ICT Disaster Recovery and Crisis Management. The big difference was that I had attendees both in the classroom (wearing masks and adequately socially distanced) plus, online attendees simultaneously connecting using Zoom. Is this the future for commercial training?

13.8 The lost school productions

Author's note

I can remember missing my youngest son's school Christmas nativity play when he was about five years old. I was abroad on business at the time, but when I next spoke to him on the phone he said "Daddy, you missed my play". The disappointment he conveyed because I had not been there was not lost on me. If nothing else, it made me feel very guilty as, despite his young age, that school play was really important to him, particularly as he was hoping both his parents would be there to support him. And so it is for children everywhere.

With that sentiment in mind, I was unsure whether to place this section within the 'Impact on education' chapter or 'Performing arts'. However, by placing it here, I believe I have got as close as I can to straddling the two.

Westbourne House School is a co-educational day and boarding preparatory school located near Chichester in the UK. It caters for children ranging from age 2½-13 years old, and the pupils are split into year groups according to age. Margo Dodd (see section 14.5.4) is a freelance production manager, a role that includes wardrobe and prop design/management, set design, stage management, plus make-up and hair design. She has been involved in most of the school's theatrical productions for the 7-13 year olds over a 12-year period.

Years 3, 4, 7 and 8 had been rehearsing all term for their respective school productions. They were scheduled to be performed in front of their parents and grandparents, four before and two after the 2020 Easter holidays. As we now know, these plans were unwittingly on a collision course with the proliferation of the coronavirus pandemic.

Year	Ages	Year	Ages
3	7-8	4	8-9
7	11-12	8	12-13

The six productions were split among the year groups with years 3 and 4 performing two each and years 7 and 8 just one a piece.

Year	Planned productions
3	*Jack and the Beanstalk* and *Adventures of a Pirate Boarding School*
4	William Shakespeare's *The Tempest* and *A Midsummer Night's Dream (junior adaptation)*
7	*A Fawlty Towers Dining Experience*
8	*Oliver*

Except for Fawlty Towers and Oliver, which the school intended to stage in May and July respectively, all the performances were scheduled for the week commencing 16 March. However, with the country already plummeting towards lockdown and public gatherings being discouraged, the school opted to film the four performances using an iPhone, without audiences present. Copies of the recording were later sent to parents in MP4 format.

The year 3 performances were brought forward by two days, which placed extra pressure on the production manager. However, with the writing on the wall, both pupils and staff were starting to disappear and isolate, resulting in *Jack and the Beanstalk* being cancelled, at very short notice, at 8.25 am on the morning of the performance. Its remaining cast, still at school, joined the also depleted ranks of *The Adventures of a Pirate Boarding School,* which, along with the two Shakespeare plays, was one of the only three to go ahead that week. By the end of that week, the UK's lockdown became official and, with the school now closed, all the staff and pupils had left. This excluded the offspring of key workers who were permitted to remain, along with the staff and their families who live on site.

The impact of cancellation on the children

There was extreme disappointment throughout the school, especially for the year 8 pupils who were leaving the school as the 2019-2020 academic year concluded. Quite apart from their all-important common entrance exams, these children, although resilient in many ways, like all children, will have suffered badly from the missed ambition, excitement and treats of their final term at the school. The grand finale should have been their year group's annual staged musical, *Oliver*, and the much awaited prize giving at the end of it. This, and the absence of their final preparations before moving on to their senior schools, will have left a large hole in their young lives. The conclusion was that they were only given one day to return to school, collect their belongings and say farewell to all their teachers and friends before the official end of term in July. Loss of confidence, motivation and self-esteem was already in evidence, according to the school's director of music. He had been trying to put on a 'virtual' concert of songs from the cancelled musical, but had struggled to get some of the children to co-operate with that alternative project. Generally, a fear of an unseen enemy and the uncertain future, together with instructions to distance from each other, not to share their belongings and to cover their noses and mouths in certain places were bound to have an adverse psychological effect, very possibly triggering an increase in anxiety and other mental health issues. Only time will tell.

Impact on backstage staff

The decision to bring forward the production date of any performance will invariably not be without its impact on the all-important backstage activity, overseen by the production manager. Margo Dodd's business supplied many of the costumes and props for the performances.

For the year 3 productions, the two days lost meant seriously condensing the time originally planned for the final costume preparations, which literally needed round-the-clock dedication to make up that lost time. But then with *Jack and the Beanstalk* cancelled at the eleventh hour, much of the overnight effort was wasted and was replaced with a desperate a reshuffle of pirate costumes for a hastily reworked version of *The Adventures of a Pirate Boarding School*.

As costumier for the productions, Margo Dodd suffered a large financial loss, because of the 'no-show, no-fee' arrangement, particularly for the year 7 and 8 productions in the summer term, which were of course cancelled. A considerable number of costumes, shoes, props and furniture had been supplied (or were planned to be) from her own collection. This would have generated a handsome hire fee, along with costumes from two other organisations and a large quantity of props, furniture and set from the local theatre, and portable staging from another amateur group. This was lost revenue for them as well. Furthermore, other fees that were lost included the second instalment of her show fee for *Fawlty Towers* and full show fee for *Oliver*.

We find ourselves in an era where youngsters' education has been seriously disrupted. After all the effort put into rehearsing, to also be deprived of the opportunity to see their respective school productions through to a natural conclusion, must be bitterly heart-breaking.

The impact of the pandemic on the performing arts is covered in more detail in the next chapter, especially for the amateur scene.

CHAPTER 14: PERFORMING ARTS

Like our penchant for enjoying the various types of hospitality venues available, during happier and safer times many of us would also opt to visit cinemas, theatres and various live events that have been on offer. But all that has changed.

In many countries, theatres and cinemas have been forced to close their doors because of local lockdown regulations, while live events have been cancelled. Major festivals and prestigious sporting events around the world have been postponed or abandoned altogether, putting tremendous pressure on the live events industry. Behind the scenes there is a massive workforce putting in a huge amount of effort before a performer can walk out on stage and 'strut their stuff'. Sadly, many performers and supporting backstage staff have also found themselves out of work and devoid of income following lockdowns.

Notwithstanding the vital contribution the live events industry plays in society, in this chapter, I have decided to focus on the world of theatre rather than the broader concept of the performing arts. Perhaps in recent times one of the biggest shocks and disappointments was the closing of the long running and amazingly successful production of The Phantom of the Opera in both London's West End and on Broadway. Consequently, it was encouraging to learn Andrew Lloyd Webber had reopened the London Palladium on 23 July 2020 for a test pilot event to see how audiences and workers could be safely welcomed back to the theatre. The performance was led by the recording artist and musical theatre actress, Beverley Knight. She performed in front of a socially distanced audience of 640 suitably masked people, taking up around 25% of the Palladium's capacity. There have been similar exercises undertaken by other theatres. In Salford, UK, the Lowry Theatre is being used as a temporary court by the justice system to hear non-custodial crime cases plus civil and family tribunal work. While this is by no means a complete financial substitute for the loss of theatre audiences, it is helping to cover the Lowry's costs.

In November 2020, internationally renowned comedian Omid Djalili was performing in front of a socially distanced audience who were all wearing visors. He later remarked that he wasn't sure if he was at a comedy gig or was expected to address a conference of welders.

Even so, being starved of their income during lockdowns, many venues are threatened with permanent closure – some have already closed for good. Moreover, unlike the London Palladium, countless venues are just totally unsuitable for applying an appropriate standard of social distancing while still covering their costs. In the UK, the government has made provision to help the sector but, with no end in sight to the pandemic, whether that is enough remains to be seen.

Some of these threatened venues support both the professional and amateur performing arts. Any closures could also present a threat to local thespian and musical groups that also provide a source of generally less expensive, but often quality entertainment. Amateur groups may depend upon these venues as places both for rehearsal and performances, although they are unlikely to financially benefit from any government economic stimulus initiatives.

14: Performing arts

14.1 Why singers might be COVID-19 super-spreaders

The *Los Angeles Times* reported that 60 singers of the Skagit Valley Chorale turned up during March for a socially distanced rehearsal in Mount Vernon, Washington. Within three weeks, 45 had tested positive for COVID-19, three had been hospitalised and two had died. Writing in *Elemental*[+], Sara Austin claims that:

> *"The louder you are, the more particles you emit and the greater risk you would infect the people near you."*

(Austin, 2020)

The CDC was involved in a follow-up investigation. The findings included the statement:

> *"This outbreak of COVID-19 with a high secondary attack rate indicates that SARS-CoV-2 might be highly transmissible in certain settings, including group singing events. This underscores the importance of physical distancing, including maintaining at least 6 feet between persons, avoiding group gatherings and crowded places, and wearing cloth face coverings in public settings where other social distancing measures are difficult to maintain during this pandemic."*

(Hamner, et al., 2020)

A chilling thought for all performers and audiences alike, although additional research is still ongoing. Initial findings have suggested that anyone singing quietly would create no more of a threat than if they were just talking to someone. But this could be good news as well as bad, as there is an abundance of music that has been written with quiet singing in mind. Conversely, there is also a plethora that has not, and one piece that immediately comes to mind that I have often sung is 'The Peers Chorus' from Gilbert and Sullivan's operetta 'Iolanthe'. A chorus with the opening words of "Loudly let the trumpets bray" can hardly be sung 'pianissimo'.

14.2 Online productions

Although this offers little consolation to theatre venues, some performers, both professional and amateur, have been able to make the transition to online performances. In the UK, the BBC has been broadcasting a socially distanced production entitled *Staged*. It stars Michael Sheen and David Tennant, with a cameo appearance from Dame Judi Dench. Sheen and Tennant play fictitious versions of themselves whose West End play has been put on hold because of the pandemic, but their director has persuaded them to continue rehearsing online.

I have come across a number of very slick, online musical productions that I have thoroughly enjoyed. To begin with, I would certainly like to applaud the *One Voice Children's Choir* from Salt Lake City, Utah. Their cover version of Memories (Maroon 5) is sublime.

I also discovered the Phoenix Chamber Choir from Vancouver, and their magical COVID-19 public announcement messages. In what was termed a "social distance sing project", to the tune of Queen's Bohemian Rhapsody, they sang '*Wash Your Hands*' and to Billy Joel's Longest Time they sang '*The Longest Time – Quarantine Edition*'.

I was also delighted to discover that my old school, the Royal Hospital School, Holbrook had recorded its own online 'Lockdown Sanctus' based on the Sanctus from Joseph Haydn's Missa brevis.

But things have moved on, and although traditional venues have been struggling to operate as the waves of the pandemic ebb and flow, fee-charging virtual performances have been gathering momentum. I was delighted to discover that tickets for one of my own favourites, Andrea Bocelli, were available via one of the global event promoting platforms. Tickets can also be obtained for virtual performances for a multitude of other genre, including the traditional British pantomime, radio plays and concerts featuring a variety of artists. It all helps to generate some income while the more conventional route to market for the performing arts remains hampered by the pandemic.

Not being able to go to the theatre during lockdown was something that I greatly missed. However, in August 2021, I got to join mask wearing audiences when I saw live performances of South Pacific at the Chichester Festival Theatre, and a few days later, Hairspray at the Liverpool Empire. I can tell you that the feel good factor was immense, and I am sure it was shared by audience and performers alike. Before 2021 ended, I also got to see an excellent 'Rat Pack' tribute act and marvellous classical concert with an excellent soprano and tenor accompanied by over sixty musicians.

But as the pandemic ebbs and flows, restrictions on live performances of just about every kind, including their audiences, will inevitably fluctuate. In fact, the London Theatre reported that various performances of over thirty West End shows had been cancelled during December 2021 due to COVID-19 (London Theatre, 2021).

14.3 Personalised videos on the rise

In recent times, we have seen a 300% rise in celebrities creating personalised videos for their fans using Apps such as memmo and Cameo. Although some charge modest fees, others can command thousands of dollars at a time for the service. The average length of video would typically be under two minutes.

The process works by fans sending a script to the celebrity who films it on their mobile and returns it to the fan. People use the service for any one of a number of reasons, such as birthday surprises, get well soon messages, recognising an achievement or perhaps just to cheer someone up.

14.4 Impromptu Opera

It was while I was exploring some online productions that I came across Impromptu Opera. Some 25 years ago I was attending a residential opera workshop, when I met a very competent young professional pianist called Martyn Parkes. During the course of the week we studied two works, Gilbert and Sullivan's *The Mikado* and Johann Strauss' *The Gypsy Baron,* under the baton of the late John Brophy and accompanied by the extremely proficient, Martyn.

Earlier this year, our paths crossed again when I stumbled across @impromptuopera, which Martyn runs with his wife, the Icelandic opera singer, Hrafnhildur Björnsdóttir. Posted on Impromptu Opera's Facebook page, he was accompanying her while she sang 'We Can't Meet Again' – a COVID-19 #StayatHome number based upon 'We'll meet again', the song immortalised by the late Dame Vera Lynn. This was one of several pandemic information flavoured songs that the duo have recorded. Their pandemic information flavoured repertoire includes 'O Sole Corona', which uses Giovanni Capurro's classic 'O Sole Mio' and 'Just Stay In', an adaptation of the classic song from the Les Miserables 'Bring Him Home'.

Before the pandemic, Impromptu Opera had a busy schedule, which included regular appearances at a number of restaurants in the Carluccio chain. They were also invited to perform at restaurant founder, Antonio Carluccio's 80th birthday celebration.

Figure 39: Impromptu Opera perform for Carluccio's 80th birthday

When they are not closed because of a total lockdown, restaurants in the UK are having to observe social distancing. Along with unresolved concerns relating to the potential risks of spreading COVID-19 by singing, Impromptu Opera, like so many other performers, must bide their time. Moreover, with the Carluccio Italian restaurant chain being forced into administration as the pandemic exacerbated its financial difficulties, only 30 of its 90-strong list of restaurants are expected to survive.

14.5 The am-dram scene

The amateur dramatic theatre and musical societies cannot compete with the glitz and big name performers that you expect from a multi-million pound production on Broadway or London's West End. But, they not only provide entertainment for their localities, but they can also be an amazingly therapeutic source of enjoyment for their members. As a teacher friend once told me, *"after a tough day at school, group singing can really help you unwind and be far more relaxing than going home and just kicking the cat"* (incidentally, she didn't actually have a cat). The downside for amateur groups is that within the UK, at least, they do not qualify for any government funding.

Having been a serious amateur thespian myself who has also sung in many light opera productions over the years, I wanted to understand how the pandemic was affecting the world of amateur drama and musical productions.

The last show I performed in was with CAOS Musical Productions, a society that celebrated its 100th anniversary in 2011. It was over ten years ago now when I played the title role in Johann Strauss' operetta *Die Fledermaus*. It was performed in the Minerva Theatre, Chichester, and I seem to recall the cost of putting on this production was in excess of £30,000 (circa $40,000). Pictured below in that 2008 performance of '*Die Fledermaus*' as Rosalinda and Gabriel Eisenstein are Amanda Crehan and David Russell.

Figure 40: CAOS Musical Productions – Die Fledermaus, 2008

The major expenses for a production of this nature would typically include theatre hire, music royalties, costumes and possibly an orchestra. We had an eight-piece mix of percussion, strings and woodwind musicians. So, with social distancing in mind, calculating realistic prices for tickets that are not going to frighten away your audience but still cover your costs is a tough one. It may even be unachievable, meaning some productions could go ahead but only at a loss.

I approached members of Facebook's Gilbert and Sullivan group to see how they were faring. I had various responses from the UK and one from Puerto Rico.

14.5.1 *Princess Ida is kept waiting*

When the lockdown intervened, one North of England amateur operatic society was just a few days away from the dress rehearsal of its production of Gilbert and Sullivan's

Princess Ida. This society uses its local community centre. The scenery was painted, props waiting in the wings, costumes completed, tickets sold and having rehearsed twice weekly over a six-month period, the cast were good to go.

By relying on piano accompaniment for the rehearsals and the show, with no royalties to pay as *Princess Ida* is out of copyright, and the costumes being made by society members, the total cost was kept to well under £1,000.

With the world still trying to understand the full implications of the pandemic, the society had hoped to reschedule *Princess Ida* for later in the year. But, social distancing constraints could still apply not only to the audience but also to the cast, which could demand a total choreography rethink. Moreover, while the cast had committed to be available for the original show dates, some may have other commitments that clash with any re-arranged alternatives. In fact, at least two members of the original *Princess Ida* cast are expected to be missing from any future rearranged programme. Moreover, some older members may have got used to not going to rehearsals, and could see this as a suitable time to 'retire'.

This is a concern very much shared with other societies whether, after a lengthy absence from the commitment of regular rehearsals, all the members will be willing to come back. Some may have found other interests in between times.

14.5.2 *Carousel grinds to a halt*

Still in the UK, Fiona Aucott is a member of Bournemouth Gilbert and Sullivan Productions (GaSP). She is also the first cousin three times removed of Richard D'Oyly Carte, the great nineteenth-century theatrical impresario. Richard built the state-of-the-art Savoy Theatre in London to host the

Gilbert and Sullivan operettas or the Savoy Operas as they became known.

GaSP had planned to put on three music hall performances in May 2020, which ultimately had to be cancelled. Although the costs involved were fairly minimal, the society's outlay for printing, publicity, rehearsal rooms and pianists was fortunately covered by insurance. It was also in May that the auditions for their big October production of *Carousel* were scheduled. These were postponed until June, and then till July, but were ultimately cancelled when it became clear the production could not go ahead.

Based upon my own experience of *Die Fledermaus* and allowing for inflation, a show of this nature would cost the best part of £40,000 to put on, a major outlay for just about any amateur thespian society. Theatre cost alone can be in the order of 25% of that figure, while the licence fee for performing a show such as *Carousel* would be as much as 16% of the box office takings. This is a massive financial commitment for any amateur society.

GaSP has decided to postpone *Carousel* for two years. In the meantime, they have opted to put on *The Pirates of Penzance* in October 2021, for which they will have no royalties to pay as, like *Princess Ida*, the show is also out of copyright.

Many Gilbert and Sullivan patrons are elderly and may continue to be reluctant to venture out all the time the COVID-19 threat exists. Societies must also remain mindful that social distancing measures and its impact on audience numbers may also need to be factored into their production business cases.

In addition to GaSP, Fiona is a member of the Bournemouth Symphony Chorus, whose activities have also been curtailed by the pandemic. However, they have not been idle and, under the baton of conductor Gavin Carr, have recorded and posted on YouTube a superb virtual version of Thomas Tallis' 'If Ye Love Me' with more than 70 performers taking part. It is testament to its quality that it has since been featured by Martin Handley, the host of *Breakfast on BBC Radio 3* – the BBC's classical music channel. In addition to the extremely high standard of the singing, what I also liked was if at any point not everyone was singing, it seemed as if a spotlight came on over each singer who was. Nice touch.

14.5.3 The first virtual 'The Mikado'?

David Claypoole is based in Puerto Rico and is the founder and artistic director of the Virtual Light Opera Company (ViLOC). He formed the company more or less a day or so after Puerto Rico was locked down.

ViLOC's first production was an ambitious virtual creation called '*The Staykado*' (based on '*The Mikado*') complete with libretto. Described as a virtual performance of Gilbert & Sullivan's timeless classic with an international cast!

It was posted on Facebook/YouTube in mid-May, with the intention of reaching out to all those Gilbert & Sullivan fans out there in the land of 'Lockdown'. Within a few days of being uploaded onto YouTube, it had already had well over 2,000 views.

Having selected his principals from US-based performers he had worked with before, he opened the project up to anyone else who might be interested in joining using the Gilbert and Sullivan Facebook page. On the first day, he had 200 interested parties contact him. However, when they discovered that it wasn't just a sing-along but a serious project, some lost interest and jumped ship. The final chorus was made up of performers from Canada, the US, New Zealand and Israel.

This COVID-19 Productions, as it was styled, was performed under the baton of Musical Director, John Centenaro. He entered the proceedings wearing a railway conductor's hat, something that most definitely appealed to my sense of humour.

I talked earlier about some of the online song recordings that I have come across, but most lasted no more than a few minutes. *'The Staykado'* runs for over two hours and 20 minutes, which by comparison is so much more complex and challenging than a virtual group recording just a single piece of music.

Figure 41: Musical Director

Figure 42: Virtual Light Opera Company's 'The Staykado'

Corresponding with the Zoom images above, '*The Staykado*' principal performers were:

Sam Shaw Pooh Bah	David Claypoole Ko Ko	Eileen Mager Katisha
Jessica Walch Yum Yum	Heath Weisberg Phish Tush	Illyanna Weisberg Peep Bo
Peter O'Malley *Staykado*	Alexa Ortiz Pitti Sing	Christopher Cantu Nanki Pooh

David Claypoole also looks upon this as a learning exercise in putting together such a full-blown Gilbert and Sullivan production in this fashion. He also told me that:

"We've had lots of fun, produced an artistic product we are proud of while providing an outlet for many people who were feeling lonely and isolated. We learned a lot doing The Mikado. The production of Trial by Jury,

VILOC's next production, is going to be much more polished and musically perfect."

What was also commendable about this production was the inclusion in the chorus of 24-year-old Chicago-based Julia Willems who has the genetic disorder Williams Syndrome. Sometimes referred to as the 'musical syndrome', like many others who suffer with this condition, she is drawn to music and Gilbert and Sullivan operettas are her favourite. Julia has long dreamed of performing in a Gilbert and Sullivan operetta, but given her condition, this has not been possible – until now! Her dream came true when she performed in *The Staykado* production along with 40 plus performers from around the world. Her performance has since been viewed by thousands.

The principal parts for VILOC's follow-up production of *Trial by Jury* were filled by performers from Scotland, England, Canada, India and the US. The finished performance has now been uploaded to YouTube and listed as: *'ViLoc's Trial by Jury.'*

14.5.4 Performing arts portfolio

Based in West Sussex, in the UK, Margo Dodd has developed something of a portfolio of business interests in the world of music, dance and theatre. This section considers the impact that the pandemic has had on each of those activities.

Figure 43: Prison governor 'Franke' meets Ida in Die Fledermaus

Pictured above is Margo Dodd with the late John Warner in the aforementioned 2008 production of *Die Fledermaus*.

Margo showed a penchant for dancing when she was barely walking, and later attended a North London dance school. Despite also singing from an early age, voice training only commenced in her late teens. Margo went on to join several amateur musical societies in Hampshire and West Sussex, which helped her to gain a wide experience in musicals, operetta and plays. She has taken leading roles, cameo roles, understudies, chorus and danced in a variety of shows from *The Pirates of Penzance* and *Titanic The Musical* to *Die Fledermaus* and *See How They Run*.

14.5.4.1 Music agency

Margo launched a music agency in 1992 to meet a growing demand for soloists, choirs, ensembles and solo instrumentalists at events, mainly key celebrations in church (weddings and funerals in particular) locally and further afield.

As mentioned in section 14.2, many commendable virtual productions have been created through the wonders of modern technology. But, nothing compares to the thrill and quality of live performances, both for the performers and audiences alike. The only obvious upside of lockdown is that it has given most musicians extra time to study their art and expand their repertoire. Margo describes how:

"With cancellations of, or the limitation of attendees at weddings and funerals plus the restrictions on singing, all business and enquiries through my music agency has disappeared over night."

She believes that there really is no suitable replacement for live performance. Even so, opportunities in this aspect of Margo's portfolio are currently at rock bottom.

14.5.4.2 Choreographer

For Margo, of all the disciplines in the performing arts, dance is her main passion. Ballet initially, then tap, modern, salsa, tango and flamenco. She started in choreography, firstly with her own children dancing together, moving on to groups of 20 or so children in school competitions, and then for all preparatory school children aged 7-13 in school productions. The various school shows choreographed required a mix of different styles and genres of dance. These included *Fiddler on the Roof, Singing in the Rain, Bugsy Malone, Little Shop of Horrors, The Sound of Music* and *Beauty & The Beast.*

She also choreographed adult amateurs from concert pieces and incidental dancing in productions including William Shakespeare's *Much Ado about Nothing* to all musical numbers and both overtures in *The Pirates of Penzance.*

14: Performing arts

The pandemic has meant that dancers all over the world, professional and amateur, are struggling to keep up their fitness, exercising in their homes, gardens and balconies. Venue lockdowns have impacted their rehearsal space and restrictions placed on personal contact represent a disaster for most dancers. However, she says *"there is a limited opportunity for distanced movement and dance or, as my Argentinian tango tutor is suggesting, with a hula hoop between couples!"* Again, the wonders of technology have made it possible for dance teachers to continue their work by offering classes via online platforms, such as Zoom. But, many people lack the space at home to take part effectively, and it is certainly no substitute for physical classes and training. Restrictions place many obstacles in the way, not to mention the closure of rehearsal studios, halls and theatres.

As for choreography, there is no impact on an individual's scope and ability to design the dancing and movement. But, the design itself is invariably limited by social distancing restrictions, and so is the execution of those designs, especially dances that involve couples. It would be impossible, for example, to teach the Bottle Dance in *Fiddler on the Roof* or the Ländler in *The Sound of Music* without being able to touch the dancers, not to mention the dancers being unable to touch each other! Contact and physical interaction between dancers can be critical for the effective emotional expression of the art.

Much of Margo's work has involved working with up to 50 children in a hall at one time. Although it is technically possible to work with smaller groups to comply with social distancing restrictions, it is not financially viable or necessarily logistically feasible.

14.5.4.3 Costumier

Margo has had a lifelong interest in clothing and fashion. She had a tendency in early adult life to collect and hoard garments and objects from bygone eras, initially inspired by the wardrobes of deceased grandparents, great aunts and parents-in-law! The ever-expanding collection was eventually kept in empty rooms at her widowed father-in-law's apartment and her husband's home office space.

The early collection expanded as it was complemented by 'donations' from retiring wardrobe mistresses, and eventually the amassed costumes outgrew the original storage arrangements. A purpose-built construction replaced an old garage in the garden, and in 2016 the collection was consolidated and rehoused in new premises.

The pandemic has resulted in the costume hires for three shows and two small private hirers being cancelled. For businesses such as Margo's, the future is precarious, and they are entirely dependent on the entertainment industry being allowed to get back on its feet. No performance means no fee, even if costumes have been on loan for approval, fitting and alteration.

On the positive side, she has no business accommodation overheads. Moreover, her stock may well benefit from the unfortunate sad closure of some struggling local amateur drama societies. She has already received enquiries from a few requiring new homes for their costume and props.

CHAPTER 15: THE PSYCHOLOGICAL IMPACT

When I wrote the prequel to this book, apart from acknowledging the 'fear factor', which can be an intrinsic part of being caught up in a pandemic, I have to confess that I didn't give much thought to the wider psychological issues. I hope by including this chapter, I will have gone someway in redressing the balance.

I was recently listening to what was termed a 'Healthcare Special' series of webinars organised by the British Computer Society. The coronavirus pandemic has necessitated some rapid changes in the UK's National Health Service and information technology has been at the forefront.

One of the panellists pondered about whether once the pandemic is over, will it be followed by a mental health pandemic caused by a plethora of psychological disorders generated by the stress and anxiety of living with COVID-19. A chilling thought. But there is evidence of mental disorders following the 1918-1919 Spanish flu pandemic. Dr Greg Eghigian is professor of history at Penn State University and specialises in the history of psychiatry and mental health. Writing in the *Psychiatric Times*, he says:

"Spanish flu survivors reported sleep disturbances, depression, mental distraction, dizziness, and difficulties coping at work."

(Eghigian, 2020)

Now, 100 years on, I would like to think that we have a far greater awareness of, and are much more capable of effectively dealing with, mental health issues.

15: The psychological impact

15.1 The fear factor

I read a Facebook post a friend had shared that was attributed to Trey Gowdy, an American television news personality, former politician and former federal prosecutor. Gowdy had allegedly written about COVID-19 in the following post:

> *"The common flu has killed more people this year already and the media is SILENT! A handful of deaths out of 320 million Americans and we are in panic tearing down our society and costing our economy billions in the wake."*

Although Gowdy has apparently since claimed the post was fraudulent, a claim supported by Snopes (Mikkelson, 2020), I traced the post back to 23 April 2020. On that date the US had registered more than 700,000 COVID-19[33] cases, along with around 51,000 deaths – a fatality rate of 7.3%. Seasonal flu can kill as many as half a million people globally each year.

But, whether you have an issue with their comparison of the statistics or not, I feel that the author, whoever they may be, does make a good point about panic. Each year, health services around the world prepare to deal with seasonal flu, whether it is vaccinating the vulnerable or treating patients needing hospitalisation. But, I personally have never been aware of any associated panic. It is certainly something the media does not seem to be overly concerned about. However, with the combined threat of COVID and seasonal flu joining

---

[33] Eight months later, by 31 December 2020, we now know that the total COVID-19 case count for the US had passed 22 million, while the death toll was approaching 400,000.

forces with Respiratory Syncytial Virus (RSV), perhaps the media may take more than just a passing interest.

As part of the research I did for the masterclass I mentioned earlier, as well as for my original pandemic book published in 2016, I visited Hong Kong, Singapore and Vietnam. They were three of the six global 2002-2003 SARS hotspots. The others were Beijing, Toronto and Taiwan. I spoke to a variety of people and the one thing they all had in common was the sense of fear that they associated with SARS, even though compared with COVID-19, SARS was just a drop in the ocean.

"In 1918 fear moved ahead of the virus like a bow wave before a ship."

(John M. Barry, 2004)

I later came across John Barry's quotation and although it is a reference to the Spanish flu, it could equally apply to just about any pandemic caused by a novel contagion. Thinking about Barry's quotation and Gowdy's alleged post made me ask myself the question – "Why is there no panic over seasonal flu?"

On reflection, I believe that because we have lived with the threat of flu for hundreds of years and, in principle, we understand it. That does not mean we like it – we have just learned to live with it. Moreover, every year there is a seasonal flu vaccine available.

However, when a nasty novel virus comes along and starts killing people, human nature demands that we panic, especially as we invariably don't know what we are dealing with. In recent times, we have seen that with SARS, HIV/AIDS and now with COVID-19. While Barry's quotation had the Spanish flu in mind, (which was also a novel virus), it could be applied to just about any new killer contagion. Unlike seasonal flu, there is still no vaccine for SARS and, despite efforts to find one, two decades on from the initial outbreak, SARS could still make a comeback.

There are already concerns that post traumatic stress disorder (PTSD) may well develop among frontline health workers, paramedics and care home workers, along with food store employees, the police, etc. In the UK, during the lockdown that commenced in March 2020, unlike other countries, public transport kept running. The Office of National Statistic (ONS) has since flagged that outside of the health and care services, bus, coach and taxi drivers, plus chauffeurs, in addition to sales and retails assistants, are the professions particularly vulnerable to COVID-19 (Windsor-Shellard & Kaur, 2020). These are the people on the front line who put their personal safety at risk every day.

We must not also forget the stress that people will have experienced in following their respective government's lockdown instructions and staying at home for most if not all of the time. Some will be able to WFH, others have been furloughed, and of course there will be those who have lost their jobs. Here in the UK, the lockdown has been far less draconian than the measures applied in some other countries.

People forced into a lockdown and who suddenly found they had time on their hands have reacted in many different ways.

There has been an abundance of sad stories. But, there have been many accounts of volunteers in the community finding ways of helping the isolated and distressed. That said, there are those people for whom lockdown has felt like a prison sentence. The front door of their homes has seemed more like the door of a cell, even though it is, in effect, the door to their sanctuary from the virus. Sections 16 and 16.5 have some examples of how the community has come together to help those less fortunate individuals.

I talked about employers remembering their home working staff who would normally work in the 'office' in section 7.4. I know from my own personal experience, albeit back in the 1990s, that the transition from office based to WFH can be challenging. Every effort should be made to make those who unexpectedly find themselves in WFH mode still able to feel a valued part of the organisation.

There are those unfortunate individuals who have lost their jobs, and, on that point, I can emphasise having been made redundant three times in my career. On the first occasion, I'll be honest, I was desperate, and felt as though the world was coming to an end. But, on the second and third times, I just took it in my stride. A good friend of mine has been made redundant a total of eight times, and we joke that he has made a career out of redundancy.

Joking aside, if you have found yourself in this position, you may need some serious advice in terms of the steps to take to get yourself back into employment. The advice available will of course vary from country to country. But, to provide you with some food for thought, I have included a link on my website entitled 'Lost your job? Been furloughed?':

www.bcm-consultancy.com/pandemicthreat

This will direct you to a UK government website that is part of the National Careers Service and, although you may not be UK based, it might provide you with some ideas about the way forward. Obviously, if your own government provides a similar service, it makes more sense to refer to that.

15.2 Domestic abuse

I wanted to complete this section by talking a little about domestic abuse (DA). It is a rather sad indictment of society that DA seems to be an integral part. In the days before COVID-19 arrived on the scene, regular cases of DA were brought before the various magistrates' courts up and down the UK. Between March and June of 2020, UK police recorded a 7% rise in DA cases as compared with the same period in 2019. That said, the ONS has been reluctant to point the finger of blame at COVID-19 for being solely responsible, since DA offences have been steadily rising over recent years. However, as a magistrate friend of mine told me:

"From the bench, we see things from a different perspective than perhaps the ONS can. With people unnaturally locked down together and sometimes with little chance of escaping from each other's company, it is highly probable that, in some relationships, friction can result in partners and children suffering physical as well as mental abuse."

The charity, National Domestic Abuse Helpline, received approaching 50,000 calls during the initial three-month lockdown period in the UK. The charity calculated that this was over 80% higher than normal, with many of the victims, the majority being women, looking for refuge to escape from their abusers, (Gov.UK, 2021).

CHAPTER 16: SOME PERSONAL STORIES

16.1 Captain Sir Tom Moore

Since the coronavirus pandemic started, there have been many wonderful stories about people doing extraordinary feats to help raise money for various charitable causes. There is possibly none more inspiring than the story of 100-year-old retired British army Captain Sir Tom Moore. Captain Tom set out to raise £1,000 (approximately $1,250 USD) for the UK's National Health Service charities. With the support of a walking frame, Captain Tom's objective was to complete 100 laps of his garden before the arrival of his centenary birthday.

His feat not only captured the hearts of the British people, but donations came from far and wide, while his efforts accumulated a staggering figure in excess of £32 million ($40 million USD). In recognition of this amazing achievement, he has been appointed the first Honorary Colonel of the Army Foundation College in Harrogate. Maybe the icing on the cake was receiving a Knighthood from Her Majesty, Queen Elizabeth. When his 100th birthday arrived, the Post Office delivered well over 140,000 birthday cards from well-wishers.

So, it was particularly sad to learn that on 2 February 2021, Captain Sir Tom Moore died after having tested positive for COVID-19 a week earlier. It had not been possible to vaccinate him against the virus because of the treatment he was receiving for a pre-existing pneumonia condition. The Queen led the tributes, and many world leaders were also quick to honour Capitan Sir Tom. UK Prime Minister Boris Johnson said:

"Captain Sir Tom Moore was a hero in the truest sense of the word. In the dark days of the Second World War, he fought for freedom and in the face of this country's deepest post-war crisis, he united us all, he cheered us all up and he embodied the triumph of the human spirit. It's quite astonishing that at the age of 100 he raised more than 32 million pounds for the NHS on his own and so gave countless others their own chance to thank the extraordinary men and women who have protected us throughout this pandemic. He became not just a national inspiration but a beacon of hope for the world."

(BBC, 2021)

One of many inspired by Captain Sir Tom Moore, and certainly, worthy of mention, is 5-year-old Tony Hudgell who walked 10 kilometres on prosthetic legs. He had to have both legs amputated when he was a baby, resulting from the abuse he suffered at the hands of his birth parents. They both received 10- year prison sentences in 2018 for child cruelty.

Tony was adopted by Paula Hudgell and her husband Mark, and they supported him as he set out to raise £500 for Evelina London Children's Hospital, which had saved his life. The final figure achieved incredibly was over £1 million.

To watch Boris Johnson's speech or learn more about Tony Hudgell, please visit *www.bbc.co.uk/news/uk-england-beds-bucks-herts-55881753* and *www.bbc.co.uk/news/uk-england-kent-53138706* respectively.

16.2 Sally – An essential shop worker's story

Based in London, Sally is a team leader working for one of the largest supermarket chains. To begin with, when the pandemic broke, most supermarkets did not have a full complement of staff, as several were considered vulnerable and were shielding at home. Sally's team consequentially lost several very experienced people, and although the company recruited temporary replacements, initially they placed a further burden on the remaining team members as they learned the role. One industry journal statistic she remembers seeing was estimating anything up to 20% of supermarket workers would need to take time off at the height of the pandemic.

Sally recalls that it was late March 2020, and the UK was heading towards its first lockdown. Panic buying had gripped the nation and products such as flour, pasta, rice, soap and hand sanitisers were disappearing from the supermarket shelves often faster than employees could replenish them. So too were toilet rolls, with an estimated 145 million bought during the initial pandemic buying period. One major lesson learned by supermarkets is how the public is likely to behave when a lockdown is imminent.

Additionally, supermarket food delivery services have experienced a surge in demand, as people stay at home – customers have been placing 'unusually large orders', according to Ocado UK.

In the store, Sally explained that although the vast majority of customers have been behaving reasonably, her experience since COVID-19 reached the UK has still been far from positive, having often had to tolerate hostility. She and her colleagues have been frequently verbally abused by customers; sometimes had things thrown at them, one has been physically abused, while a couple have been racially abused. They have also been spat at while being threatened by shoplifters they have confronted.

Things certainly started to become even more difficult when panic buying began, especially when limits were applied to how many items customers could buy. When faced with empty shelves, some customers even unfairly blamed Sally and her team. She also witnessed elderly people being pushed over, customers taking products out of other customer's baskets, which in some cases resulted in blows being exchanged and the police being summoned.

Cages containing products for restocking shelves have often been ambushed by customers and stripped bare before they have reached their designated shelves.

This is reminiscent of the localised panic buying that occurred in the UK during the 2007 flooding. Water supplies had been disrupted because of a pumping station being flooded, leaving people temporarily without potable water. With an angry looking mob gathering outside his supermarket, one store manager refused to open until police arrived to control the crowd (Dakin, 2014).

Sally also reported that some people just totally ignored social distancing regulations. This left her and her colleagues trying to deal with complaints from other customers upset by the regulations being flouted. Moreover, when it became compulsory for customers to wear face masks, it was not unusual to see customers confronting other customers for not complying. Again, customers often direct their complaints at staff, expecting them to resolve the issue. Sally noticed one regular customer who had a very distinctive and unique hairstyle, who was always wearing his mask under his chin, leaving his mouth and nose completely exposed. Then came the day that she pointed out to him that two policemen had entered the shop and suddenly he adjusted the mask so just his eyes were peering out over the top. Thereafter, she was pleased to see that he was always in compliance with the regulations.

She has found it unbelievable how a small minority of customers have demonstrated such a lack of awareness and consideration to others. Sally cited one customer's behaviour as not just disgusting, but in light of the threat from COVID-19, it was positively menacing. He had sneezed into his hand, which he then wiped on his trousers before offering her a cash payment with the same hand. She felt she had no option but to temporarily close the till while she washed her hands and the checkout area was disinfected.

Similar to Sally's experience, albeit in another supermarket, a customer was caught on CCTV reacting violently to being requested to follow the one-way system and protective social distancing protocols that had been put in place. The customer promptly started throwing bottles of wine and spirits onto the floor, smashing many of the bottles, before storming out of the shop (Kay & Munchetty, 2020).

As Sally also pointed out, with customers wearing masks, it can be difficult to identify them. Consequently, you never know if the person you are serving today is the one who was abusing you yesterday.

Looking back, she has felt almost 'betrayed' by her employer, as it was several weeks before any form of physical protection was provided. Even when people entering a shop are were legally obliged to wear face masks unless they were medically exempt, some didn't bother, claiming that they have an exemption from their doctors, although she had never seen one. It is clear that other shoppers who are following the rules don't like it either, and she has seen arguments start. Although she hadn't witnessed it personally, she had heard of an instance when a mask-less woman was chased out of the shop by other, law-abiding shoppers.

As if one were needed, an independent verification of Sally's story has been provided first by Jo Causon, and secondly by Jo Whitfield.

Jo Causon, Chief Executive of the Institute of Customer Service explains:

> *"Given what has been going on in the wider world, there is a time when we all get a bit frustrated with things but some of the examples we are starting to see are: compromising social distancing, situations where people have been spat at and also threatening language – and the majority of cases, most customers are reasonable but there is a significant minority where we are seeing this and really that is what our campaign is all about: helping to address that."*

(Causon, 2020)

Meanwhile, Jo Whitfield, Chief Executive of Co-op Foods, has said her organisation is one of 23 UK food outlets that is supporting this initiative, especially as over 400 UK shop workers are being threatened by abuse every day (Kay & Munchetty, 2020).

16.3 Philip's story

My son, Philip, teaches English as a foreign language in Hangzhou, China, approximately 750 kilometres east of Wuhan, the initial epicentre of the COVID-19 outbreak. With the Chinese New Year holiday period approaching he had made plans to fly to the US for a few days to visit friends, returning to China for the start of the new school term. But, with the pandemic intervening, things did not go according to plan.

Instead of being away from Hangzhou for just a few days, he finally returned five weeks later than intended. During this time, in addition to visiting the US as planned, he spent time in the UK and the Netherlands, plus transiting through Moscow Airport twice. On two occasions, Phil has presented COVID-19 like symptoms, – once in the UK and a second time in China. Thankfully, he tested negative on both occasions. At the time of his UK test on 8 February 2020, he was one of around only 4,000 people who had been tested at that time.

Here is a chronological account of his story, which emphasises China's 'no-nonsense' approach to managing the pandemic.

"26 Jan China case count: 2,744, death toll: 80

In Hangzhou, there were no official restrictions in place, although an increase in the wearing of masks was noticeable. Some shopping malls had started to check temperatures and so too had railway stations before entry was permitted.

Travelled by train to Shanghai. Temperature was checked at metro stations and at the hotel. The metro was uncharacteristically quiet. Many malls were offering hand sanitiser upon entry. Museums, galleries and non-essential shops and services had closed.

27 Jan China case count: 4,515, death toll: 106

Full day in Shanghai. Many restaurants chose to close except for delivery or take away, although this was not mandated.

Personal experience – While in Starbucks at 2 pm, they informed all patrons they were closing, along with all other branches in the city.

During this time, the temperature checking of all take away delivery people started. They needed to have that information available via an app should the customer request it. (This has remained in place since.)

28 Jan China case count: 5,974, death toll: 132

Flew to Hong Kong. Temperature checks at each stage of the journey – before entering the metro, airport and upon entering the plane.

Hotel insists upon previous travel history and temperature check. Visible use of face masks.

Personal experience – Locally based friends' fiancée reportedly reluctant for us to meet (my friend and I).

29 Jan *Flew Hong Kong to New York (2 days before President Trump restricts travel from China. First confirmed coronavirus case in USA – 20 Jan).*

Temperature and document checks before entering Hong Kong Airport and passing through immigration. Clear use of masks by majority of people.

Upon arrival in New York, I was asked where in China I was travelling from. Border guard not wearing PPE, although some airport staff were wearing masks.

Not aware of health or temperature checks being taken.

Travelled to Boston by train.

Several attempts to buy masks failed. This aside, there was little evidence of a problem. Few people wearing masks, no temperature checks or health questions were conducted.

16: Some personal stories

No apparent social distancing measures in place.

Personal experience – The friends I was due to stay with were reluctant to have someone who lived in mainland China visit due to a new pregnancy.

6 Feb *Return to China not possible as flight restrictions had been imposed. Only had USA health insurance for limited period – opted to return to UK.*

Flew Aeroflot to London via Moscow to avoid paying extortionate direct air fare.

7 Feb *No special measures in place in either Moscow or London and no incidents to report.*

Checked-in to hotel in London.

8 Feb *On the morning of my second day, I developed a cough and called 111 because of my residential history. I was advised to stay in my hotel room and wait for an ambulance.*

I informed hotel staff of the situation, who were very helpful in the days that followed. Ambulance arrived 12 hours later with paramedics in full PPE. I was taken to a local hospital. A doctor, also with full PPE, including face guard, swabbed me after questioning me. She concluded it was unlikely that I had the still yet to be named new coronavirus, but I had to self-isolate in the hotel until the test results were available.

I received the results around 60 hours later confirming that my test was negative on the same day the virus was named SARS-CoV-2 and the disease it causes COVID-19.

12 Feb *Travelled by train to Manchester. No checks and no masks being warn.*

Split time in the North of England between Manchester and Sedbergh.

21 Feb *Flew from Manchester to Amsterdam and onward by train to Groningen. No checks, no masks.*

Personal experience – At the airport in Amsterdam, I needed to change money. Upon producing RMB (Chinese yuan), the Bureau de Change assistant had to ask me a series of questions to ascertain if the money could be a potential source of infection. These included, when it was taken out, from which city, how long had it been in my possession while still in China.

I remained in the Netherlands, where there were no checks and no masks worn. No COVID-19 cases had been identified in the country at this time.

All venues open, including a football match which I attended.

25 Feb *UK case count: 13, death toll: 0*

Flew Amsterdam to Southampton, where I was asked some additional questions when UK Border Force official noticed my Chinese residence permit.

Remained on UK South Coast visiting friends.

No checks, no masks. All venues open, including bars and restaurants. This included places with communal seating, such as Wagamama. Attended football match at Portsmouth.

During this period, Hangzhou School starts period of online learning for students using DingTalk. Teachers who are abroad are able to produce pre-recorded lessons.

Teachers, including those outside of China, had to start submitting a daily self-assessed health check to send to the education board.

3 Mar *UK case count: 49, death toll: 0*

Took train to Manchester via London. Still no apparent checks or wearing of face masks.

9 Mar *UK case count: 293, death toll: 3*

Returned to London via train. Greater level of awareness among public for social distancing was noticeable, although London Underground and city centre pubs and restaurants were still busy. Hand sanitiser, masks and other PPE difficult to find.

11 Mar *UK case count: 419, death toll: 11*

Russia case count: 28, death toll: 0

Flew Aeroflot from London to Moscow.

Temperature check before departure. Some wearing of masks, especially noticeable among flight crew. Upon arrival at Moscow Airport, the frequency of mask wearers was clearly higher than in the UK. Although as a transit hub for China this is probably not a true reflection of the general populace outside of the airport.

12 Mar *China case count 80,813; death toll: 3,176*

Flew Aeroflot Moscow to Shanghai.

The majority wore masks, no pre-boarding temperature check. Although, as it was a connecting flight, I had not needed to go through security.

Upon arrival in Shanghai, the flight was disembarked by groups based on airport/country of origin. Passengers who connected through Moscow from Italy/Iran were taken off first, then the USA, Germany, France, and next my group, other European countries. Each being checked for symptoms before leaving the plane and having to complete a health declaration and wear a mask.

After leaving the plane, passengers were required to sit down with a health professional in full PPE to discuss their health declaration. They also had their temperature checked and electronically register with the local CDC.

Anyone showing any symptoms was required to be securely transferred to hospital for a series of tests.

From the airport, people were being transported via buses to their home districts in neighbouring cities, then from there to their local communities, which were closed to non-residents/non-authorised personal. Once there, all new arrivals were required to follow the 'not one step' quarantine policy. This meant residents couldn't leave their apartments/hotel rooms for 14 days.

In my individual case I was allowed to take the train from Shanghai to Hangzhou after a mix up between the Shanghai and Hangzhou CDCs. Upon arrival I was taken to my local community and the local social workers performed a shop for me. I was asked for the things I needed, and every two/three days they would complete an additional shop for me. Later in my quarantine it was confirmed that I could have delivery drivers come directly to my home. During this two-week period, I was also required to submit a daily temperature check.

Note: I arrived in China at a time when the authorities did not require people finishing their 'not one step' quarantine to complete any COVID-19 testing. However, my colleagues who arrived a few days later were required to do so. They had a fully PPE clad crew turn up and check them and received results within 12 hours

25 Mar *My quarantine period ended.*

16: Some personal stories

In Hangzhou, there were no restrictions on movements, although initially all entertainment venues were closed, many restaurants, cafes, etc. only offered take away.

All businesses, communities (most residential areas in Chinese cities are groups of tower blocks with places available for security at the entrances), hospitals, and so on require a green health code to enter. This is provided via an 'Alipay app' on the user's phone. The code turns red for those who should be in a quarantine period and yellow/orange for those awaiting test results or who have been tagged as in contact with confirmed cases.

During this period, all communities only had a single entrance operating, where the guards can check the health code status and temperature of anyone wishing to enter. Patrons were also required to wear masks. Some supermarkets provided staff with full PPE, including overalls and masks.

6 Apr The government launched a website showing city by city and district, as low-, medium- and high-risk areas. In low-risk areas, people were advised there was no need to wear masks in open areas and many indoor venues relaxed the rules on entry. Although the aforementioned health code was still generally required by businesses.

Many residential communities stopped requiring this as a prerequisite for entry.

My school reopened initially for staff training, followed by a staggered return to school for students.

26 Apr onward, Further reduction of mask and health code regulations.

Personal experience – Having felt unwell during the morning of April 26th, and as I had some concerns about my temperature, I went to see the school nurse. On discovering that my temperature was 37.9 degrees, I was taken to hospital and tested for COVID-19. Despite the diagnosis of a gastric infection, I was told I could not return to school until the third day after my temperature had normalised. The process was relatively simple. I entered the hospital, was given three tests; Blood, nasal swab and MRI body scan. Once the initial information was available, I was told I was able to go home without a need for quarantine. Within 24 hours I had received the all-clear.

I subsequently learned that my classes had been quarantined until the school was notified that I wasn't a risk. This apparently happened within 2 hours.

22 Jun Note: *Change of policy observed.*

One of my students had presented a high temperature in the morning. However, they were allowed to return to class after lunchtime. While there had not been an official change in the school's policy on high temperatures, this action was contrary to my experience of being unable to return for at least 48 hours.

23 Jun Hangzhou: *While no major new restrictions have been put in place, the re-emergence of the virus in a Beijing wet-market saw restrictions slightly tighten again. More places were once again requiring masks and all were checking each individuals' health code.*

9 Jul *Short trip to Shanghai. Much relaxed travel process. Masks are required in the train station, although not while on the train.*

Differences between Shanghai and Hangzhou. More businesses require masks in SH than HZ. Although few request or require the health code upon entry, most are still testing for temperature. A higher proportion of people are wearing face coverings in the street.

Compared to my previous visit, there seems to be a notable number of smaller businesses that have closed permanently."

16.4 Elizabeth and Gordon's story

I have been friends with Gordon and Elizabeth for many years and, along with my late wife, Vivienne, we have shared many happy times together.

They were married in 1967 and celebrated their 50th wedding anniversary in 2017. Over a period of a couple of years, Gordon, a former Royal Naval officer, underwent a noticeable decline in health, and the symptoms pointed towards some kind of neurological problem.

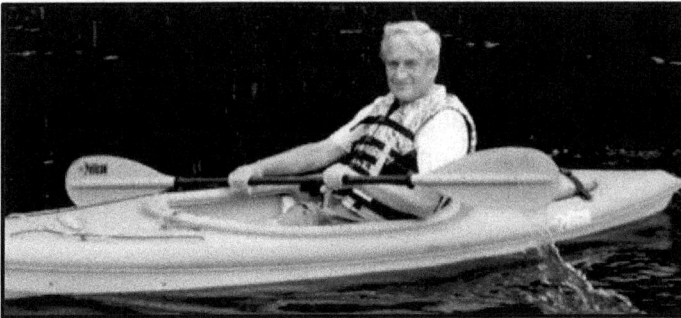

Figure 44: Gordon Peacock in happier times

Then in June 2019, the day after his 75th birthday, he suffered a transient ischaemic attack (TIA), also known as a mini stroke. He spent two weeks in hospital undergoing various tests to establish the reason for his decline. The diagnosis was Motor Neurone Disease (MND), an incurable, life-shortening, degenerative condition.

With support from their family doctor, MND nurses and the local hospice, initially Elizabeth was able to look after Gordon at home, acting as his primary carer for four months. Their grandson, Ashley, who for someone in his early 20s most definitely has an old head on young shoulders, also moved in with them to provide some additional help for his grandparents. His presence was a great comfort to them both.

As 2019 was drawing to a close, it became more difficult to support Gordon's needs at home, especially as he could no longer do anything for himself. He was admitted to the local hospice to allow Elizabeth a break while he had a few days respite care. He actually remained there for several weeks and, after taking medical advice, in February 2020, Elizabeth arranged for Gordon to be transferred to a residential care home.

Life was difficult enough even before COVID-19

Then came the coronavirus and on 11 March 2020, the residential care home went into lockdown, two weeks before the rest of the UK and a lot sooner than many other care homes. Visits were stopped to reduce the risk of patient and staff being infected with the virus. With Gordon initially on the first floor, even window visits were not possible. However, at least contact could be made using video facilities through social media, which provided some small measure of comfort. This also allowed his son, David, who lives in Canada, the opportunity to join in, too. Even so, video calls became more difficult as Gordon's ability to communicate verbally had all but ceased.

16: Some personal stories

Much heartbreak was caused for many patients and families alike as hospitals as well as care homes closed their doors to visitors. At the height of the pandemic, visitor entry was denied to loved ones, even for end-of-life situations, regardless of whether the patient was being treated for COVID or not. However, it has been acknowledged that these lockdown precautions often created loneliness among the care home residents and psychological suffering was often experienced by both them and their families.

Several weeks after the lockdown was imposed, Gordon was relocated to a ground floor room, and at least the family could see him again, albeit through the window, but this did bring some small measure of comfort. Gradually, as the first pandemic wave subsided the restrictions were eased. By this time, Elizabeth was permitted to sit by Gordon's room's open French windows, but physical contact was still not permitted.

Since relocating to the nursing home, Gordon had several near death experiences, and at the end of August, Elizabeth, their two daughters and their Rector were permitted to make brief visits. But, on each of these occasions, he pulled back from the brink. That was until 21 December 2020, when he finally passed away with his family beside him.

Gordon and Elizabeth's story is similar to so many others since the pandemic took hold. Regardless of whether patients were suffering with COVID-19 or had some totally unrelated terminal condition, hospitals and care homes have had to close their doors to visitors to protect staff, patients and visitors from the virus. Consequently, many patients have had to face their final hours without the comfort of having their loved ones beside them.

16.5 'Pompey' in the Community (PiTC)

Anyone who has the slightest interest in football (that will be soccer if you live on the far side of the pond), will have undoubtedly heard of clubs like Manchester United, Liverpool, Inter and AC Milan, Real Madrid, Barcelona and Bayern Munich. These are not only examples of well-known clubs that have been very successful over the years, but they carry a great deal of financial clout, too.

With the resources they have at their disposal, it will probably not come as a surprise that they, along with many other large clubs, have been active in supporting their respective communities during the pandemic. But I don't want to talk about them, I rather recount the efforts of a smaller club, albeit with a proud history, that is close to my own heart. Pompey in the Community (PiTC) is an independent charitable trust affiliated to my own team, Portsmouth Football Club (PFC).

PiTC harnesses the motivational power of PFC to promote education, healthy living, sporting participation and achievement among participants of all ages.

In the season preceding the pandemic outbreak, across Portsmouth and the surrounding areas, more than 35,000 people directly benefitted from its programmes. All its coaches are FA qualified, hold enhanced DBS, as well as Emergency Aid and Safeguarding Children certificates. With a staff of 45 full time, six part time and 40 casual employees, plus 150 volunteers, PiTC operated on an annual turnover of £2 million, being funded by multiple sources. When the UK-wide lockdown was announced in March 2020, PiTC's mission more or less changed overnight.

16: Some personal stories

PiTC's Director of Community Projects, Clare Martin, takes up the story:

"When the Prime Minister announced the initial lockdown, my immediate reaction was to panic a little, our core business is delivering football and school sport – both were stopping with immediate effect. However, we had a predominantly young, fit and healthy staff as well as a fleet of seven liveried vans. Within an hour I'd put a proposal to Portsmouth City Council to support the COVID-19 food relief initiative. If successful, we felt we may be able to sustain some form of existence.

The government then announced the Furlough scheme, and we breathed a sigh of relief that structured support would be in place. As a community organisation we still felt we needed to do something to support our community. We furloughed the majority of our staff and asked them to consider volunteering for The Hive, a third sector umbrella organisation that works to link community organisations with each other as well as with Portsmouth City Council. Within 24 hours, the majority of staff were signed up as volunteers and our response was born.

Our staff were split into 3 core teams that volunteered for a week in the centre, two weeks off, so if anyone became ill we could continue to function. During their weeks 'off' they all volunteered to support the deliveries, but they didn't enter the building. Our Head Office became a food and supply warehouse almost overnight. The Hive would take referrals and forward them on to us and the City Council procured the food.

The closing of pubs and restaurants meant that all coming to date food couldn't be utilised, so we were collecting donations from a huge variety of outlets, from cafes and chip shops to McDonalds outlets and cross-channel ferries.

The first delivery was from Portsmouth Football Club itself; they had, that same day, taken delivery of all the food required for home matches on the following Saturday and again on the Tuesday after; none of it would be needed as fans were now banned from attending matches. We collected £5,000 worth of pies, froze what we could knowing there would be increased need and delivered the rest to soup kitchens and hostels. The Royal Navy then came on board and lent us a full sized freezer container, so we had plenty of storage space. We were also able to provide treats, confectionery from the Isle of Wight Ferries, Easter Eggs as so many went unsold in supermarkets and tray bakes from Quattro, a catering company that went above and beyond to support.

During the first week we delivered 200 food parcels to those either isolating or who were unable to purchase food. The Government Food Parcels for the Shielding scheme had yet to begin so there were some very vulnerable people quite desperate for support. We also were accepting donations from supermarkets and individuals, which supplemented the procurement routes.

There were some harrowing stories such as the 83-year-old lady caring for her husband who was dying of cancer. In more usual times he would be in hospital, but then COVID-19 restrictions would have prevented her from being with him. She could hardly walk so our volunteers had to mask up simply to help her carry her food indoors and unpack it for her. I spoke to another lady who was calling about a donation; I asked her if she needed it that afternoon. Her reply still stays with me "Don't worry love, we have a tin of peas left in the cupboard, we can share that if you can bring it tomorrow!" By April we were delivering over 400 food parcels each week; each one sufficient to feed an individual for a week. We also had to take into account dietary needs; vegetarians, diabetics, coeliacs, etc. Another learning curve for my staff!

Over the first few weeks of lockdown, footballers were receiving bad press; the amount they were earning and being perceived to be doing little. Determined to help, Christian Burgess, who at the time was a defender for Portsmouth Football Club (PFC) and a PiTC Trustee, called me to find out how the PFC players could support PiTC. He arranged a weekly timetable with players volunteering every day to support deliveries. At that time, the PFC players were determined to help; they all donated and contributed to the fund as well as purchasing care packages for all wheelchair dependent disabled Pompey fans.

They then personally delivered them to the fans, which had an incredibly positive impact. As word of what Pompey in the Community were doing spread, more PFC staff became involved. Kev McCormack, the PFC kitman, collected 150 meals each day that the Queens Hotel were cooking for the food parcels. Alan Knight, our Player Ambassador, also volunteered daily as well as staff from all other departments of the club.

We also partnered with Enable Ability, a disability charity in the Landport area of the city. They were cooking 80 meals a day for the isolated and needy in the middle of Portsmouth. They were keeping their centre open simply to cook the meals so we moved their function into our classroom kitchen. PFC players became involved in this also, supporting the cooking, packaging and distribution of meals.

Ramadan also took place during lockdown and our local Muslim community became involved, The Akash cooked 500 meals for distribution and the Headteacher of the Madani Academy donated regular meals as well. The whole city seemed to come together to support the response.

Throughout Lockdown we submitted funding bids and were lucky to successfully bid for £73,000 of Defra funding to purchase food, £100,000 from Barclays 100x100 Fund. This then enabled us to purchase the food required rather than rely on the City Council. Of course, there were other necessities, such as toilet rolls and pet food; no point in providing food if households had to venture out for pet food or other necessities.

PiTC deliver numerous programmes for youngsters, many who live in apartments in the centre of the city, so we felt we needed to also support them too. We put together activity packages for them with treats and activities as well as Pompey paraphernalia. This then led to 'Blue Kitchen'. Youngsters would sign up to have ingredients delivered and then we would create a film teaching them how to cook, from pizzas to cup-cakes. This was picked up by Community Integrated Care, a national charity who run care homes for adults with special needs, so we now run weekly 'Zoom cooking' sessions for residents.

The PiTC Director of Community Projects, Clare Martin, summed up her story by adding:

> *"One of the most memorable features were the 'thank you' phone calls on a Friday; not from the recipients of food parcels but from numerous volunteers who wanted to say how much they appreciate being able to help or simply how it was helping them through lockdown. I cannot stress enough of how so incredibly proud I was, and I still am, of all my staff."*

16.6 Long COVID – Claire and Sarah's stories

Regardless of how mild or severe their symptoms may have been, people who have had COVID-19 can experience symptoms that linger for several weeks or even months. This is known as post-COVID-19 or 'long COVID'. There are several typical symptoms that can be presented, which have been listed in section 3.

Claire and Sarah both live in the Middle East, one in Dubai, the other in Riyadh. Both were diagnosed with COVID-19 and, while they are clear of the infection, they are now suffering with long COVID.

Claire's story

Claire is an ex-pat based in Dubai. In early September, along with a party of 15 friends (eight couples) she had dined in a Mexican restaurant. Conscious of the local COVID-19 restrictions, including the need for social distancing, they had checked in advance that the restaurant could safely accommodate them. They found themselves seated on tables with place settings for six people which, in principle, complied with regulations. However, the distance between couples was some way short of the recommended minimum, and there was nothing to discourage diners wandering around the restaurant, which some did.

Two days later, news broke that authorities had closed down the restaurant, although its management was rather coy about the reason. Claire had discovered this via a local news broadcast and initially the justification for the closure remained a mystery. Eventually she learnt the truth through her various local connections that several of the restaurant staff had in fact tested positive for COVID.

Being susceptible to chest infections and having suffered with both pneumonia and bronchitis in the past, Claire did not worry too much when she developed a cough. However, after a fever materialised a couple of days later, she subsequently tested positive for COVID-19. So too did 13 others in Claire's restaurant party, with two needing hospitalisation, though thankfully they all recovered. Later, when they were comparing their experiences, the group were surprised to discover some significant variations in the respective symptoms they had each presented.

After the positive test result, Claire was contacted by a Dubai health service track and trace team wanting to know who she had been in contact with during the previous 14 days. She was instructed to isolate at home for a further 14 days, although if her condition deteriorated, she was to call '999'. The track and trace team also called periodically to ensure that she was still isolating.

Claire had already been WFH and continued to do so as much as her condition allowed. She actually found that trying to focus on her job helped take her mind off the discomfort she was experiencing. Even so, she had to pace herself carefully as her energy levels were at a very low ebb.

At the end of her isolating period, Claire was considered to be no longer infectious. However, a number of symptoms have persisted, including extreme tiredness and lack of stamina, shortness of breath, especially after walking upstairs, coughing and difficulty in concentrating. Although not listed as a typical long COVID symptom, Claire has also experienced hair loss.

As I write this section, it is now several months since Claire's visit to the restaurant. She has not noticed any easing of the symptoms and has now got to the point where she endeavours to manage the condition. Employers should be sympathetic towards long COVID sufferers and they need to remember the condition is real and not just 'a state of mind'.

Sarah's story

Sarah is the Business Continuity Manager for HSBC Bank based in Riyadh, Saudi Arabia. She was attending hospital for a non-COVID related procedure where she remained for one day. Sarah believes she was infected while in the waiting room before surgery. She experienced a post-operation fever, which was initially diagnosed as a reaction to the surgical procedure. As more symptoms presented, she had a COVID-19 test, which proved positive on 2 July 2020. Further testing on 18, 27 and 28 July showed Sarah remained positive until she finally received a negative result on 13 August 2020.

Isolating at home, the symptoms that Sarah experienced during this time were typical of COVID-19, including headaches, fever, dry cough, aches and pains, along with waves of tiredness. She also experienced loss of appetite and sense of smell, plus a high fever, although paracetamol did provide some relief to the latter.

Prior to being infected, Sarah had been receiving treatment for high blood pressure (BP), but the infection resulted in a significant drop in BP, which was accompanied by bouts of dizziness. Of particular concern was her difficulty breathing and shortness of breath. Moreover, when showering she also found steam affected her breathing, by creating a choking sensation. Having checked into hospital, x-rays revealed severe chest congestion and inhaling steam was recommended despite her experience of showering.

Sarah, who describes herself as both a 'work-aholic' and a 'gym-aholic', was keen to get back to the gym once she had tested negative. However, she discovered that her energy levels remained very low, rendering her unable to exercise.

By the beginning of November 2020, Sarah's husband started presenting possible COVID-19 symptoms, and she accompanied him to the testing station. With the exception of a returning headache, her COVID-19 legacy symptoms had not changed, but she decided to take the test again anyway. Her husband tested negative, while she was positive.

Sarah recalls the mental trauma she felt following her original positive test back in July. That same sense of foreboding returned with the positive result in November, especially with the array of symptoms she had already experienced. Thankfully, a further test returned a negative result. Even so, she decided to self-isolate again.

Apart from the November 'blip', Sarah continues to suffer from the legacy of COVID-19. While her sense of taste and smell has returned, more than five months since originally testing negative, long COVID continues to leave its mark. For her, this has meant aches and pains, especially in her back and neck, which needs regular physiotherapy, memory loss, plus shortness of breath, especially after walking upstairs, chest pains and hair loss, in addition to the return of her high BP.

On the plus side, the HSBC has remained both understanding and supportive throughout. During her period of isolation, it would call regularly to see how she was and whether it could help in any way. They say that you only find out how good your insurance company is when you need to make a claim. The same is certainly true of one's employer – will it be there for you when you really need help and support?

CHAPTER 17: TIME YET FOR A REVIEW?

It was about two months after the WHO had declared COVID-19 to be a pandemic that a colleague suggested that the time was possibly approaching when we should consider starting a review. He argued that the pandemic would soon be over and we needed to capture the lessons to be learned regarding the damage the SARS-CoV-2 coronavirus outbreak had caused. He was considering not only the obvious mounting human cost, but the disruption to the global economy and business communities.

Despite his expression of positivity at the time, unfortunately a potentially discouraging word of caution was perhaps more fitting. We should be circumspect about allowing ourselves to be lured into what may be a premature false sense of optimism, despite various countries having commenced their vaccination programmes. Even former US President Trump has long since curbed his initial enthusiastic 'it will all be over by Easter 2020' stance, especially as confirmed COVID-19 cases in the US continued to increase with alarming momentum.

The reality is that there continues to be a lot more we need to learn about this virus. Every country can invariably learn from other countries in terms of both actions that had positive outcomes and those that didn't.

History tells us that pandemics can last for as long as two years, and they can come in waves. Furthermore, the UN Secretary General Antonio Guterres warned us that if countries cannot learn to unite against coronavirus, the pandemic could last for as many as 5-7 years (Guterres,2020). Despite his unambiguous warning, there certainly has been no shortage of nationalistic isolation examples around the world. However, we should certainly be collecting information that may ultimately prove useful when the time is right to look back and create an honest appraisal of how we did.

- What did we do well?
- What could we have done better?
- What was a total disaster?
- What opportunities did we miss and what opportunities did we exploit?
- Is there something that perhaps one country did or didn't do that made a significant difference (which could have a positive or negative outcome)?

This will apply to every business, every country and its leaders, and more importantly to global civilisation itself. It is only a matter of time before another pandemic will come our way and next time there will not be any justification in asking: "Why did no one warn us?"

In conclusion, although there is absolutely no harm in keeping a record of how the pandemic affects your organisation, to reiterate, it really is too soon to start a formal review until the pandemic is over. In the meantime, remember that despite any encouraging statistics that may emerge in terms of a reduction in new cases and fatalities, this coronavirus is likely to be with us for some time to come. We need to accept that COVID-19 may well continue to loiter with intent for some time to come.

When the time is right, in looking back in hindsight, it would be useful to have documented what went well, what perhaps could have been done better and even what was a complete disaster. For some organisations there may even be some unexpected opportunities created and better ways of going about their business. But for those who are keen to see what lessons are being learned and what conclusions are already coming downstream, there are a number of trustworthy forums that they can tap for information. Of particular note is The Lancet COVID-19 Commission. In addition to being a major report, it is also providing real-time commentary and assessment of responses by making its publications available in peer-reviewed journals (Lancet, 2021).

CHAPTER 18: COMPANION BOOK CONTENTS

For those readers of this book who have not enjoyed the benefit of reading this book's bestselling prequel, *Business Continuity and the Pandemic Threat – Potentially the biggest survival challenge facing organisations*, for your convenience, its contents list has been included in the following pages:

Part I: Understanding the Threat
Chapter 1: Introduction
Chapter 2: Anatomy of a Pandemic
Chapter 3: SARS – Case Study
Chapter 4: Spanish Influenza 1918–19 Overview
Chapter 5: Are the Spanish Flu and SARS Comparable?
Part II: Preparing for the Inevitable
Chapter 6: That Was Then
Chapter 7: Critical National Infrastructures
Chapter 8: Health Services Contingency Plans
Chapter 9: Pandemic Plan Considerations
Chapter 10: Creating a Healthier Environment
Chapter 11: Validating Your Pandemic Plan
Chapter 12: Conclusion
Chapter 13: Additional Reference Material
Chapter 14: Works Cited
Chapter 15: Glossary of Terms
Chapter 16: Free Template Downloads

For more information, please visit:
www.itgovernancepublishing.co.uk/product/business-continuity-and-the-pandemic-threat.

CHAPTER 19: SUMMARY

With the WHO endeavouring to locate the origin of coronavirus, along with the identity of 'patient zero', that search has initially focused on Wuhan. Its results and conclusions, unsatisfactory as they may have been considered by some, were published in March 2021 (WHO, 2021). In fact, I believe it fair to say that the results of the WHO convened *Global study of the origins of SARS-CoV-2* were inconclusive. Conversely, those calls for formal reviews of what the world did well, and what it did badly in responding to the crisis are somewhat premature. As the end of 2021 approached, in terms of the pandemic's duration, we have not even reached 'half-time' yet. Moreover, all the time we continue to wrestle with COVID-19, it would be dangerous to distract frontline staff from focusing on fighting the virus for such a purpose. Even so, there are still some interim lessons that we can take away from our experience so far.

When compared with the three influenza virus pandemics of the twentieth century, in terms of fatalities, with the death count at the end of December 2021 approaching 5.5 million, SARS-CoV-2 is already second only to the Spanish flu, the deadliest flu in history. However, the speed of its proliferation around the world has been arguably second to none. Furthermore, with the arrival of the Omicron variant, the spread of the disease clearly accelerated. Without the aid of commercial aviation, Spanish flu had taken around two years to cover the globe, a feat that coronavirus achieved in a matter of weeks.

19: Summary

Since the turn of the millennium, we have had various warning signs of an impending pandemic, which much of the world chose to ignore. Some, to be fair, had opted to prepare for a pandemic when it was clear that one was imminent. But, by the time we got that warning, it may have already been too late. Realistically, it is far from being a five-minute job to put together a reliable pandemic plan. Moreover, if you try to procure any products you will need, such as PPE, laptops or computer tablets, you will invariably find the shelves are already empty. Consequently, one of the first lessons we need to take away is that we cannot rely on the luxury of time to prepare once a pandemic has been declared by the WHO, we need to be ready.

Those countries that have so far tended to perform better are, in the main, those countries that have had first-hand experience of previous coronaviruses. You could argue that they have had the benefit of a dress rehearsal when having to deal with SARS or MERS, something that the rest of the world have not. That was until now. But, this in itself provides us with an important lesson to take away, insofar as we ignore the pandemic warning signs at our peril from a global, national and an organisational perspective.

Organisations that, for whatever reason, had previously abstained from engaging in preparing to face a pandemic, should now appreciate the inherent dangers of this course of inaction, always assuming that they actually survive the pandemic. Moreover, their very survival and the well-being of their employees could be placed in serious jeopardy by procrastination, especially when there is an urgent need for positive action. Furthermore, they should also realise that undertaking an appropriate degree of planning in itself is not enough. Like business continuity and emergency preparedness plans, your pandemic plan needs to be regularly rehearsed and exercised. Even a few hours each year could serve to renew and improve an organisation's state of readiness.

The debate has raged in some countries as to whether it is better to lockdown and saves lives but at the expense of the economy, or to protect the economy but sacrifice lives. Some countries chose to adopt a protectionist policy by closing their borders, which has resulted in varying degrees of success and failure. Global consolidation in the fight against COVID-19 has been the thing of dreams, while countries have opted for nationalistic isolation. At one extreme, China has practised totalitarian authority and surveillance to counter the march of the virus. Other countries have been hampered by the expectation that civil liberties will be respected and protected. This has often appeared to be regardless of the cost to the economy or the cost in lives lost. Meanwhile, citizens of democracies expect to be able to reserve the right to protest against any pandemic countermeasures they find unpalatable. Ironically, the frequent non-observance of mask wearing and social distancing that are noticeable during these protests can only serve to proliferate the virus.

Regardless of the various national strategies, there will always be those industries that will bear the brunt of a pandemic. We have seen hospitality, tourism, events and non-essential retail, among others, all suffer at the hands of COVID-19. Schools and universities have closed, and in some instances, public transport has been suspended. In the case of tourism and in line with the nationalistic posturing, some countries have banned non-nationals from entering. Until October 2021, Australia even banned its own nationals from traveling home. Others have applied strict quarantine measures when they do arrive. Evidence that travellers have been tested negative within two or three days before travelling is often mandatory. Maybe we will see a COVID-19 vaccination passport as a future pre-requisite for crossing country borders. Travel companies have folded, and many airlines have grounded their aircraft and laid off their crews as the demand for travel reduced dramatically. This has also had a knock-on effect on those supply chains that depend upon using aircraft cargo holds to transport products around the world.

Hardly had the pandemic got underway when China started locking down. This had an immediate effect on global supply chains, especially when the scramble to obtain PPE started. Initially, many frontline health workers and care home staff could not source the PPE they needed. But, seizing the initiative, local companies, schools and individuals started making gowns, visors and face masks to help plug the gap. Some distilleries, having had their route to market cut off, with restaurants, cafés and bars having to close, switched from making their traditional products, such as gin, to manufacturing hand sanitising gels.

Information technology has certainly played its part in providing the capability for some public and private sector staff and school pupils to be home based. But, with so many consigned to WFH, hospitality outlets relying upon city and town centre footfall have suffered, even when they have been permitted to remain open. Those that have been able to service the ever-growing food take-away and delivery market have certainly increased their chances of survival. Also reliant on that footfall are the non-essential retail outlets, particularly if they have no online presence. We have started to see numerous outlets heading for bankruptcy, especially when they do not offer their customers an online shopping option. Conversely, some online only outlets have seen their profits soar.

For those organisations considered to be essential and which have been able to continue working, loss of resources has often been a major inhibitor. Organisations should always plan for staff absenteeism in a pandemic, the cause of which can be varied and sometimes over extended periods, too. When staff cannot WFH, social distancing becomes essential, which in turn can reduce efficiency in the workplace. We have certainly seen several examples where questionable social distancing practices combined with concentrations of risk, have intensified localised proliferation of the virus. By contrast, on opening up again, some industries, and most notably hospitality, have found themselves facing staff shortages. In some cases, it has been because of a dependency on foreign workers who have returned home, although in other instances, former hospitality workers have found alternative opportunities and left the industry.

Overall, testing and tracing operations have had very mixed success, and numerous countries certainly got off to a rocky start. Even as we entered 2021, there were those countries still struggling to get on top of this crucial activity. However, just as information technology facilitated home working and schooling, I would expect the continuing evolution of the smartphone to certainly make testing and tracing easier during future pandemics. Moreover, I am afraid that any individuals concerned that greater use of smartphones in this respect may compromise their privacy and liberties, will just have to simply get over it.

Viruses cannot spread on their own, they need our help to be able to transfer from human to human. It is crucial that we all recognise the importance of applying the preventative measures of washing hands, wearing face masks and practising social distancing. Moreover, when faced with a lockdown, we should endeavour to remember that the door to our house or apartment is not a prison door, but it provides us with a sanctuary from the pandemic. It is certainly disappointing to see so many people across the world contravening lockdown regulations, with the forces of law and order often seeming powerless to apprehend them.

The pandemic threat has presented the world with a massive civil emergency. Several countries are known to have declared a state of emergency activating legislation that empowered their ability to manage the situation. I would certainly like to see them reviewing the effectiveness of this legislation in the face of the multi-faceted issues that a pandemic can present.

Social media has transformed the way in which the world communicates, and it offers many positive aspects. But, it also has its dark side, too, which, in the case of the pandemic, has been promoting misinformation and conspiracy theories. WHO Director-General, Dr Tedros Adhanom Ghebreyesus, referred to it as an 'infodemic', and we must learn to make the distinction between genuine and fake news.

Major social media platforms have become more proactive in marking posts as misinformation, often removing them all together. One Facebook group in the UK, populated by pandemic sceptics and dedicated to sharing pictures and videos of empty hospitals, had more than 13,000 members. Facebook took this group down on 8 January 2021. A similar group was immediately set up, but it too was removed by Facebook three days later. In extreme cases, social media platforms have suspended or even cancelled the accounts of individuals recognised as persistent offenders which has even included high profile politicians.

As the pandemic progressed, several more easily spreading variant virus mutations were detected. Many countries were experiencing a massive new pandemic wave, with consequential lockdowns becoming commonplace. For some it was their second wave, for others, their third. In some instances, this made the initial waves experienced in the first and second quarters of 2020 look comparatively insignificant. The immediate consequence was health services were being overwhelmed by the needs of the growing numbers of COVID-19 patients. By mid-January 2021, with hospitalisations spiralling, the then Secretary of State for Health, Matt Hancock, suggested that the UK had reached what he believed to be the worst point of the pandemic (BBC News, 2021). But twelve months later, the worrying Omicron variant generated spikes that were being observed that could ultimately challenge Hancock's statement.

With vaccines now being rolled out across the world, there is genuine cause for a controlled measure of optimism, although continued vigilance will be essential, certainly in the shorter term. Even so, it is very probable that it will be well into 2023, perhaps even beyond, before sufficient stocks of vaccines are available to provide protection for citizens of the poorest of nations. The WHO also believes that herd immunity will not be achieved in 2022, as it reiterates that it would take time to produce and give enough shots to halt the virus spread.

It is likely that COVID-19 will always be with us, although it may ultimately head off into comparative obscurity. When the current crisis finally draws to a close, that will be the time to look back, gather all the lessons to be learnt and continue our preparations for the next pandemic.

It is not that we should have really needed one, but this coronavirus has just provided yet another massive wake-up call. However, they say a week is a long time in politics and it concerns me that once we immerge from this crisis, the political will to act upon the lessons learnt may prove weak. As soon as the experience of COVID-19 starts to become just a distant memory, will the focus of political agendas be switched to other, non-pandemic related issues, risking us again being left unprepared for the next pandemic?

There is no doubt that there will certainly be specific lessons that organisations and countries must learn. Even so, I believe that a global consensus is what the world should be looking to accomplish. However, my fear is that without good organisation, strong leadership and above all, genuine all-round commitment, it could degenerate into a pointless, finger-pointing, talk-shop that achieves precious little. Conversely, writing in the British Medical Journal, Nick Stern and Bob Ward are attempting to draw attention to, what could be described as, an 'even bigger picture' which certainly resonated with me:

"We are at a critical moment in history, facing growing crises in climate change, biodiversity, and environmental degradation – as well as covid-19. But we also have an enormous opportunity to transform the global economy and usher in an era of greater wellbeing and prosperity."

(Stern & Ward, 2021)

Perhaps coming at the problem from a different angle, Dr Jonathan Quick, MD, expresses similar concerns in his book *The End of Epidemics*. In chapter 2, he focuses on:

19: Summary

"The Bush: Lessons from Ebola, AIDS and Zika – How deforestation, climate change and population movement are turning wildlife into pandemic incubators"

(Quick, 2018)

Let us hope that arguments like Quick, Stern and Ward's strike a chord with leaders the world over, galvanising a groundswell of positive thinking and above all, positive actions.

APPENDIX A: OTHER PUBLICATIONS BY THE AUTHOR

In Hindsight – A compendium of Business Continuity case studies

---

This book went to number one on the Amazon bestsellers lists when first launched.

"I wanted to send you a note of congratulations on your book, which I've just had the pleasure of reading. I think it is a very useful contribution to available literature and hopefully will lead to an appreciation of why BCM is essential."
Dr Kevin Pollock MBCI

"Not just BCM, I would also recommend this book to Emergency Planners and any public event planners. It is well researched, authenticated information, and contains a treasure trove of collective experience that will aid the planning process."
John Ball AFBCI

"I am constantly amazed by the number of executives who dismiss potential disasters as being too unlikely to consider, or who put off dealing with known risks because they have other things to worry about. This book is full of these people, and what happens in the case studies provides ample evidence to counter their complacency."
Martin Caddick LLB MBA FBCI MIOR

Validating Your Business Continuity Plan – Ensuring your BCP actually works

---

"If there exists a warm, friendly book about business continuity, then this is it. Reading this book is like having an elderly but very experienced uncle teaching you about the subject, sharing their experience, the lessons they have learned and (business continuity) war stories."
Charlie Maclean-Bristol FBCI FEPS

"I wish I'd had a copy of this book when I started out in Business Continuity. It certainly deserves the 'must read' tagline and should form part of the essential library of anyone involved in the validation of Business Continuity Plans."
Mark Fenech BSc MBA CRISC MBCI

"I found your book very interesting and am happy that I could add to its great value. I wish you all the success in publishing it."
Abdullah Al-Hour FBCI

Business continuity and the Pandemic Threat — Potentially the biggest survival challenge facing organisations

---

A world bestseller

"I thoroughly enjoyed reading Clark's book which is written in a style that makes it easy for anyone to understand without requiring a background in medicine or business. I have been involved in disaster management

planning for the past ten years and yet I still found this book both enlightening and extremely informative."
Dr Tanya Mellilo MD, MSc (Dist) PhD

"Having known Rob Clark for several years, and spoken to him on numerous occasions about the many aspects of the business continuity world – the breadth of knowledge, analysis of the subject and the well-balanced presentation of this volume comes as no surprise. This informative book is written in an easy going and conversational manner, but the message it brings to the table is critical to understanding the meaning of any forthcoming pandemic threat and considerations of how to mitigate the effects, where possible, to you and your organisation." ."
Owen Gregory MSc BA (Hons) MBCI MBCS

"Bob Clark is the real deal. His book demonstrates a predictive understanding of our current threat environment as well as our personal & corporate vulnerabilities to it. Knowledge is power ... read and prevail."
Robert Preininger CBCP

Crisis Management – Is Social Media its new best friend or its worst nightmare?

"I have known Robert Clark for over 10 years, and I am very familiar with the other books he has written. Even though he has already reached the Number One position on the Amazon bestsellers lists with his book In Hindsight: A compendium of Business Continuity case studies, I firmly believe that this is his best work to date."
Catherine Feeney MSc FIH JP

"I read your book and I am enthusiastic about the content in regard to social media, social media behaviour and

crisis management. Business Continuity managers, crisis or social media team members should read this book to better prepare themselves to face a crisis thereby enabling themselves to make social media a friend. If they don't appreciate the potential for disruptive power that social media has, it can result in a nightmare for their organization during a crisis. The case studies are very relevant and useful."
Joop Franke (Hon) FBCI

ICT Disaster Recovery – Entering the 5th Age of Computing

Clark is the author of the book with the working title *'ICT Disaster Recovery – Entering the 5th Age of Computing'*.

From a commercial perspective, ICT Disaster Recovery used to be solely the domain of large organisations and the concept was almost exclusively embraced by the financial sector. The sheer magnitude of the financial investment required simply made it inaccessible to just about everyone except the corporate giants.

Today, advances in technology means that every organisation from the one-man-band upwards can now easily and inexpensively protect and recover their information technology environments.

This book will examine ICT disaster recovery, the origin of business continuity management and how it has evolved from its embryonic state in the late 1960s and early 1970s through to the modern era. It will go on to consider how IT disaster recovery is being influenced by the arrival of the 5th generation of computing.

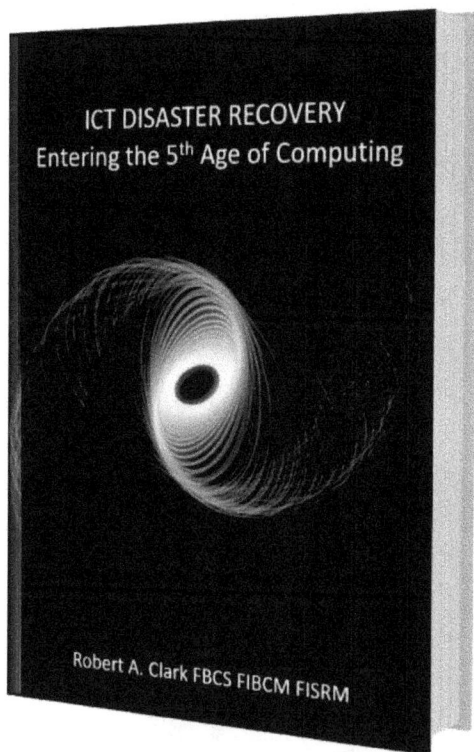

With his career in IT starting long before the expression 'BCM' had even been coined, the author has seen the evolution of BCM from its origins in ICT disaster recovery, through to its coming of age with the launch of the international standards ISO 22301 and ISO 27031. With his substantial hands-on IT experience, as well as a being a Fellow of the British Computer Society and a Fellow of the Institute of Business Continuity Management, he is well placed to take the reader by the hand through this fascinating journey.

APPENDIX B: USEFUL FREE RESOURCE DOWNLOADS

Please visit the author's website at *www.bcm-consultancy.com/pandemicthreat* and take advantage of some free resources that include sample plans, videos and articles.

APPENDIX C: PANDEMIC TRAINING

In conjunction with Meirc Training & Consulting, I am delighted to offer both virtual learning and classroom courses in:

Business continuity and crisis management during pandemic threats:

This course will provide participants with a full understanding of the threats and issues that are synonymous with pandemics. It takes into account both the business and human aspects of this threat, and does not just consider businesses in isolation, but as part of a greater supply chain.

Participants will learn how to evaluate and deliver the content of a pandemic plan for their organizations. No prior knowledge of pandemics is required.

Organizations that are unprepared to face the inevitability of a pandemic are at risk. A pandemic is far more than just about absenteeism caused by illness. In fact, it presents organizations with a multi-faceted threat capable of affecting just about every aspect of their business and crippling their operational ability. Even organizations located in parts of the world that have not been directly affected by a contagion, may still find supply chain failures that become major issues.

In addition, I am also pleased to be working with Meirc Training & Consulting to provide virtual and classroom courses in:

- Certified Crisis Management Professional
- Certificate in IT Disaster Recovery Planning

Appendix C: Pandemic training

For more information about these courses and other training opportunities, please visit: *www.meirc.com/plus*.

APPENDIX D: GLOSSARY OF TERMS

Item	Explanation
Administration	Going into administration is when a company becomes insolvent and is put under the management of licensed insolvency practitioners. This is similar to a company entering chapter 11 in the US.
Affiliate marketing	An arrangement by which an online retailer pays commission to a third party when its website sends traffic to the retailer or generates sales from referrals.
Anti-vaccine agenda	COVID-19 vaccines have faced a varied and powerful misinformation movement online.
ASU	Arizona State University.
BAME	Black, Asian and Minority Ethnic groups.
BCI	The Business Continuity Institute based in UK has a global reach and over 8,000 members.
BCM	Business Continuity Management.

BCP	A Business Continuity Plan is a document that outlines how a business will continue operating during an unplanned disruption in service.
BII	Business Interruption Insurance which some organisations were able to make a claim for COVID-19 related lost profits.
BMJ	British Medical Journal.
BYOD	Bring Your Own Device refers to organisations allowing employees to use their own personal electronic devices for work purposes.
CBRN	This refers to the threat presented by **C**hemical, **B**iological, **R**adiological and **N**uclear weapons which, collectively, are referred to as weapons of mass destruction.
CCTV	Closed circuit television.
CDC	(US) Centre for Disease Control and Prevention.
CFR	The Case Fatality Ratio is the proportion of deaths from a certain disease compared to the total number of people diagnosed with the disease over a given period.

CMT	Crisis Management Team is usually drawn from an organisation's senior management who would typically come together to manage a serious event which has occurred, and which threatens the continued viability of that organisation.
C-Suite	Usually acknowledged as the executive level managers within an organisation.
DNCC	Daily New Case Count identifies, by country, state or territory how many new COVID-19 cases have been detected.
DA	Domestic Abuse is defined by the UN *"as a pattern of behavior in any relationship that is used to gain or maintain power and control over an intimate partner."*[34]
Ebola	Ebola virus disease is a rare but severe, often fatal, illness in humans. The virus is transmitted to people from wild animals and spreads in the human population through human-to-human

---

[34] For more information, visit: *www.un.org/en/coronavirus/what-is-domestic-abuse*.

	transmission. The average EVD case fatality rate is around 50%.
Epidemiology	The science that studies the patterns, causes and effects of health and disease conditions.
Eureka moment	Aka the 'lightbulb moment' or the 'Aha! moment', refers to suddenly understanding a previously unintelligible problem.
FCA	Financial Conduct Authority is the conduct regulator for around 51,000 financial services firms and financial markets in the UK and the prudential supervisor for 49,000 firms, setting specific standards for around 18,000 firms.
FFP3	This the European safety standard, including UK, for protective masks and is suitable for most dangerous working environments including for front line health workers.
Footfall	The number of people that might visit a location (e.g., a town centre, a washroom, etc.) in a given time.
GCHQ	Government Communications Headquarters, commonly known as GCHQ, is the UK's intelligence,

	security and cyber agency. Its mission is to help keep the country safe.
GPG	The Good Practice Guidelines is produced by the BCI and is considered by some as the definitive guide for business continuity and resilience professionals.
HSJ	Heath Service Journal.
Herd immunity	Often associated with population immunity, which can be the result of everyone being vaccinated against a virus or everyone who has had the virus and has developed immunity.
JIT or (J-i-T)	Just In Time is a supply chain management methodology aimed at reducing flow times and costs while an organisation aims to achieve zero inventory.
ICT DR	Information and Communication Technology Disaster Recovery.
Index case	The first identified case of a communicable disease. Sometimes referred to as 'patient zero'.
The Lancet	The Lancet is a highly respected medical journal, which since 1823 has been committed to applying scientific

	knowledge to improve health and advance human progress.
MERS	Middle East Respiratory Syndrome.
Microcephaly	A neurological disorder that causes underdevelopment of the brain in unborn children.
NaCTSO	National Counter Terrorism Security Office is a UK based police unit. It is funded by, and reports to, the Home Office, which advises the British government on its counter-terrorism strategy.
NGO	A Non-Governmental Organisation is a not-for-profit group that is independent of any government.
NRR	National Risk Register. The UK NRR is used as a reference point throughout this book and available in the public domain.
NORAD	North American Aerospace Defense Command.
ONS	The Office of National Statistics is the UK's largest independent producer of official statistics and its recognised national institute.

PPE	Personal Protective Equipment which should protect the wearer in their respective work environment. For example, front line health workers, pathologists, firemen and police forensic teams etc.
PTSD	Post-Traumatic Stress Disorder.
RSV	Respiratory Syncytial Virus is a common respiratory virus that usually causes only mild symptoms lasting one to two weeks. However, RSV can be dangerous for infants and the elderly.
SAR	Special administrative region – a term applied to the former British and Portuguese colonies of Hong Kong and Macau, which were returned to China at the end of the twentieth century.
SARS	Severe Acute Respiratory Syndrome.
Soccer	Association football, often referred to as soccer, is a team sport that uses a spherical shaped ball.
Shangri-La	A fictional mystical, harmonious place described in the 1933 novel Lost Horizon by the British author, James Hilton.
SME	Small and medium size enterprise.

SoE	When their increasing COVID-19 cases gave rise for concern, some countries declared a 'State of Emergency' which in most cases would constitutionally permit the respective governments to use additional powers for managing the situation.
Super-spreader	A highly infectious person who spreads the agent of an infectious disease to an unusually large number of people.
The 'R' number	The reproduction number (R) is the average number of secondary infections produced by a single infected person. An R number of one means that on average every person who is infected will infect one other person, meaning the total number of infections is stable. If R is two, on average, each infected person infects two more people. If R is 0.5 then on average for each two infected people, there will be only one new infection. If R is greater than one the epidemic is growing, if R is less than one the epidemic is shrinking.
TIP	The Independent Panel (for Pandemic Preparedness and Response).
TTI	Testing, tracing and isolating

WFH	Work From Home.
WHO	The World Health Organization.
WMD	Weapons of mass destruction.
Zika	Zika is an infection spread mainly by mosquitoes found in parts of the Americas, the Caribbean, Africa and Asia. It can be harmful to pregnant women.
Zoonosis	A disease that can be transmitted from animals to people.

APPENDIX E: BIBLIOGRAPHY

ABI, 2020. [Online] Available at:
www.abi.org.uk/products-and-issues/topics-and-issues/coronavirus-hub/business-insurance/
[Accessed 08 08].

Aizenman, N., 2019. *Why Health Workers In The Ebola Hot Zone Are Threatening To Strike.* [Online] Available at: *https://text.npr.org/717079729*
[Accessed 13 12 2020].

Allen, N. & Landauro, I., 2020. *Coronavirus traces found in March 2019 sewage sample, Spanish study shows.* [Online]
Available at: *https://uk.reuters.com/article/us-health-coronavirus-spain-science/coronavirus-traces-found-in-march-2019-sewage-sample-spanish-study-shows-idUKKBN23X2HQ* [Accessed 26 08 2020].

Annett, T., 2020. *Fauci Calls White House Ceremony a 'Super-Spreader Event'.* [Online] Available at: *www.bloomberg.com/news/articles/2020-10-09/fauci-calls-white-house-ceremony-a-super-spreader-event*
[Accessed 11 08 2021].

Apolone, G. et al., 2020. *Unexpected detection of SARS-CoV-2 antibodies in the prepandemic period in Italy.*
[Online] Available at: *https://journals.sagepub.com/doi/pdf/10.1177/0300891620974755*
[Accessed 14 12 2020].

Arena, J., 2020. *1,300 English-language teaching jobs on the line.* [Online]
Available at: *https://timesofmalta.com/articles/view/1300-*

english-language-teaching-jobs-on-the-line.825598
[Accessed 19 10 2020].

Asahi Shimbun, 2020. *Experts ponder why cruise ship quarantine failed in Japan.* [Online] Available at: *www.asahi.com/ajw/articles/13140946*
[Accessed 11 08 2021].

ASU (Arizona State University), 2020. *ASU releases first comprehensive survey on how companies are protecting their employees from COVID-19.* Available at: *https://news.asu.edu/20201119-discoveries-asu-first-comprehensive-survey-how-companies-protect-employees-covid-19.* [Accessed 02 06 2020]

ASU (Arizona State University), 2021. *Back to the Workplace: Are we there yet? (A key insight from Employers One Year into the Pandemic).* Available at: *https://issuu.com/asuhealthsolutions/docs/asu_workplace_c ommons_phase_2_report?fr=sZGIwZjE5NTg1NjM.*
[Accessed 02 06 2020]

Austin, S. 2020. *Why Singers Might Be Covid-19 Super-Spreaders.* [Online]
Available at: *https://elemental.medium.com/why-singers-might-be-covid-19-super-spreaders-57607ed71b9b*
[Accessed 14 09 2020].

Bangkok Post, 2020. *HTMS Bhumibol escorting cruise ship.* [Online]
Available at:
www.bangkokpost.com/thailand/general/1856089/htms-bhumibol-escorting-cruise-ship [Accessed 06 07 2020].

Baraniuk, C., 2020. *What the Diamond Princess taught the world about covid-19.* [Online] Available at: *www.bmj.com/content/369/bmj.m1632*
[Accessed 07 07 2020].

Barber, K., 2020. *Portsmouth trio save thousands of chilli plants from waste after city chilli and gin festival is cancelled.* [Online] Available at: *www.portsmouth.co.uk/business/consumer/portsmouth-trio-save-thousands-chilli-plants-waste-after-city-chilli-and-gin-festival-cancelled-2996258* [Accessed 08 10 2020].

Barras, V. & Greub, G., 2014. *History of biological warfare and bioterrorism.* [Online] Available at: *www.sciencedirect.com/science/article/pii/S1198743X1464 1744#:~:text=Contagious%20diseases%20and%20other% 20biological,to%20weaken%20them%20%5B3%5D.* [Accessed 13 09 2020].

Barry, John M., 2020. *The Great Influenza: The Story of the Deadliest Pandemic in History.* Penguin.

BBC News, 2020. *Amazon's £250,000 for bookshops fund stuns trade.* [Online] Available at: *www.bbc.co.uk/news/business-52400911* [Accessed 30 08 2020].

BBC News, 2020. *Asos adds three million customers as profits soar amid pandemic.* [Online] Available at: *www.bbc.co.uk/news/business-54535775* [Accessed 04 01 2021].

BBC News, 2021. Captain Sir Tom Moore: 'National inspiration' dies with Covid-19. [Online] Available at: https://www.bbc.co.uk/news/uk-england-beds-bucks-herts-55881753 [Accessed 04 01 2021].

BBC News (Wales), 2020. *Coronavirus: 'Covidiots' criticised on Tui quarantine flight.* [Online] Available at: *www.bbc.co.uk/news/uk-53970217* [Accessed 31 08 2020].

BBC News, 2020. *Coronavirus: Hong Kong on verge of 'large-scale' outbreak, says Carrie Lam.* [Online] Available

at: *www.bbc.co.uk/news/world-asia-china-53575875*
[Accessed 30 07 2020].

BBC News, 2020. *Coronavirus: How did Cambodia's cruise ship welcome go wrong?*. [Online] Available at: *www.bbc.co.uk/news/world-asia-51542241* [Accessed 05 07 2020].

BBC News, 2020. *Covid-19: Oxford vaccine rolled out to hundreds of GP sites in England.* [Online] Available at: *www.bbc.co.uk/news/health-55567421.* [Accessed 26 11 2020].

BBC News, 2020. *Ruby Princess: New South Wales premier apologises over cruise ship outbreak.* [Online] Available at: *www.bbc.co.uk/news/world-australia-53802816*
[Accessed 17 08 2020].

BBC News, 2020. *Sir Ian McKellen 'euphoric' to receive Covid-19 vaccine.* [Online] Available at: *www.bbc.co.uk/news/entertainment-arts-55345131*
[Accessed 22 02 2022].

BBC News, 2021. *Covid: Uk at 'Worst Point' of Pandemic,* Says Hancock. [Online] available at: *www.bbc.co.uk/news/uk-55621228*
[Accessed 31 12 2021].

BBC Our World – Coronavirus Cruising. 2020. [Film] Directed by Nick London. s.l.: Make Waves.

BCI, 2020. *BCI Horizon Scan Report.* 2020 – An examination of the risk landscape for resilience professionals Edition 2020. The BCI.

BCI, 2021. *BCI Horizon Scan Report.* 2021 Edition 2021. The BCI.

BCI, 2018. *Good Practice Guidelines – 2018 Edition.* 2018 Edition ed. s.l.:The BCI.

Beaumont, P, 2021. *UK and US criticise WHO's Covid report and accuse China of withholding data.* [Online]
Available at:
www.theguardian.com/world/2021/mar/30/who-criticises-chinas-data-sharing-as-it-releases-covid-origins-report
[Accessed 02 06 2021].
Bendix, A, 2021. *A year and a half after Sweden decided not to lock down, its COVID-19 death rate is up to 10 times higher than its neighbors.* [Online]
Available at: *www.businessinsider.com/sweden-covid-no-lockdown-strategy-failed-higher-death-rate-2021-8?r=US&IR=T* [Accessed 15 09 2021].
BGMEA, 2020. *Bangladeshi and Garment Manufacturers Exporters Association (BGMEA).* [Online] Available at:
www.bgmea.com.bd/
[Accessed 30 08 2020].
Billion Pound Cruises – All at Sea. 2020. [Film] Directed by Page Shephered. s.l.: Ttitle Role Products (for ITV).
Blackford, M. G., 2007. *Pathway to the Present : US Development and its Consequences in hte Pacific.*
Honolulu: University of Hawaii Press.
Bostickson, W. & Ghannam, Y. 2021. *Proposed Forensic Investigation of Wuhan Laboratories*; Researchgate, Google Scholar.
Brahmbhatt, M. & Dutta, A., 2008. *On SARS Type Economic Effects during Infectious Disease Outbreaks..*
[Online] Available at:
https://openknowledge.worldbank.org/handle/10986/6440
https://openknowledge.worldbank.org/ [Accessed 11 02 2016].
Brean, J., 2021. *Omicron variant likely in global circulation for 'weeks if not months' as Canada discovers more cases.* [Online]

Available at: *https://nationalpost.com/news/canada/covid-19-testing-system-is-working-ontario-top-doctor-says-after-four-suspect-cases-omicron-variant-discovered-in-canada* [Accessed 01 12 2021].

Brett, E. (2003). *Attacks of Terror: Surviving the Unthinkable*. Lincoln, NE: iUniverse.

Brinch, P., 2020. *Annual Report 2020*. [Online] Available at: *http://cdn.shopify.com/s/files/1/0016/2617/7647/files/FINAL_Annual_Report_2020.pdf?v=1604655179* [Accessed 02 01 2021].

Brocklehurst, S., 2020. *The woman who discovered the first coronavirus*. [Online] Available at: *www.bbc.co.uk/news/uk-scotland-52278716* [Accessed 19 06 2020].

Bryant, N., 2020. *BBC News at One*. [Online] Available at: *www.bbc.co.uk/iplayer/episode/m000qqxv/bbc-news-at-one-30122020* [Accessed 30 12 2020].

Burns, H., 2020. *Tesco online sales grow 48% during coronavirus lockdown*. [Online] Available at: *www.insider.co.uk/company-results-forecasts/tesco-online-sales-grow-48-22255555* [Accessed 20 08 2020].

Business Interruption Group, 2020. *1 The Business Interruption Group Represents Thousands Of Businesses, Employing Millions Of Americans Across Every Sector Of The Economy*. [Online] Available at: *https://werbig.org/* [Accessed 24 08 2020].

Cain, A., 2020. *NHS Resilience Manager* [Interview] (27 June 2020).

Campbell, D., 2020. *NHS to enlist 'sensible' celebrities to persuade people to take coronavirus vaccine*. [Online] Available at:

www.theguardian.com/society/2020/nov/29/nhs-enlist-sensible-celebrities-coronavirus-vaccine-take-up [Accessed 13 12 2020].

Carvalho, C., 2015. *Raising the steaks': Louis' restaurant, opened in 1970s, forced out due to rising rents – but family tradition will be continued by son's new venture.* [Online] Available at: *www.scmp.com/news/hong-kong/article/1860897/raising-steaks-louis-restaurant-opened-1970s-forced-out-due-rising* [Accessed 05 06 2017].

Causon, J., 2020. *Institute's CEO, Jo Causon, was on BBC Breakfast News launching our campaign 'Back our Essential Workers – Service with Respect'.* [Online] Available at: *www.instituteofcustomerservice.com/jo-causon-bbc-back-essential-workers/* [Accessed 20 07 2020].

CBRE, 2015. *Research and Reports Search..* [Online] Available at: *http://www.cbre.com* [Accessed 05 06 2017].

CDC, 2018. *Bioterrorism Agents/Diseases.* [Online] Available at: *https://emergency.cdc.gov/agent/agentlist-category.asp* [Accessed 10 09 2020].

CDC, 2020. *Cruise Ship Guidance.* [Online] Available at: *www.cdc.gov/quarantine/cruise/index.html* [Accessed 15 07 2020].

CDC, 2020. *Human Coronavirus Types.* [Online] Available at: *www.cdc.gov/coronavirus/types.html* [Accessed 28 06 2020].

Chan, H., 2020. *Pervasive personal data collection at the heart of South Korea's COVID-19 success may not translate.* [Online] Available at: *https://blogs.thomsonreuters.com/answerson/south-korea-covid-19-data-privacy/* [Accessed 19 07 2020].

Chavarria-Miró, G. et al., 2020. *Sentinel surveillance of SARS-CoV-2 in wastewater anticipates the occurrence of COVID-19 cases.* [Online]
Available at:
www.medrxiv.org/content/10.1101/2020.06.13.20129627v1.full.pdf
[Accessed 10 09 2020].
Cheng, M., 2005. *WHO Handbook for Journalists: Influenza Pandemic.* [Online] Available at:
www.who.int/csr/don/Handbook_influenza_pandemic_dec05.pdf
[Accessed 26 03 2021].
Cheng, Yamaguchi, M., 2020. *Quarantined cruise ship Diamond Princess became incubator for coronavirus.*
[Online] Available at:
www.stuff.co.nz/travel/news/119631986/quarantined-cruise-ship-diamond-princess-became-incubator-for-coronavirus [Accessed 18 02 2022].
Cheung, J., September 2015. *We're done: Steak house shutters on high rent.* Hong Kong: The Standard.
[Accessed 16 09 2021].
Clark, C., 2007. Current and improved biodefences costs – benefit assessment. In: H. Richardson, P. Gordon & J. Moore, eds. *The economic impacts of terrorist attacks.* Cheltenham, UK: Edward Elgar Publishing Limited.
Clark, R.A., 2012. *A Business Response to Terrorism.* [Unpublished master's dissertation]. Available from Buckinghamshire New University library.
Clark, R., 2016. *Business Continuity and the Pandemic Threat.* First ed. Ely, UK: ITGP.
Clark, R., 2018. *Criris Management – Is social media its new best friend or its worst nightmare?.* s.l.:KDP.

Clark, R. A., 2014. *In Hindsight – a compendium of business continuity case studies.* Ely, UK: ITGP.

CLIA, 2020. *Ocean Cruise Line Ships.* [Online] Available at: *https://cruising.org/-/media/research-updates/research/state-of-the-cruise-industry.pdf* [Accessed 03 07 2020].

Cole, L., 1988. *Clouds of Secrecy : The army's Germ Warfare Tests over Populated Areas.* Oxford: Rowman and Littlefield Publishers Inc.

Cole, L. A., (2007). *Terror – How Israel Has Coped and What America Can Learn.* Bloomington: Indiana University Press.

Costgliola, V., & Quaqliata, F. (2008). *Bioterrorism: a Potential Weapon for Terrorist Attacks Through Food and Water Contamination: Evolution of Our Understanding of the Use of Chemical and Bacteriological Weapons. In M. V. Magni (Ed.), Detection of Bacteria, Viruses, Parasites and Fungi (p. 7).* Dordrecht: Springer.

Crichton, G., 2007. The Glasgow airport attack from a business continuity and crisis management point of view.. *Business Continuity Journal,* Two (Three).

Curson, P., 2003. *Monster of man's making.* [Online] Available at: *www.smh.com.au/national/monster-of-mans-making-20030402-gdgjc5.html* [Accessed 29 06 2020].

Dakin, C., 2014. The Gloucestershire Floding – 2007. In: R. A. Clark, ed. *In Hindsight – a compendium of business continuity case studies.* Ely: ITGP.

Davidson, P., 2020. *COVID-19: Psychological Impact, Wellbeing and Mental Health – Discussion Panel.* [Online] Available at: *www.youtube.com/watch?v=V2L1YPAzyBQ* [Accessed 21 07 2020].

Department for Education, 2020. *Government scheme to help universities in financial difficulties – New government scheme launched to support English universities at risk of insolvency.* [Online] Available at: *www.gov.uk/government/news/government-scheme-to-help-universities-in-financial-difficulties* [Accessed 30 12 2020].

Deslandes, A. et al., 2020. SARS-CoV-2 was already spreading in France in late December 2019. *International Journal of Antimicrobial Agents,* 25 April.

Diver, T., 2020. *Patients without medical conditions ask GPs for sick notes to exempt them from mask rules.* [Online] Available at: *www.telegraph.co.uk/news/2020/07/19/patients-without-medical-conditions-ask-gps-sick-notes-exempt/* [Accessed 09 08 2020].

Djudjic, D. 2020. *Photographer Speaks Up After Her Photo Was Used In Disgraceful Uk Government Ad: "I Was Devastated".* [Online] Available at: *www.diyphotography.net/photographer-speaks-up-after-her-photo-was-used-in-disgraceful-uk-government-ad-i-was-devastated/* [Accessed 14 09 2021].

Dorminey, B., 2014. *Ebola as ISIS Bio-Weapon?* [Online] Available At: *www.forbes.com/sites/brucedorminey/2014/10/05/ebola-as-isis-bio-weapon/?sh=4d64e8b07319* [Accessed 16 02 2022].

Drayton, E. & Waltmann, B., 2020. *Will universities need a bailout to survive the COVID-19 crisis?.* [Online] Available at: *www.ifs.org.uk/publications/14919* [Accessed 30 12 2020].

Du, L. & Huang, G., 2020. *Japan May Have Beaten Coronavirus Without Lockdowns or Mass Testing. But How?.* [Online] Available at: *https://time.com/5842139/japan-beat-coronavirus-testing-*

lockdowns/
[Accessed 08 01 2021].
Duncan, A., 2014. A Tale of Three Cities – The bombingg of Madrid (2004), London (2005) and Glasgow (2007). In: R. A. Clark, ed. *In Hindsight – A compendium of business continuity case studies.* Cambridge, UK: ITGP.
Earth, M, 2021. *Meet the teens that 'make Suffolk proud' after going extra mile in Covid.* Online] Available at: *www.eadt.co.uk/news/suffolk-teenagers-in-covid-hope-awards-announced-8260264?fbclid=IwAR01BNaEmFG5qR_FIHlTAVn2XWZ MIq04E8uw0CfDFycTcSnFEXYl4Mr5bnY* [Accessed 16 09 2021].
Edwards, P., Vincent M., 2016. *Disposable surgical face masks for preventing surgical wound infection in clean surgery.* [Online] Available at: *www.cochrane.org/CD002929/WOUNDS_disposable-surgical-face-masks-preventing-surgical-wound-infection-clean-surgery* [Accessed 31 08 2020].
Eghigian, G., 2020. *The Spanish Flu Pandemic and Mental Health: A Historical Perspective.* [Online] Available at: *www.psychiatrictimes.com/view/spanish-flu-pandemic-and-mental-health-historical-perspective* [Accessed 07 08 2020].
Ejinsight, 2015. *High rent forces another Hong Kong steakhouse to close.* [Online] Available at: *www.ejinsight.com/20150923-high-rent-forces-another-hong-kong-steakhouse-close/* [Accessed 05 06 2017].
Elemental, 2020. *Why Singers Might Be Covid-19 Super-Spreaders.* [Online] Available at: *https://elemental.medium.com/why-singers-might-be-covid-19-super-spreaders-57607ed71b9b,* [Accessed 26 11 2021].

Europol, 2021. *EUROPOL WARNING ON THE ILLICIT SALE OF FALSE NEGATIVE COVID-19 TEST CERTIFICATES.* [Online] Available at: *www.europol.europa.eu/newsroom/news/europol-warning-illicit-sale-of-false-negative-covid-19-test-certificates* [Accessed 03 02 2021].

Farge, E,; Revill, J,; 2020. *'Test, Test, Test': Who Chief's Coronavirus Message To World.* [Online] Available at: *www.reuters.com/article/us-healthcare-coronavirus-who-idUSKBN2132S4* [Accessed 20 08 2021]

Federal Bureau of Investigation. (2011, 11 01*). North Georgia Men Arrested, Charged in Plots to Purchase Explosives, Silencer and to Manufacture a Biological Toxin.* Retrieved 12 01, 2011, from Federal Bureau of Investigation: *www.fbi.gov/atlanta/press-releases/2011/north-georgia-men-arrested-charged-in-plots-to-purchase-explosives-silencer-and-to-manufacture-a-biological-toxin*

Feeney, C., 2014. The Devastating Effect of the SARS Pandemic on the Tourist Industry. In: R. Clark, ed. *In Hindsight – a compendium of business continuity case studies.* Ely, UK: ITGP.

Feuer, WK., 2020. *A package addressed to Trump containing the deadly poison ricin was intercepted.* [Online] Available at: *www.cnbc.com/2020/09/19/a-package-addressed-to-trump-containing-the-deadly-poison-ricin-was-intercepted-this-week* [Accessed 20 16 09 20210].

Fisher, L., Elliott, F., Hamilton, F. & Blakely, R., 2020. *Vaccine hack was detected by spies who saw it coming.* [Online] Available at: *www.thetimes.co.uk/article/vaccine-hack-was-detected-by-spies-who-saw-it-coming-jfzpxmcxh* [Accessed 13 12 2020].

Fisher, L. & Smyth, C., 2020. *GCHQ in cyberwar on anti-vaccine propaganda.* [Online] Available at: *www.thetimes.co.uk/article/gchq-in-cyberwar-on-anti-vaccine-propaganda-mcjgjhmb2* [Accessed 21 11 2020].

Forces Net, 2019. *Salisbury Decontamination Work 'Completed' After Nerve Agent Attack.* [Online] Available at: *www.forces.net/news/salisbury-be-declared-decontaminated-novichok* [Accessed 17 08 2020].

Frandino, N., 2020. *3D printers forge face shields for fight against the coronavirus.* [Online] Available at: *https://uk.reuters.com/article/uk-health-coronavirus-3d-printing-volunt/3d-printers-forge-face-shields-for-fight-against-the-coronavirus-idUKKBN21L1F6* [Accessed 18 08 2020].

Freifeld, K., 2020. *Harvey Weinstein free of coronavirus symptoms, spokesman says.* [Online] Available at: *https://uk.reuters.com/article/us-people-harvey-weinstein/harvey-weinstein-free-of-coronavirus-symptoms-spokesman-says-idUKKCN21S00A* [Accessed 16 07 2020].

Frodsham, I., 2020. *Coronavirus: Cheltenham Festival and Liverpool v Atletico Madrid 'led to spike' in COVID-19 deaths.* [Online] Available at: *https://news.sky.com/story/coronavirus-cheltenham-festival-and-liverpool-v-atletico-madrid-led-to-spike-in-covid-19-deaths-11994875* [Accessed 10 08 2020].

Fullfact, 2020. *Fake stories wrongly claim Elisa Granato, one of the UK's first Covid-19 vaccine trial participants, has died.* Available at: *https://fullfact.org/online/elisa-granato-fake/* [Accessed on 19 08 2021].

Furnari, C., 2020. *Online Alcohol Sales Surge Amid Coronavirus Pandemic.* [Online] Available at:

www.forbes.com/sites/chrisfurnari/2020/12/01/online-alcohol-sales-surge-amid-coronavirus-pandemic/ [Accessed 04 01 2021].

Gates, B., 2020. *Coronavirus: Bill Gates interview @BBC Breakfast.* [Online] Available at: *https://youtu.be/ie6lRKAdvuY* [Accessed 18 07 2020].

Gates, B., 2015. *The next outbreak? We're not ready.* [Online] Available at: *www.youtube.com/watch?v=6Af6b_wyiwI* [Accessed 18 07 2020].

Gates Foundation, 2020. *What We Do.* [Online] Available at: *www.gatesfoundation.org/What-We-Do* [Accessed 18 07 2020].

Ghebreyesus, D. T. A., 2020. *International Day for Epidemic Preparedness.* [Online] Available at: *www.who.int/news-room/events/detail/2020/12/27/default-calendar/international-day-of-epidemic-preparedness* [Accessed 12 08 2021].

Giles, C. & Samson, A., 2020. *UK public debt exceeds 100% of GDP for first time since 1963.* [Online] Available at: *www.ft.com/content/57974640-8bea-448c-9d0b-32f34825f13e* [Accessed 14 10 2020].

Gill, E., 2020. *Covid cases have now been confirmed at more than 40 Greater Manchester schools.* [Online] Available at: *www.manchestereveningnews.co.uk/news/greater-manchester-news/covid-cases-now-been-confirmed-18907137* [Accessed 10 09 2020].

Godlee, F., 2020. Covid 19: Christmas relaxation will overwhelm services. 15 12.371(4847).

Gov.UK, 2021. *Domestic abuse: how to get help.* [Online] Available at: *www.gov.uk/guidance/domestic-abuse-how-to-get-help.* [Accessed 11 09 2021].

Gracie, C., 2020. *Panorama, China's Coronavirus Cover-Up (2020),* s.l.: s.n.

Graham-Harrison, E. & Kuo, L., 2020. *China's coronavirus lockdown strategy: brutal but effective.* [Online] Available at: *www.theguardian.com/world/2020/mar/19/chinas-coronavirus-lockdown-strategy-brutal-but-effective* [Accessed 30 07 2020].

Green, A., 2020. *Obituary – Li Wenliang.* [Online] Available at: *www.thelancet.com/journals/lancet/article/PIIS0140-6736(20)30382-2/fulltext* [Accessed 22 09 2020].

Guardian, 2020. *'Test, test, test': WHO calls for more coronavirus testing – video.* [Online] Available at: *www.theguardian.com/world/video/2020/mar/16/test-test-test-who-calls-for-more-coronavirus-testing-video* [Accessed 26 11 2020].

Guenthier, L., 2020. *Little Red Riding Hood.* [Online] Available at: *www.dltk-teach.com/rhymes/littlered/story.htm* [Accessed 18 07 2020].

Guterres, A. 2020. *Global Wake-Up Call.* [Online] Available at: Global Wake-Up Call | United Nations [Accessed 11 09 2021].

Haill, O., 2020. *Profiting from coronavirus: which companies are benefiting, how investors should act.* [Online] Available at: *www.proactiveinvestors.co.uk/companies/news/914223/profiting-from-coronavirus-which-companies-are-benefiting-how-investors-should-act-914223.html* [Accessed 21 08 2020].

Halterbeck, M., Conlon, G., Williams, R. & Miller, J., 2020. *Impact of the Covid-19 pandemic on university finances.* [Online] Available at: *https://londoneconomics.co.uk/wp-content/uploads/2020/04/LE-Impact-of-Covid-19-on-university-finances-FINAL.pdf* [Accessed 30 12 2020].

Hamner, L. et al., 2020. *High SARS-CoV-2 Attack Rate Following Exposure at a Choir Practice — Skagit County, Washington, March 2020.* [Online] Available at: *www.cdc.gov/mmwr/volumes/69/wr/mm6919e6.htm* [Accessed 15 08 2020].

Hancock, A., 2020. *Coronavirus: is this the end of the line for cruise ships?.* [Online] Available at: *www.ft.com/content/d8ff5129-6817-4a19-af02-1316f8defe52* [Accessed 13 07 2020].

Hansen, R. B., 2020. *Featured Insights and Interviews* [Interview] (11 11 2020).

Harari, Y. N., 2020. *Yuval Noah Harari: the world after coronavirus | Free to read.* [Online] Available at: *www.ft.com/content/19d90308-6858-11ea-a3c9-1fe6fedcca75* [Accessed 07 01 2021].

Hawley, C., 2021. *One year since first coronavirus lockdown,* Salford: BBC Breakfast TV.

Hay, L., 2020. *Do insurers have Covid-19 covered?.* [Online] Available at: *https://home.kpmg/xx/en/home/insights/2020/03/do-insurers-have-covid-19-covered.html* [Accessed 09 08 2020].

Holland America, 2020. *Updated Statement Regarding Westerdam.* [Online] Available at: *www.hollandamerica.com/blog/ships/ms-*

westerdam/statement-regarding-westerdam-in-japan/
[Accessed 05 07 2020].

Hong Kong CHP, 2020. *Latest Situation of Coronavirus Disease (COVID-19) in Hong Kong.* [Online] Available at: *https://chp-dashboard.geodata.gov.hk/covid-19/en.html* [Accessed 03 07 2020].

Hossain, A., 2020. *Coronavirus: Two million Bangladesh jobs 'at risk' as clothes orders dry up.* [Online] Available at: *www.bbc.co.uk/news/world-asia-52417822* [Accessed 30 08 2020].

ILO, 2020. *ILO Monitor – COVID-19 and the world of work. Sixth edition.* [Online] Available at: *www.ilo.org/wcmsp5/groups/public/---dgreports/---dcomm/documents/briefingnote/wcms_755910.pdf* [Accessed 24 09 2020].

Independent School Parent, 2020. *Coronavirus: Royal Hospital Begins Remote Lessons Around the Globe.* [Online] Available at: *www.independentschoolparent.com/education-news/coronavirus/* [Accessed 19 08 2020].

ITV, 2020. *Boris Johnson very very exciting to witness first covid vaccinations.* [Online] Available at: *www.itv.com/news/london/2020-12-08/boris-johnson-very-very-exciting-to-witness-first-covid-vaccinations-at-guys-hospital-in-london* [Accessed 09 12 2020].

Jack, S., 2020. *Tesco recruits 16,000 to support online shopping growth.* London: BBC Nws.

Johns Hopkins University, 2019. *Global Health Security Index.* [Online] Available at: *www.ghsindex.org/wp-content/uploads/2019/10/2019-Global-Health-Security-Index.pdf* [Accessed 21 11 2020].

Johnson, B., 2021. *Captain Sir Tom Moore: 'National inspiration' dies with Covid-19.* [Online] Available at: *www.bbc.co.uk/news/uk-england-beds-bucks-herts-55881753* [Accessed 11 09 2021].

Kay & Munchetty. 2020. [Film] UK: BBC Breakfast Television – 2020/09/25.

Knaus, C., 2020. *More than 130 Australian companies ready to boost PPE stock of coronavirus masks, gowns and gloves.* [Online] Available at: *www.theguardian.com/world/2020/mar/23/more-than-100-australian-companies-ready-to-boost-ppe-stock-of-coronavirus-masks-gowns-and-gloves* [Accessed 18 08 2020].

Koonin, L. M., 2020. Novel coronavirus disease (COVID-19) outbreak: Now is the time to refresh pandemic plans. *Journal of Business Continuity & Emergency Planning,* 13(4).

Lakhani, N., Singh, M. & Salam, E.., 2020. *We may have to ration': US food banks face shortages as demand surges.* [Online] Available at: *www.theguardian.com/us-news/2020/apr/17/us-food-banks-over-budget-demand-coronavirus* [Accessed 02 08 2020].

Lancet, 2021. *Correcting COVID-19 vaccine misinformation.* Volume 33, 100780, March 01, 2021

Lee, B, 2021. *New CDC Warning: Avoid Cruise Ship Travel, Regardless Of Covid-19 Vaccination Status* [Online] Available at: *www.forbes.com/sites/brucelee/2021/12/30/cdc-warns-avoid-cruise-ship-travel-regardless-of-covid-19-coronavirus-vaccination-status/* [Accessed 31 12 2021].

Lee, D., 2020. *Amazon doubles quarterly profit despite Covid-19 costs.* [Online] Available at:

www.ft.com/content/7a42b1d8-9ca7-4827-aaae-729fdb7637f5 [Accessed 30 08 2020].

Lee, G. & Warner, M., 2008. *The politcal economy of the SARS epidemic – The impact in human resources in East Asia.* London and New York: Routledge.

Liberty, 2021. *PROTECTING EVERYONE DURING THE CORONAVIRUS CRISIS.* [Online]
Available at:
www.libertyhumanrights.org.uk/fundamental/coronavirus/
[Accessed 17 12 2020].

London Theatre, 2021. *Which West End shows have cancelled performances due to Covid-19?* [Online]
Available at: *www.londontheatre.co.uk/theatre-news/west-end-features/which-west-end-shows-have-cancelled-performances-in-2021-due-to-covid* [Accessed 23 12 2021].

LSHTM, 2021. *Bio Detection dogs identify COVID-19 with up to 94% accuracy.* [Online] Available at:
www.lshtm.ac.uk/newsevents/news/2021/bio-detection-dogs-identify-covid-19-94-accuracy
[Accessed 01 12 2021].

Luscombe, R., 2020. *Coronavirus: stranded ship to dock in Oakland as sister ship in Florida ordered to wait.* [Online]
Available at:
www.theguardian.com/world/2020/mar/08/coronavirus-cruise-ship-dock-oakland-us-death-toll-climbs [Accessed 04 07 2020].

Ma, J., 2020. *Coronavirus: China's first confirmed Covid-19 case traced back to November 17.* [Online] Available at:
www.scmp.com/news/china/society/article/3074991/corona virus-chinas-first-confirmed-covid-19-case-traced-back
[Accessed 17 08 2020].

Machell, B., 2020. *Virus expert Nathan Wolfe: the cost of Covid – and the next pandemic.* [Online] Available at:

www.thetimes.co.uk/edition/magazine/virus-expert-nathan-wolfe-the-cost-of-covid-and-the-next-pandemic-070hqknfh?utm_medium=Social&utm_source=Twitter#Echobox=1595074366
[Accessed 19 07 2020].
Makhovsky, A., 2020. *Nobody will die from coronavirus in Belarus, says president.* [Online] Available at:
https://uk.reuters.com/article/us-health-coronavirus-belarus/nobody-will-die-from-coronavirus-in-belarus-says-president-idUKKCN21V1PK [Accessed 21 07 2020].
Martin, M., 2021. *Vaccine nationalism.* London: BBC – Andrew Marr Show.
Maruthappu, M. et al., 2016. Economic downturns, universal health coverage, and cancer mortality in high-income and middle-income countries, 1990–2010: a longitudinal analysis. *The Lancet,* 388(10045).
Mason, C., 2020. London: BBC News.
Maruffi, F., 2020. *COVID-19 and the raise of business interruption disputes and new legislative proposals.* [Online] Available at:
www.lexology.com/library/detail.aspx?g=88e9311a-b5f3-4e28-88c1-1467ee042446 [Accessed 24 08 2020].
McClellan, A., 2020. Government must stop household mixing this Christmas. *Health Service Journal,* 15 12.
McCurry, J., 2020. *Cruise ship refused port over virus fears to dock in Cambodia – operator.* [Online] Available at:
www.theguardian.com/world/2020/feb/12/westerdam-cruise-ship-with-2000-onboard-refused-port-by-four-countries-amid-coronavirus-fears
[Accessed 04 07 2020].
McLeigh, C., 2017. Evolving Biosecurity Framework. In: R. Dover, H. Dylan & M. Goodman, eds. *The Palgrave*

Handbook of SEcurity, Risk and Intelligence. London: Springer Nature.

MI5, 2020. *TERRORIST METHODS.* [Online] Available at: *https://www.mi5.gov.uk/terrorist-methods* [Accessed 11 08 2021].

Micallef, J., 2020. *State Of The Cruise Industry: Smooth Sailing Into The 2020's.* [Online] Available at: *www.forbes.com/sites/joemicallef/2020/01/20/state-of-the-cruise-industry-smooth-sailing-into-the-2020s/* [Accessed 06 07 2020].

Mikkelson, David, 2020. Did Former U.S. Rep. Trey Gowdy Suggest COVID-19 Was a Conspiracy Against Trump? . [Online] Available at: *https://www.snopes.com/fact-check/gowdy-covid19/* [Accessed 06 07 2021].

Moorcraft, B., 2020. *Retroactive business interruption measures could bankrupt US insurers in two months. Insurance Business.* [Online] Available at: Moorcraft B. (2020) Retroactive business interruption measures *www.insurancebusinessmag.com/us/news/breaking-news/retroactive-business-interruption-measures-could-bankrupt-us-insurers-in-two-months-225240.aspx* [Accessed 10 08 2021].

Morrin, S., 2020. *20 Big Ideas that will shape the world in 2021.* [Online] Available at: *www.linkedin.com/pulse/20-big-ideas-shape-world-2021-siobhan-morrin/?trackingId=bAQq5mGdRmyW0yRe8Yd2bQ%3D%3D* [Accessed 04 01 2021].

Mosely, H., 2020. *BBC Click -.* [Online] [Accessed 10 10 2020].

Murray, A. & Parkinson, G., 2020. *Adapt and survive: How economies and businesses are changing to combat COVID-19.* [Online]
Available at: *www.nytimes.com/2020/03/01/business/china-coronavirus-surveillance.html* [Accessed 16 09 2021].
Murray, A. & Parkinson, G., 2020. *Adapt and survive: How economies and businesses are changing to combat COVID-19.* [Online]
Available at: *https://newseu.cgtn.com/news/2020-04-29/pandemic-playbook-7-adapt-resources-PIJheKuD72/index.html* [Accessed 22 12 2020].
Mozur, P; Zhong, R; & Krolik, A., 2020. *In Coronavirus Fight, China Gives Citizens a Color Code, With Red Flags.*
Available at: *www.nytimes.com/2020/03/01/business/china-coronavirus-surveillance.html* [Accessed 22 12 2020].
National Counter Terrorism Security Office. (2010). *Hazardous Materials. Retrieved 01 12, 2012, from National Counter Terrorism Security Office:*
www.nactso.gov.uk/AreaOfRisks/Hazardous.aspx
Nebehay, S., 2021. *Omicron cases doubling in 1.5 to 3 days in areas with local spread – WHO* [Online] Available at:
www.reuters.com/business/healthcare-pharmaceuticals/omicron-cases-doubling-15-3-days-areas-with-local-spread-who-2021-12-18/ [Accessed 31 12 2021].
Needleman, S. E. & Tilley, A., 2020. *Store Shelves Stripped of Laptops as Coronavirus Increases Working From Home.* [Online] Available at:
www.wsj.com/articles/store-shelves-stripped-of-laptops-as-coronavirus-increases-working-from-home-11584534112 [Accessed 04 01 2021].
Newberry, C., Dawley, S., 2019. *How to Manage a Social Media Crisis: A Practical Guide for Brands.* [Online]

Available at: https://blog.hootsuite.com/social-media-crisis-management/ [Accessed 16 02 2022].

NHS England, 2020. *Amazing Covid dogs trial at KGH.* [Online]
Available at: *www.kgh.nhs.uk/news/covid-dogs-1573/*
[Accessed 22 12 2020].

NHS, 2021. *Long-term effects of coronavirus (long COVID).* [Online]
Available at: *www.nhs.uk/conditions/coronavirus-covid-19/long-term-effects-of-coronavirus-long-covid/* [Accessed 25 01 2021].

Nix, E. 2015. 9 *Things You May Not Know About Isaac Newton.* [Online] Available at: www.history.com/news/9-things-you-may-not-know-about-isaac-newton [Accessed 14 09 2021]

Norris, B., 2020. *Risk managers fare well in pandemic but fell short on risk identification.* [Online] Available at: *www.commercialriskonline.com/risk-managers-fare-well-in-pandemic-but-fall-short-on-risk-identification/*
[Accessed 26 09 2020].

Noyes, J., 2020. *Ruby Princess passengers say onward flights no excuse for rush to disembark2.* [Online] Available at: *www.smh.com.au/national/ruby-princess-passengers-say-onward-flights-no-excuse-for-rush-to-disembark-20200611-p551ly.html*
[Accessed 07 07 2020].

NSCS, 2020. *UK and allies expose Russian attacks on coronavirus vaccine development.* [Online] Available at: *www.ncsc.gov.uk/news/uk-and-allies-expose-russian-attacks-on-coronavirus-vaccine-development*
[Accessed 11 12 2020].

NTI, 2015. *THE BIOLOGICAL THREAT.* [Online]
Available at: *www.nti.org/learn/biological/* [Accessed 13
09 2020].

NYSE, 2020. *Market Summary.* [Online] Available at:
www.nyse.com
[Accessed 07 07 2020].

Obama, B. & Lugar, R., 2005. *Grounding a Pandemic.*
[Online]
Available at:
*www.nytimes.com/2005/06/06/opinion/grounding-a-
pandemic.html* [Accessed 30 06 2020].

ONS, 2020. *Coronavirus (COVID-19) related mortality
rates and the effects of air pollution in England.* [Online]
Available at:
*www.ons.gov.uk/economy/environmentalaccounts/methodol
ogies/coronaviruscovid19relatedmortalityratesandtheeffect
sofairpollutioninengland* [Accessed 24 08 2020].

ONS, 2020. *Coronavirus and homeworking in the UK:
April 2020.* [Online]
Available at:
*www.ons.gov.uk/employmentandlabourmarket/peopleinwor
k/employmentandemployeetypes/bulletins/coronavirusandh
omeworkingintheuk/april2020*
[Accessed 22 12 2020].

*Our World Data 2021. Coronavirus (COVID-10)
Vaccinations.* [Online] Available at:
https://ourworldindata.org/covid-vaccinations
[Accessed 31 12 2021].

Parker, B., 2020. *Cruise line reveals suspension costing
$150 million a month, with fewer than half of customers
seeking cash refunds.* [Online]
Available at:
www.telegraph.co.uk/travel/cruises/news/royal-caribbean-

cruise-suspension-costs-bookings-refunds/ [Accessed 13 07 2020].

Parker, K., 2020. *Without support, training providers won't survive.* [Online]
Available at: *www.tes.com/news/without-support-training-providers-wont-survive* [Accessed 13 08 2020].

Parker, T., 2020. *Meet the companies manufacturing face masks to plug coronavirus shortages.* [Online] Available at: *www.nsmedicaldevices.com/analysis/companies-manufacturing-face-masks/* [Accessed 18 08 2020].

Paumgarten, N., 2020. *The Price of the Coronavirus Pandemic.* [Online]
Available at:
www.newyorker.com/magazine/2020/04/20/the-price-of-the-coronavirus-pandemic [Accessed 21 08 2020].

Pinsent Masons, 2020. *Coronavirus: FCA brings test case on business interruption insurance.* [Online] Available at:
https://www.pinsentmasons.com/out-law/news/coronavirus-fca-test-case-business-interruption-insurance
[Accessed 24 08 2020].

Professor Kontopantelis, E., 2020. *Excess death toll in care homes from Covid-19 'hugely underestimated'.* [Online]
Available at: *www.manchester.ac.uk/discover/news/excess-death-toll-in-care-homes-from-covid-19-hugely-underestimated/* [Accessed 29 12 2020].

Putzier, K., 2017. *Here are the most expensive office markets in the world.* [Online] Available at:
www.businessinsider.com/the-most-expensive-office-markets-in-the-world-2017-9?IR=T [Accessed 31 01 2018].

PwC, 2021. *Global Crisis Survey - Building resilience for the future.* March 2021. PwC

Quick, J. D., 2018. *The End of Epidemics - The looming threat to humanity and how to stop it.* London, UK: Scribe.

Ralph, O. & Vincent, M., 2020. *Why fate of many small businesses rests on court fight with insurers.* [Online] Available at: *www.ft.com/content/5baa13c1-ce48-4820-a69f-a3df68b01507*
[Accessed 24 08 2020].

Ramakrishna, K. & Tan, S. S., 2003. *After Bali: the threat of terrorism in Southeast Asia.* Singapore: Institute of Defense and Strategic Studies.

Ramnath, S., 2020. What is Business Interruption Insurance and How is it Related to the Covid-19 Pandemic?. *Federal Reserve Bank of Chicago: Letter No 440*, May.

Ratner, G., 1991. *Gerald Ratner – Famous Gaffe.* [Online] Available at: *www.ft.com/content/5baa13c1-ce48-4820-a69f-a3df68b01507*
[Accessed 31 12 2021].

Reuters, 2010. *BP CEO apologizes for "thoughtless" oil spill comment.* [Online] Available at: https://www.reuters.com/article/us-oil-spill-bp-apology-idUSTRE6515NQ20100602 [Accessed 16 02 2022].

RHS, 2020. *About the Royal Hospital School.* [Online] Available at: *www.royalhospitalschool.org/about/about-us*
[Accessed 30 06 2020].

RHS, 2020. *ONLINE AND HYBRID LEARNING.* [Online] Available at:
www.royalhospitalschool.org/academic/online-and-hybrid-learning
[Accessed 30 12 2020].

Richardson, H., Gordon, P. & Moore, J., 2007. Introduction. In: *The Economic Impacts of Terrorist Attacks.* Cheltenham: Edward Elgar Publishing Limited.

Roberts, M., 2020. *Flu virus with 'pandemic potential' found in China.* [Online]

Available at: *www.bbc.co.uk/news/health-53218704*
[Accessed 01 07 2020].
Robson, S., 2020. *Four arrested as hundreds turn up to 'utterly ridiculous' Manchester lockdown protest – police vow organiser will get a £10,000 fine.* [Online] Available at: *www.manchestereveningnews.co.uk/news/greater-manchester-news/four-arrested-hundreds-turn-up-19245241* [Accessed 08 11 2020].
Rothgang, H. et al., 2020. *Care Homes and COVID-19: Results of an Online Survey in Germany.* [Online] Available at: *https://ltccovid.org/wp-content/uploads/2020/07/Care-homes-and-Covid19-survey-of-care-homes-in-Germany-16-July-2020.pdf* [Accessed 29 12 2020].
Sacker, S., 2020. *HardTalk* [Interview] (29 04 2020).
Sandalls, K., 2020. *School pupils send letters to 800 alumni.* [Online] Available at: *www.ipswichstar.co.uk/news/royal-hospital-school-pupils-letter-writing-1-6713077* [Accessed 19 08 2020].
Schwab, K. & Malleret, T., 2020. *COVID-19: The Great Reset.* [Online] Available at: *https://straight2point.info/wp-content/uploads/2020/08/COVID-19_-The-Great-Reset-Klaus-Schwab.pdf* [Accessed 27 11 2020].
Sharpe, O., 2020. *Cruise Line Reveals How Much Money It Has Lost Amid Coronavirus Outbreak.* [Online] Available at: *www.worldofcruising.co.uk/norwegian-cruise-line-reveals-money-lost-amid-coronavirus-outbreak/* [Accessed 13 07 2020].
Shaw, N., 2020. *Woman sacked for self-isolating wins £7,000 at employment tribunal.* [Online] Available at: *www.leicestermercury.co.uk/news/uk-world-news/woman-*

sacked-self-isolating-wins-4517016
[Accessed 16 09 2020].

Sherwell, P., 2021. *Scientists cast doubt on WHO's China mission to find virus origin.* [Online] Available at: *www.thetimes.co.uk/article/scientists-cast-doubt-on-whos-china-mission-to-find-virus-origin-ftbtnbj9t?shareToken=cd0d95321423ba440a222376d90fcb 23*
[Accessed 03 01 2021].

Ship Technology, 2020. *Covid-19: Australia starts criminal inquiry into Ruby Princess.* [Online] Available at: *www.ship-technology.com/news/covid-19-australia-criminal-inquiry-ruby-princess/* [Accessed 04 07 2020].

Shukman, D., 2020. *Covid-19 Vaccines* [Interview] (09 12 2020).

Sky News, 2020. *Coronavirus: Black box seized from Ruby Princess ship at centre of Australia outbreak.* [Online] Available at: *https://news.sky.com/story/coronavirus-black-box-seized-from-ruby-princess-ship-at-centre-of-australia-outbreak-11970925* [Accessed 06 07 2020].

Smith, N., 2020. *The giants of the video game industry have thrived in the pandemic. Can the success continue?.* [Online] Available at: *www.washingtonpost.com/video-games/2020/05/12/video-game-industry-coronavirus/* [Accessed 04 01 2021].

Smith, O., 2020. *Revealed: The countries that rely most on your money.* [Online] Available at: *www.telegraph.co.uk/travel/maps-and-graphics/Mapped-The-countries-that-rely-most-on-your-money/* [Accessed 07 09 2020].

Sørensen, B; Susrund, A. & Dalgleish, A. 2021. *A Reconstructed Historical Aetiology of the SARS-Coronavirus-2 Spike*; Immunor & St Georges University of London.

Spring, M., 2020. *The Rise Of Misinformation – BBC Click.* [Online]
Available at: *www.youtube.com/watch?v=3blKFEDcuIo*
[Accessed 03 10 2020].
START, 2019. *National Consortium for the Study of Terrorism and Responses to Terrorism (START). Global Terrorism Database.* [Online]
Available at: *www.start.umd.edu/gtd* [Accessed 18 08 2020].
Statista, 2021. *Do you personally use a smartphone?* – by age.* [Online]
Available at: *www.statista.com/statistics/300402/smartphone-usage-in-the-uk-by-age/*
[Accessed 04 02 2021].
Stempel, J., 2020. *Ghislaine Maxwell seeks bail, citing coronavirus, and denies Jeffrey Epstein charges.* [Online]
Available at: *https://www.reuters.com/article/us-people-ghislaine-maxwell/ghislaine-maxwell-seeks-bail-citing-coronavirus-and-denies-jeffrey-epstein-charges-idUKKBN24B2KN* [Accessed 16 07 2020].
Stern, N & Ward, B. 2021. *Covid-19, climate change, and the environment: a sustainable, inclusive, and resilient global recovery.* [Online] Available at:
www.bmj.com/content/375/bmj.n2405 [Accessed 31 12 2021].
Sunak, R. 2020. *Chancellor's statement on coronavirus (COVID-19): 26 March 2020.* [Online] Available at:
www.gov.uk/government/speeches/chancellor-outlines-new-coronavirus-support-measures-for-the-self-employed
[Accessed 15 09 2021].
TASW, 2011. *Beyond pandemics: a whole-of-society approach to disaster preparedness.* [Online] Available at:

www.towardsasaferworld.org
[Accessed 12 01 2014].

Tegnell, A., 2020. *BBC HARDtalk* [Interview] (19 May 2020).

The BMJ, 2020. *Covid-19: Russia admits to understating deaths by more than two thirds.* [Online] Available at: *www.bmj.com/content/371/bmj.m4975*
[Accessed 29 12 2020].

The Economist, 2021. What is the economic cost of covid-19? *The Economist,* January.

The Guardian, 2003. China Accused of Sars Cover-Up. [Online] Available at: *www.theguardian.com/world/2003/apr/09/sars.china*
[Accessed 22 02 2022].

The New York Times, 2020. *'This Is All Beyond Stupid.' Experts Worry About Russia's Rushed Vaccine.* [Online] Available at: *www.nytimes.com/2020/08/11/health/russia-covid-19-vaccine-safety.html.* [Accessed 26 11 2021].

The WHO, 2013. *Pandemic Influenza Risk Management : WHO Interim Guidance.* [Online] Available at: *www.who.int/influenza/preparedness/pandemic/GIP_Pande micInfluenzaRiskManagementInterimGuidance_Jun2013.p df* [Accessed 02 04 2015].

The WHO, 2020(a). *Disease outbreaks.* [Online] Available at: *www.who.int/emergencies/diseases/en/* [Accessed 12 09 2020].

TIP, 2021. *COVID-19: Make it the Last Pandemic - A Summary.* [Online] Available at: *https://theindependentpanel.org/wp-content/uploads/2021/05/Summary_COVID-19-Make-it-the-Last-Pandemic_final.pdf* [Accessed 02 06 2021].

Thomas, D., 2020. *Coronavirus: 'We've spent £10,000 on invalid insurance'.* [Online] Available at:

www.bbc.co.uk/news/business-53465972
[Accessed 21 08 2020].
Thomson, B., 2021. *Review 2020 – The Business Year: BBC Breakfast.* [Online]
www.bbc.co.uk/iplayer/episode/m000qtld/review-2020-4-the-business-year [Accessed 03 01 2021].
Three Years in Wuhan. 2020. [Film] Directed by Ma Shengkang, Wenlan Peng. China: Sandouotang Media Co Ltd.
Tiwari, N, 2020. *Coronavirus: Why we touch our faces and how to stop.* [Online] Available at:
www.youtube.com/watch?v=doqS8Y0ZuUQ [Accessed 12 09 2021].
Togoh, I., 2020. *'I Can't Save Every Job' Warns British Chancellor With Plan To Help Millions Of Furloughed Workers.* [Online]
www.forbes.com/sites/isabeltogoh/2020/09/24/i-cant-save-every-job-warns-british-chancellor-with-plan-to-help-millions-of-furloughed-workers. [Accessed 26.11.2021].
Triggle, N., 2020. *Covid: Twelve charts on how Covid changed our lives.* [Online] Available at:
www.bbc.co.uk/news/uk-55214991?xtor=ES-211-[39246_PANUK_DIV_50_NCA_Covidvaccine_RET_ABC]-20201217-[bbcnews_howcovidchangedourlives_coronavirus]
[Accessed 18 12 2020].
UK Cabinet Office, 2015. *UK National Risk Register of Civil Emergencies.* [Online] Available at:
https://assets.publishing.service.gov.uk/government/uploads/system/uploads/attachment_data/file/419549/20150331_2015-NRR-WA_Final.pdf
[Accessed 28 06 2020].

UK Cabinet Office, 2017. *National Risk Register of Civil Emergencies.* [Online] Available at: *https://assets.publishing.service.gov.uk/government/upload s/system/uploads/attachment_data/file/644968/UK_Nationa l_Risk_Register_2017.pdf* [Accessed 28 06 2020].

United Nations, 2020. *5 ways the UN is fighting infodemic of misinformation* [Online] Available at: *www.un.org/en/un-coronavirus-communications-team/five-ways-united-nations-fighting-%E2%80%98infodemic%E2%80%99-misinformation* [Accessed 13 09 2020].

United Nations, 2017. *The Biological Weapons Convention.* [Online] Available at: *www.un.org/disarmament/wmd/bio/* [Accessed 13 09 2020].

US Department of Homeland Security based at the University of Maryland, 2019. *Global Terrorism Database (GTD).* [Online] Available at: *www.start.umd.edu/data-tools/global-terrorism-database-gtd* [Accessed 10 09 2020].

US Department of Justice, 2021. *Correctional Populations in the United States, 2019 – Statistical Tables.* [Online] Available at: *https://bjs.ojp.gov/sites/g/files/xyckuh236/files/media/docu ment/cpus19st.pdf* [Accessed 31 12 2021].

Vallance, P., 2021. Coronavirus: Dowing Street briefing, London: s.n.

Verna Yu., 2020. *Hero who told the truth': Chinese rage over coronavirus death of whistleblower doctor.* [Online] Available at: *www.theguardian.com/global-development/2020/feb/07/coronavirus-chinese-rage-death-whistleblower-doctor-li-wenliang* [Accessed 12 09 2021].

Walsh, F., 2020. *Fergus Walsh: Was coronavirus here earlier than we thought?*. [Online] Available at: *www.bbc.co.uk/news/health-52935644* [Accessed 17 08 2020].

Waters, R., 2020. *Advanced Micro Devices.* [Online] Available at: *www.ft.com/content/844ed28c-8074-4856-bde0-20f3bf4cd8f0* [Accessed 04 01 2021].

Watson, K., 2020. *Coronavirus: Brazil's Bolsonaro in denial and out on a limb.* [Online] Available at: *www.bbc.co.uk/news/world-latin-america-52080830* [Accessed 21 07 2020].

Whiting, K., 2020. *These are the top 10 job skills of tomorrow – and how long it takes to learn them.* [Online] Available at: *www.weforum.org/agenda/2020/10/top-10-work-skills-of-tomorrow-how-long-it-takes-to-learn-them/* [Accessed 03 01 2021].

Whitten, S., 2015. *Rumors and misinformation circulate on social media following Paris attacks..* [Online] Available at: *www.cnbc.com/2015/11/14/rumors-and-misinformation-circulate-on-social-media-following-paris-attacks.html* [Accessed 07 12 2017].

Whitty, C., 2020. *The NHS is absolutely open for business.* [Online] Available at: *www.facebook.com/10downingstreet/videos/professor-chris-whitty/788834461908150/* [Accessed 17 08 2021].

WHO, 2020(a). *Why do the virus and the disease have different names?.* [Online] Available at: *www.who.int/emergencies/diseases/novel-coronavirus-2019/technical-guidance/naming-the-coronavirus-disease-(covid-2019)-and-the-virus-that-causes-it* [Accessed 01 07 2020].

WHO, 2020. *Coronavirus.* [Online] Available at: *www.who.int/health-topics/coronavirus#tab=tab_3* [Accessed 30 06 2020].

WHO Director-General's opening remarks at the media briefing on COVID-19 - 28 February 2020. [Online] Available at: *www.who.int/director-general/speeches/detail/who-director-general-s-opening-remarks-at-the-media-briefing-on-covid-19---28-february-2020* [Accessed 15 09 2021].

WHO, 2020. *Listings of WHO's response to COVID-19.* [Online] Available at: *www.who.int/news/item/29-06-2020-covidtimeline* [Accessed 26 03 2021].

WHO, 2020. *WHO Statement regarding cluster of pneumonia cases in Wuhan, China.* [Online] Available at: *www.who.int/china/news/detail/09-01-2020-who-statement-regarding-cluster-of-pneumonia-cases-in-wuhan-china* [Accessed 26 03 2021].

WHO, 2020. *Zoonoses.* [Online] Available at: *www.who.int/topics/zoonoses/en/#:~:text=A%20zoonosis%20is%20any%20disease,zoonotic%20infections%20in%20n ature* [Accessed 01 07 2020].

WHO, 2021. *WHO-convened Global Study of Origins of SARS-CoV-2: China Part.* [Online] Available at: *www.who.int/publications/i/item/who-convened-global-study-of-origins-of-sars-cov-2-china-part* [Accessed 02 06 2021]

Windsor-Shellard, B. & Kaur, J., 2020. *Coronavirus (COVID-19) related deaths by occupation, England and Wales: deaths registered up to and including 20 April 2020.* [Online] Available at: *www.ons.gov.uk/peoplepopulationandcommunity/healthand*

*socialcare/causesofdeath/bulletins/coronaviruscovid19relat
eddeathsbyoccupationenglandandwales/deathsregisteredup
toandincluding20april2020* [Accessed 05 09 2020].

Wingfield-Hayes, R., 2020. [Online] Available at:
www.bbc.co.uk/news/world-asia-52466834 [Accessed 22
07 2020].

Wolfe, J. & Takenaga, L., 2020. *The stigma of Covid travel.*
[Online]
Available at: *www.nytimes.com/2020/08/28/us/coronavirus-
briefing-travel-stigma.html* [Accessed 29 08 2020].

WP, 2020. *An inside look at Trump's failed coronavirus
response.* [Online]
Available at: *www.youtube.com/watch?v=Atxdfrj3zEk*
[Accessed 04 12 2020].

Yamey, G. & Walensky, R. P., 2020. *Covid-19: re-opening
universities is high risk.* [Online] Available at:
www.bmj.com/content/370/bmj.m3365
[Accessed 10 09 2020].

Zhang, K., 2020. *Coronavirus: Hong Kong resident denies
he is 'patient zero' of Diamond Princess cruise ship
outbreak.* [Online] Available at:
*www.scmp.com/news/hong-
kong/society/article/3074698/coronavirus-hong-kong-
resident-denies-he-patient-zero* [Accessed 02 07 2020].

Zimmer, C., 2020. *'This Is All Beyond Stupid.' Experts
Worry About Russia's Rushed Vaccine.* [Online] Available
at: *https://www.nytimes.com/2020/08/11/health/russia-
covid-19-vaccine-safety.html* [Accessed 16 02 2022].

APPENDIX F: PERMISSIONS AND LICENCES

Appendix F.1: Text and images

- Some of the quoted text used in this book has been used in accordance with the *Copyright, Designs and Patent Act 1988*. The author of this book owns the copyright for some of the figures, has received permission from various personal friends/organisations to include a copy of their photographs and other figures have been obtained from the royalty free Author Academy Photo Database/Pixabay.

Appendix F.2: Open Government Licence

Some of the information used in this book was extracted from the UK National Risk Register of Civil Emergencies 2017 plus other publications and was done so under the terms of the Open Government Licence.

This publication is available for download at: *www.gov.uk/government/publications/national-risk-register-of-civil-emergencies-2017-edition*. It is also available from Cabinet Office, 70 Whitehall, London SW1A 2AS.

To view this the associated licence, please visit:

- *www.nationalarchives.gov.uk/doc/open-government-licence/* or write to the Information Policy Team, The National Archives, Kew, London TW9 4DU.

APPENDIX G: USEFUL RESOURCES

- **WHO:** *www.who.int/emergencies/diseases/novel-coronavirus-2019*
- **US CDC Centers for Disease Control and Prevention:** *www.cdc.gov/flu/pandemic-resources/index.htm*
- **UK National Health Service (NHS):** *www.nhs.uk/conditions/coronavirus-COVID-19/*
- **European Commission:** *ec.europa.eu/education/resources-and-tools/coronavirus-online-learning-resources_en*
- **Australia:** *www.australia.gov.au*
- **Canada:** *www.canada.ca/en/public-health/services/diseases/2019-novel-coronavirus-infection/awareness-resources.html*
- **New Zealand:** *www.health.govt.nz/our-work/diseases-and-conditions/COVID-19-novel-coronavirus/COVID-19-resources-and-tools*
- **South Africa:** *www.gov.za/Coronavirus*

FURTHER READING

IT Governance Publishing (ITGP) is the world's leading publisher for governance and compliance. Our industry-leading pocket guides, books, training resources and toolkits are written by real-world practitioners and thought leaders. They are used globally by audiences of all levels, from students to C-suite executives.

Our high-quality publications cover all IT governance, risk and compliance frameworks and are available in a range of formats. This ensures our customers can access the information they need in the way they need it.

Our other publications about business continuity include:

- *Business Continuity and the Pandemic Threat - Potentially the biggest survival challenge facing organisations* by Robert A. Clark, *www.itgovernancepublishing.co.uk/product/business-continuity-and-the-pandemic-threat*
- *Validating Your Business Continuity Plan – Ensuring your BCP actually works* by Robert A. Clark, *www.itgovernancepublishing.co.uk/product/validating-your-business-continuity-plan*
- *ISO 22301:2019 and business continuity management – Understand how to plan, implement and enhance a business continuity management system (BCMS)* by Alan Calder, *www.itgovernancepublishing.co.uk/product/iso-22301-2019-and-business-continuity-management-*

understand-how-to-plan-implement-and-enhance-a-business-continuity-management-system-bcms

For more information on ITGP and branded publishing services, and to view our full list of publications, visit *www.itgovernancepublishing.co.uk*.

To receive regular updates from ITGP, including information on new publications in your area(s) of interest, sign up for our newsletter at *www.itgovernancepublishing.co.uk/topic/newsletter*.

Branded publishing

Through our branded publishing service, you can customise ITGP publications with your company's branding.

Find out more at *www.itgovernancepublishing.co.uk/topic/branded-publishing-services*.

Related services

ITGP is part of GRC International Group, which offers a comprehensive range of complementary products and services to help organisations meet their objectives.

For a full range of resources on business continuity visit *www.itgovernance.co.uk/shop/category/bcm-and-iso-22301*.

Training services

The IT Governance training programme is built on our extensive practical experience designing and implementing management systems based on ISO standards, best practice and regulations.

Our courses help attendees develop practical skills and comply with contractual and regulatory requirements. They also support career development via recognised qualifications.

Learn more about our training courses in business continuity and view the full course catalogue at *www.itgovernance.co.uk/training*.

Professional services and consultancy

We are a leading global consultancy of IT governance, risk management and compliance solutions. We advise businesses around the world on their most critical issues and present cost-saving and risk-reducing solutions based on international best practice and frameworks.

We offer a wide range of delivery methods to suit all budgets, timescales and preferred project approaches.

Find out how our consultancy services can help your organisation at *www.itgovernance.co.uk/consulting*.

Industry news

Want to stay up to date with the latest developments and resources in the IT governance and compliance market? Subscribe to our Weekly Round-up newsletter and we will send you mobile-friendly emails with fresh news and features about your preferred areas of interest, as well as unmissable offers and free resources to help you successfully start your projects. *www.itgovernance.co.uk/weekly-round-up*.

EU for product safety is Stephen Evans, The Mill Enterprise Hub, Stagreenan, Drogheda, Co. Louth, A92 CD3D, Ireland. (servicecentre@itgovernance.eu)

www.ingramcontent.com/pod-product-compliance
Lightning Source LLC
Chambersburg PA
CBHW060424220326
41598CB00021BA/2283